The Comeback

The 2024 Elections and American Politics

Andrew E. Busch
University of Tennessee, Knoxville

John J. Pitney Jr.
Claremont McKenna College

BLOOMSBURY ACADEMIC
NEW YORK · LONDON · OXFORD · NEW DELHI · SYDNEY

BLOOMSBURY ACADEMIC
Bloomsbury Publishing Inc, 1385 Broadway, New York, NY 10018, USA
Bloomsbury Publishing Plc, 50 Bedford Square, London, WC1B 3DP, UK
Bloomsbury Publishing Ireland, 29 Earlsfort Terrace, Dublin 2, D02 AY28, Ireland

BLOOMSBURY, BLOOMSBURY ACADEMIC and the Diana logo are trademarks of
Bloomsbury Publishing Plc

First published in the United States of America 2025

Cover design: Sally Rinehart
Cover images © top: Chip Somodevilla/Getty Images; bottom: Saul Loeb/Getty Images

Bloomsbury Publishing Inc does not have any control over, or responsibility for, any
third-party websites referred to or in this book. All internet addresses given in this
book were correct at the time of going to press. The author and publisher regret any
inconvenience caused if addresses have changed or sites have ceased to exist, but can
accept no responsibility for any such changes.

Library of Congress Cataloging-in-Publication Data available

ISBN: HB: 978-1-5381-9757-8
      PB: 978-1-5381-9758-5
      ePDF: 979-8-7651-5511-0
      eBook: 978-1-5381-9759-2

Typeset by Deanta Global Publishing Services, Chennai, India
Printed and bound in the United States of America

For product safety related questions contact productsafety@bloomsbury.com.

To find out more about our authors and books visit www.bloomsbury.com and sign up
for our newsletters.

We dedicate this volume to our children:
Joshua
Hannah
Kaden
Daniel
Elizabeth

Contents

Acknowledgments

We would like to acknowledge CMC for Jack's fall semester sabbatical and Lisa and Melinda for their patient forbearance as Jack and Andy mumbled to themselves about things such as seat-vote ratios and the National Popular Vote Interstate Compact.

Chapter 1

Burdened by What Has Been

Imagine time-traveling from November 6, 2024, to January 7, 2021—right after the attack on the Capitol. If you had told people that Donald Trump had just won his second term, the reaction surely would have been surprise and disbelief. If you were to go back to the 1990s, that news would have triggered laughter: the idea of a Trump White House bid was a running joke in the *Doonesbury* comic strip.[1]

As we shall see in this chapter, the 2024 election had extraordinary features, starting with Trump's comeback from near-oblivion. But the mere fact of a partisan shift in the presidency (along with the Senate) was not one of them. The election took place during a period of instability in American politics.[2] Of the 12 biennial elections between 2000 and 2022, 10 resulted in a change in party control of the House, Senate, or White House.[3] Of the previous dozen elections, the same was true of only five.

In the immediate aftermath of the 2024 election, many commentators called the outcome a "blowout." Trump won a clear victory, but his margins were modest by the standards of earlier times. His 312 electoral votes amounted to 58 percent of the total, ranking 39th among all 59 presidential elections. For the first time in his three races, he won the aggregated popular vote, but his share fell just short of a majority. This result was also in keeping with recent history. During the new century, presidential races tended to be close. In the six elections between 1976 and 1996, the winner's average margin in the aggregated popular vote was 8.63 percent (table 1.1). Between 2000 and 2020, the winner's average margin was only 2.57 percent. In two of those elections (2000 and 2016), the candidate who won the electoral vote lost the popular vote. The closeness of these elections was no guarantee of the 2024 outcome, but it did shape the strategies and expectations of politicians and their handlers.

Table 1.1. Winner's Popular Vote Margin

Winner's Popular Vote Margin, 1976–1996	
1976 Carter	2.06%
1980 Reagan	9.74%
1984 Reagan	18.21%
1988 Bush	7.72%
1992 Clinton	5.56%
1996 Clinton	8.51%
Average	**8.63%**
Winner's Popular Vote Margin, 2000–2020	
2000 Bush	−.51%
2004 Bush	2.46%
2008 Obama	7.27%
2012 Obama	3.86%
2016 Trump	−2.09%
2020 Biden	4.45%
Average	**2.57%**

Source: List of United States Presidential Elections by Popular Vote Margin, Wikipedia, January 21, 2025, https://en.wikipedia.org/wiki/List_of_United_States_presidential_elections_by_popular_vote_margin.

One reason for the voting patterns of the 21st century was increased party competition. Through the 1980s, Democrats seemed to be the natural majority party. Notwithstanding Reagan's landslides, Democrats maintained a decisive edge in party identification and kept control of the U.S. House and most state legislatures. By the millennium, however, the parties were at rough parity. The 2000 election produced a tie in the Senate and near-ties in the Electoral College and the U.S. House—hence the title of a book in this series, *The Perfect Tie.* The outlier of the 2000–2020 period was 2008—a solid win, if not quite a Democratic tsunami. That year, extraordinary circumstances hobbled the GOP: a world-historic economic crisis, an unpopular war, and an underfunded campaign. (John McCain was the last major party nominee to date who chose to rely on public funding.) Four years later, when the GOP did not suffer from such disadvantages, the outcome reverted to form. As we noted in *After Hope and Change*, Obama became the first president to win reelection while losing vote share.

Another reason for the twitchiness of electoral outcomes is that Americans vote for change when they are unhappy with the country's state. During the early 21st century, they were very unhappy indeed. Gallup has long asked respondents whether they were satisfied with "the way things are going in the United States at this time." The percentage saying they were satisfied tumbled during the early years of the century and never topped 50 percent at any point between 2003 and 2024. By 2024, only 26 percent expressed satisfaction.[4] Other survey questions have revealed parallel trends. Trust in government fell by more than half between 2005 and 2024.[5] The distrust extended to the "fourth branch." During the same period, trust in the mass media went from 50 percent to 31 percent.[6]

One need not look for mysterious psychological or cultural explanations for the souring of America. During this period, the nation suffered several historic traumas that raised reasonable doubts about the people in charge of its governmental and private institutions.

The "forever wars" in Iraq and Afghanistan made a mockery of officials who suggested that we could plant friendly democracies in hostile foreign soil. In the eyes of many Americans, these conflicts produced little for the United States except death, debt, and disillusionment.

The 2008 financial crisis plunged the nation into the worst economic turmoil since the Great Depression, throwing millions out of their jobs and homes and destroying trillions in net worth. And not a single Wall Street CEO went to prison.

Starting in 2020, COVID-19 touched nearly every household in the country. Besides killing more than a million Americans, the pandemic had social and economic effects that will be unfolding for many years to come. Before it hit, Americans took it for granted that the government knew how to contain such problems before they disrupted everyday life.

In each of these cases, experts and authorities made significant errors. Rachelle Walensky, director of the Centers for Disease Control and Prevention, said of COVID-19: "To be frank, we are responsible for some pretty dramatic, public mistakes, from testing to data to communications."[7] Walensky was being generous: one could easily add the educational and economic costs of lockdowns imposed by many states. Public health officials made the mistakes in good faith, but by the time vaccines got the pandemic under control, more and more Americans were losing confidence in the government response.[8]

In addition to these headline-grabbing maladies, traditionally minded Americans were increasingly disturbed by radical social changes that seemed to be accelerating over the previous decade, exemplified by everything from the purging of Aunt Jemima and the Washington Redskins to the sudden ascendance of land acknowledgments and transgender pronouns. From the point of view of millions of Americans, everything was topsy-turvy.

If you are a strong, consistent partisan, you will likely be happy only when your party gets its way. If the other party is either running things or thwarting your side, you will probably register dissatisfaction. If you do not have a strong attachment to either party, then partisan warfare itself will displease you.[9] So it is worth noting that a time of discontent coincided with an era of partisan sorting. The parties completed their ideological evolution during this

conservative Democrats and liberal Republicans joined the endan-
_ _ species list. As both sides became more consistently ideological, voters
were less likely to cross party lines when choosing a president. In 1988, for
instance, 17 percent of Democrats voted for the Republican winner, George
H. W. Bush. Twenty years later, Barack Obama got a slightly smaller share
of the popular vote than Bush, but only 9 percent of Republicans supported
him.[10]

Campaign geography changed with the emergence of the red state/blue
state divide. This term stemmed from media coverage of the close 2000 election. Some point to NBC anchor Tim Russert's use of the network's map
colors as shorthand for the states that Bush and Gore carried. (Previously,
network mapmakers chose the colors at random.) Others note election maps
published by the *New York Times* and *USA Today*.[11] In the late 20th century,
Republican presidential candidates could carry blue states, and Democrats
could win the red states. California went Republican in 1976, 1980, 1984, and
1988. Tennessee went Democratic in 1976, 1992, and 1996. From 2000 to
2020, most states predictably gave lopsided margins to one side or the other,
and the outcome hinged on a small number of "swing states." So one oddity
of this period is that close national tallies coincided with a series of state-level
landslides that canceled one another out.

Meanwhile, congressional elections went from split tickets to straight
tickets. In 1988, 17 senators won in states where their party's presidential
nominee lost.[12] On the House side, 148 districts had split results.[13] In the
2020 Senate election, only Susan Collins (R-ME) won a state that her party's
presidential candidate lost. Just 16 districts voted for a House candidate of
one party and a presidential candidate of the other.

All these changes affected the pursuit of office. Senators and House members came to believe that constituent service and the pursuit of pork-barrel
projects were no longer as effective in winning support from voters who
favored the other party. "Rallying the base" became even more important,
and lawmakers had to worry that deviations from the party line would invite
primary challenges. At the presidential level, candidates focused mainly on
the swing states, skipping the other side's electoral fortresses and taking their
own for granted. Each side could count on 47 percent of the vote, and relied
on "micro-targeted" smaller voter segments to get over the top.

On key issues, partisan lines hardened over time. When Joe Biden entered
the Senate in 1973, Senate colleagues included conservative Democrats
and liberal Republicans. Just weeks after Biden took his senatorial oath,
the Supreme Court handed down its decision in *Roe v. Wade*. Justice Harry
Blackmun, a Nixon appointee, wrote the majority opinion. His fellow Nixon
appointees Warren Burger and Lewis Powell and Eisenhower appointee Pot-
ter Stewart also voted for the decision. At the time, prominent Republican

officeholders supported abortion rights, and two of the nation's most permissive abortion laws bore the signatures of Republican governors: Nelson Rockefeller of New York and Ronald Reagan of California. Conversely, plenty of Democrats and progressives opposed abortion, with some civil rights leaders calling it "black genocide." Senator Biden said: "I don't like the Supreme Court decision on abortion. I think it went too far. I don't think that a woman has the sole right to say what should happen to her body."[14] By 2021, Biden had joined most Democrats in supporting *Roe*. But the presence of six Republican-appointed justices had raised conservative hopes—and liberal fears—that the Court would overturn the decision and open the way to highly restrictive abortion laws. In mid-2022, that is exactly what happened. With few exceptions, Republican and Democratic officeholders took opposite sides on the decision.

More and more voters dwelt in partisan ideological silos, holding consistently liberal Democratic or conservative Republican views across various issues.[15] The two sides increasingly saw political events through their own lenses, relying on different news sources.[16] Strong majorities of Republicans and Democrats agreed with a survey statement that voters in both parties "not only disagree over plans and policies, but also cannot agree on the basic facts."[17]

Parties in the electorate were different in other ways. In 1972, whites without four-year college degrees made up a majority of voters in both parties.[18] By 2024, they still accounted for most Republican identifiers and leaners but only 26 percent of Democrats. The latter had become a coalition of Blacks, Hispanics, and college-educated whites.[19] Christians, and especially Evangelical Protestants, were a significant part of the GOP base, while religiously unaffiliated people were increasingly prominent on the Democratic side. Rural areas had become overwhelmingly Republican, while most big cities were a deep shade of blue. (It would only be a slight exaggeration to say that one could fire a cannon through Wilshire Boulevard in Los Angeles without hitting a Republican.)

Animosity fueled discontent: the two sides disliked each other. Growing shares of Republicans and Democrats saw people in the other camp as more closed-minded, dishonest, immoral, and unintelligent than other Americans.[20] More than three-fourths of Republicans agreed with the statement that the Democratic Party had been "taken over by socialists." A similar share of Democrats said that the GOP had been "taken over by racists."[21] Opponents thought that the stakes of their conflict were high. Three-quarters of Republicans said that Democratic policies threatened the country, while nearly two-thirds of Democrats said the same of the Republican agenda.[22] Some surveys even found that a measurable number of Americans thought that resorting to political violence might be necessary.[23]

Political violence was not just hypothetical. The January 6, 2021, attack on the United States Capitol was a sign of the intense divisions in American political life. So was the matter that had sparked it. Despite dozens of court decisions and vote audits upholding the results of the 2020 election, most Republicans thought that Biden and Harris had won by fraud. They did not see them as legitimate.[24]

OUTSIDER

When people think the insiders have done them wrong, they turn to outsiders. The first book in this series, *Upside Down and Inside Out*, described the role of outsiderism in the 1992 campaign. "Outsiderism declaims against the overblown perquisites and privileges of those in office, against the systematic use of political power to keep and maintain power." Also frequently referred to as "populism," it often lacks much policy content. "But much of the time, it is not a question of position but merely positioning. What strategists and candidates understand is that with the use of a vague symbol, they can appeal to diverse positions united only by a common mood or discontent."[25] Running after the savings and loan crisis and the recession of 1990–1991, eccentric businessman Ross Perot rode outsiderism to an impressive 19 percent of the aggregated popular vote in 1992. Four years later, he tried again, but good economic times had eased national discontent, and his support dropped by half.

By most objective standards, Perot did not stand outside the political and economic elites. He had made his money selling computer services to government agencies, hence his monicker as "America's first welfare billionaire." But what matters for outsiders is less the content of their résumé than the persuasiveness of their pose.

Enter Donald J. Trump. He had inherited a family fortune deriving from federal housing programs, and he had befriended people in the top echelons of society.[26] (Bill and Hillary Clinton attended his wedding to his third wife.) But he clung to his outer-borough inflection and styled himself as a champion of regular working Americans against the elites. To Americans in "flyover country" who resented professionals and technocrats, Trump was a delight.[27] It is telling that he admired President Andrew Jackson, a pugnacious outsider who had little regard for the niceties of society. Unlike Jackson, however, Trump dueled with mean tweets instead of bullets. Disregarding political norms, he gleefully insulted his opponents with crude language and often baseless accusations. His attacks on the liberal Democratic establishment energized his followers so much that they were willing to overlook or embrace his departures from some long-standing Republican policy positions. Trump's outsiderism extended to leading figures in his own party. During the 2016 campaign, he took great pleasure in crushing the candidacy of Jeb Bush, a member of the party's leading dynasty.

Even after becoming president in 2017, Trump kept cultivating his outsider persona, railing against "fake news" and "the Deep State." The latter phrase referred to something far more extensive and sinister than the usual bureaucratic resistance that had frustrated all of his modern predecessors. The most extreme version of the idea was the QAnon conspiracy theory, which held that Trump was waging a secret war against a vast network of satanic pedophiles who controlled much of the government. Though Trump did not openly embrace QAnon, he pointedly declined to denounce it. At a 2020 press conference, he said: "Well, I don't know much about the movement, other than I understand they like me very much, which I appreciate, but I don't know much about the movement."[28]

Trump's outsiderism did not save him from a COVID-19 backlash. Though he tried to assign the blame to Democratic governors, some of whom had indeed contributed to the crisis,[29] most Americans disapproved of how he handled the pandemic.[30] He failed at overturning the 2020 election, and for a moment, it looked as if the January 6 attack on the Capitol might end his political career. But his base rallied behind him, and there were not enough Republican votes in the Senate to convict him. As we discuss more extensively in a later chapter, grassroots support helped him make a remarkable comeback.

Meanwhile, the new administration soon took center stage. Although President Biden put points on the policy scoreboard, his first two years did not impress the public. By April 2021, his Gallup approval rating had fallen below 50 percent and stayed there through 2022.[31] True, he would never reach the 67 percent approval that Nixon enjoyed at his 1973 inaugural. Since George W. Bush's second term, discontent and polarization had tended to put a low ceiling on presidential approval ratings. Moreover, Biden had to grapple with GOP doubts about his legitimacy. Nevertheless, concerned Democrats thought he could do better, and urged him to use the bully pulpit and strengthen his communications operation. In the fantasy world of the old TV series *The West Wing*, a few powerful speeches and snappy sound bites would turn the poll numbers around. But in this world, the Biden-Harris administration did not have a messaging problem. It had a reality problem. More precisely, it had several reality problems that would supercharge existing feelings of dissatisfaction and open the door to Trump's return.

REALITY PROBLEMS: COVID-19 AND THE ECONOMY

Picking up from Trump's Operation Warp Speed, the Biden-Harris administration oversaw the distribution of 100 million doses of COVID-19 vaccines
within its 100 days in office. Well into 2022, however, the virus lingered and
mutated. Because of the Delta and Omicron variants, the disease claimed
more American lives during Biden's first year than in Trump's last. (In their
June 27 debate, Trump made that point.) Vaccines helped a great deal, but
officials sometimes set unrealistic expectations. At a televised town hall in
July 2021, Biden said: "You're not going to—you're not going to get COVID
if you have these vaccinations."[32] He erred. Vaccinated people could indeed
get COVID-19, albeit with a drastically reduced chance of hospitalization
or death. Pandemic-era closures and restrictions may have saved lives, but
they came at a steep social cost, particularly when it came to learning loss in
American schools.[33]

As the economy recovered from the pandemic, some consumer goods
became scarce, and prices outpaced wages. Voters under 60 had little
memory of significant inflation, so trips to the gas pump and grocery store
were a shock. It was more than just perception: for a long time, Americans
really were losing ground. The best measure of individual economic well-
being—real disposable personal income per capita—plunged during the
administration's first year and a half and was barely edging up by the autumn
of 2022.[34] Republicans also made a plausible case that administration policies
contributed substantially to the picture. The COVID-19 relief package alone
spent three times as much as the Congressional Budget Office estimated was
necessary to fill the Keynesian "output gap."[35] The administration had also
won the enactment of a $280 billion CHIPS Act, a $1.2 trillion infrastructure
bill, and an $891 billion set of tax breaks and spending programs called the
Inflation Reduction Act (IRA). Progressives lamented (and conservatives
expressed relief) that the IRA was far less ambitious than an earlier version
called Build Back Better, which would have cost $3.5 trillion. Conservatives
noted it would increase the national debt, which is hardly the best way to
reduce inflation in the long run.

At the start of 2023, Democrats could respond that the inflation rate had
dropped since its peak in mid-2022, but Americans still worried about prices.
The catch was that ordinary voters do not think of inflation as economists do.
"Well, I know why I'm upset. Because I have GasBuddy on my phone and
I'm looking around and I'm like, 'so um, when are prices gonna get back to
where they were before? Right?'" said Lisa D. Cook, a member of the Board
of Governors of the Federal Reserve System. "Most Americans are not just
looking for disinflation. You and I as macroeconomists are looking for disinflation. They're looking for deflation. They want these prices to be back
where they were before the pandemic."[36]

As the months ticked by, there were some favorable signs for Democrats. Inflation eased, unemployment remained low, and the stock market soared. Thanks in part to record-setting domestic oil production, gasoline prices dropped from their midyear highs. Consumer confidence ended 2023 with a surge.[37] Not all was rosy, however. In January 2024, Pew found that 28 percent of Americans rated economic conditions as excellent or good, a nine-point increase from April 2023 but still a very low figure.[38] Among Democrats, the figure was 44 percent, less than a majority and far below the 81 percent of Republicans who had a positive view of the Trump economy just before the pandemic. After the election, *The Economist* would publish an index measuring economic performance for 37 wealthy countries in the year ending in November 2024. The U.S. performance was 20th of 37 overall, 23rd in inflation, and 29th in change in unemployment rate.[39]

And the experience of other countries should have been a warning to the administration: postpandemic inflation had been a problem throughout most of the world, and in 2024 elections, every incumbent party in developed countries lost vote share.[40]

REALITY PROBLEMS: IMMIGRATION AND CRIME

During the 2020 campaign, Biden vehemently denounced Trump's immigration policies. "Parents were ripped—their kids were ripped from their arms and separated," Biden said at their final debate. "And now they cannot find over 500 sets of those parents and those kids are alone. Nowhere to go, nowhere to go. It's criminal. It's criminal."[41] After becoming president, he reversed Trump's toughest restrictions and halted the construction of new border barriers between the United States and Mexico. After a COVID-19 lull, encounters between migrants and Border Patrol agents surged to record levels. In the 2022 fiscal year, there were more than 2.4 million encounters, and in the following fiscal year, there would be 2.5 million.[42] Some voters worried about harsh conditions confronting asylum seekers, while others feared an alien "invasion." Either way, voters doubted that the federal government was doing a good job with it.[43] Early on, Biden declared that Harris would be the administration's point person on immigration. Aides sought to temper the announcement with the caveat that her role would be primarily diplomatic, aimed at the "root causes" of migration.[44] Harris led a diplomatic mission to persuade Mexico and several Central American nations to stem the flow of migrants. The mission was largely symbolic, but it would later provide Republicans with an opening to tag her as a "failed border czar."[45]

Throughout 2023, the southern border continued to radiate pain. According to unofficial estimates, officials processed 302,000 migrants in December—the most ever.[46] The surge strained communities in the Southwest, and Texas governor Greg Abbott sought to export some of the hardship by transporting migrants to cities such as Chicago and New York. Florida governor Ron DeSantis piled on, sending a planeload of migrants to the posh precincts of Martha's Vineyard, home to Barack Obama's seafront mansion. Critics accused the governors of using migrants as political pawns, but they had some success in upending the political chessboard. Northern Democratic leaders started acknowledging the problem. "I hope Democrats can understand that it isn't xenophobic to be concerned about the border," said Senator John Fetterman (D-PA). "It's a reasonable conversation, and Democrats should engage."[47]

Seeing that his previous position on the border carried serious political risk and little benefit, Biden did engage. His aides worked with a bipartisan group of senators to produce what he said would "be the toughest and fairest set of reforms to secure the border we've ever had in our country."[48] Under the bill, asylum officers would decide on the asylum cases of migrants at the border, applying a higher standard of proof in the initial screening. Once illegal crossings reached a certain level, the Department of Homeland Security would have to bar migrants, except unaccompanied minors, from crossing the border between ports of entry. Unwilling to let Biden score a victory that might help his election prospects, Trump posted his opposition: "This Bill is a great gift to the Democrats, and a Death Wish for The Republican Party."[49] Following Trump's lead, and perhaps unconvinced Biden would enforce the new provisions any more rigorously than he was enforcing existing law, most Senate Republicans came out against it, and the bill died. In the spring of 2024, Biden issued a proclamation limiting asylum processing at the border with Mexico. By August, CBP recorded 58,038 migrant encounters at the border, down 77 percent from December 2023. From a policy standpoint, the move apparently was a qualified success, though it also seemed to demonstrate that lax executive enforcement had indeed been the biggest problem all along. But the policy shift may have come too late to register with the general public. The administration did not have a satisfying answer to the obvious question: why did they wait so long?

From the day he rode the golden escalator in 2015, Trump had linked illegal immigration to crime. The available evidence is mixed on the proposition that undocumented immigrants are more likely to commit crimes than citizens.[50] But a third of Americans—and two-thirds of Republicans—believe it, so it is part of the broader national conversation about crime.[51] When migrants were accused of a parade of high-profile crimes, such as the murder of nursing student Laken Riley in Georgia, the proposition gained credibility.

And that conversation was getting intense. Television news aired disturbing footage of smash-and-grab robberies and interviews with people afraid to go out at night. As defenders of the administration were quick to note, crime rates were far below the levels of the early 1990s, and an FBI report later showed that reported violent crime ticked downward in 2023.[52] Dismissing fear of crime as a partisan delusion would be a mistake, however. The Bureau of Justice Statistics (BJS) found that the violent victimization rate increased in 2022, and though it declined slightly in 2023, it was still above the 2020 level.[53] Whereas the FBI data came from police reports, BJS relied on a household survey. The latter might have picked up on crimes that victims had not reported to the police. Voters had reasons to worry about crime, a problem for the administration. After George Floyd's death in 2020, some prominent Democrats got attention for their calls to "defund the police." Despite President Biden's calls to "fund the police," Democrats continued to suffer political damage from the earlier remarks.

REALITY PROBLEMS: FOREIGN POLICY

Foreign policy seldom moves public opinion. It did so in 2021. To end American engagement in Afghanistan, the Trump administration had reached a deal with the Taliban—but not the Afghan government—to withdraw all U.S. forces. Biden announced that he would complete the withdrawal by summer. The result was chaos. The Taliban took over so fast that the United States could not evacuate all the Afghan people who helped American forces. On August 16, Biden admitted: "This did unfold more quickly than we had anticipated. So what's happened? Afghanistan political leaders gave up and fled the country. The Afghan military collapsed, sometimes without trying to fight."[54] Disastrous elements of the episode included $7 billion of military equipment left behind, televised pictures of desperate Afghans falling from American transport planes leaving the country, a late terror bombing that left 13 Marines dead, and at least a few thousand American citizens reportedly left behind to fend for themselves.[55] Some indications also leaked out that Biden had pushed the military to withdraw on a faster timetable against warnings from his generals.[56]

Democrats sought to blame Trump, noting that his withdrawal deal included the release of thousands of Taliban fighters, but the general public held the incumbent administration accountable for the final call to withdraw and the implementation. In a YouGov survey late in August of 2021, two-thirds of respondents said that the withdrawal had gone badly, and of those who gave that answer, two-thirds blamed Biden.[57] In closed-door meetings, Harris reportedly had serious questions about the withdrawal, but in keeping with vice presidential custom, she publicly supported the president's policy.[58]

In the month after the fall of Afghanistan, Biden's Gallup approval rating dropped six points.[59] Later that year, the nonprofit group More in Common surveyed veterans and nonveterans about the withdrawal.[60] The survey found that 37 percent of all Americans and 49 percent of all veterans felt "betrayed" by the outcome. Specifically among veterans of Afghanistan, that figure was 73 percent. Political scientist William Galston, a Marine Corps veteran, wrote of the survey: "As we saw in the late 1970s, similar sentiments about the end of the war in Vietnam had a powerful impact on our politics, beginning with a pervasive sense of American decline and ending with the election of a president in 1980 who was determined to reverse this decline and who campaigned on the slogan `Let's Make America Great Again.'"[61]

When it came to Ukraine, the political story was more muddled. Thanks to aid from the United States and its allies, which began under Trump and expanded significantly under Biden, Ukraine was surprisingly effective in fighting the Russian invasion that started in February 2022. From the Democrats' political viewpoint, the war was an averted disaster. Though support for Ukraine did not immediately boost the administration's political standing, a successful Russian blitz would have undercut it by fostering perceptions of American weakness and disarray. Instead, criticism fell on Donald Trump, who initially called the invasion a "genius move." Over time, as the war dragged on without a Ukrainian victory, opinion began to polarize. Though Democrats continued to support American military aid to Ukraine, Republicans increasingly became divided. The percentage of Republicans saying that the United States was providing too much support rose from 9 percent in March 2022 to 49 percent in April 2024.[62]

On October 7, 2023, Hamas and affiliated terrorist organizations broke out of Gaza to launch a surprise attack on Israel, murdering hundreds of civilians, taking hundreds more as hostages, and committing brutal acts of torture and rape. The administration declared support for Israel, and at first, most Americans seemed to agree. Israel then launched a massive counterattack against Hamas, which operated from tunnels beneath densely populated areas. Thousands of civilians lost their lives. As the death toll mounted, Democrats increasingly voiced doubts about the American position. One survey finding was especially ominous for Biden's electoral prospects: among Democrats under 30, disapproval of Biden's response to the war outweighed approval by 50–21 percent.[63] Democrats had previously relied on support from this age-group, and they worried that the war might lead some younger voters to stay home or support third-party candidates. In Michigan and other key states, Muslim and Arab American voters made up a small but potentially pivotal voting bloc. In a close election, they potentially stood to make a difference.

REALITY PROBLEMS: AGE AND INFIRMITY

In November 2023, President Biden celebrated his 81st birthday, and three-quarters of adults said he was too old to serve effectively for a second term.[64] His verbal and physical stumbles had become the stuff of comedy routines and social media memes. Some of his critics openly warned that he was already incapacitated. His supporters brushed off such concerns, pointing out that FDR had won World War II in a wheelchair. Behind the partisan rhetoric was an uncomfortable question: even if he were still mentally competent in 2024, what would be like a year or two later? Whether spoken or unspoken, this question hung over the electorate. Most adults have dealt with aging family members who declined like a Hemingway character went bankrupt: gradually, then suddenly.

Things changed suddenly on June 27, 2024. President Biden had challenged Donald Trump to the earliest-ever general election debate, hoping to shift the "narrative" of the campaign. He had assumed that a television matchup would help him by reminding voters what they disliked about his predecessor. The move backfired. From the moment Biden shuffled onto the stage, it was clear he would have a bad night. His voice was weak and hoarse, and many of his comments seemed disjointed. Even the split-screen reaction shots worked against him: his slack-jawed expression made him look like a lost old man as he listened to Trump.

After the debate, his supporters said that judging him by a single poor performance was unfair. The defense rang hollow. At 81, he had been showing signs of decline throughout the campaign, and the news media reported that his staff had covered for him.[65] A reasonable person could conclude that leading figures in the administration and Congress had failed to level with the American people about his condition. This perception played into a broader distrust of elites. For many, it was another sign that the political establishment was rife with double-talk, cover-up, and conspiracy. Naturally, Team Trump seized the opportunity. "The biggest hoax in history has been exposed," said Trump aide Stephen Miller. "Anybody who's anybody in the Democratic Party participated in, knew of and covered up Biden's cognitive dysfunction while allowing secret unnamed staffers to run the country." Vivek Ramaswamy, who ran a Trump-friendly campaign for the nomination before endorsing the 45th president, added the press to the mix: "I think now this will go down as another journalistic failure that has betrayed the public by running interference for Biden [and] obfuscating the truth that the man is in what appears to be severe cognitive decline."[66]

Biden tried to hang on for a while. He sat for media interviews, which elicited such faint praise as "not as bad as the debate." He selectively pointed to polls showing that his candidacy had not yet crashed, like a pilot telling passengers to ignore the smoke billowing from the engines because the plane is still aloft. Democratic politicians feared that Biden would have more senior moments in the future. On July 21, after internal polls showed that he was indeed crashing, he withdrew from the race and endorsed Vice President Kamala Harris as the Democratic nominee for president.

Under the circumstances, the disastrous early debate may have been the best thing that could have happened to the Democratic Party. If Biden had waited until autumn to debate Trump, his performance might have been as shaky. At that point, ballot deadlines would have passed in many states, making it practically impossible to switch candidates. Although a deeply polarized nation would not have given Trump the 49-state sweep that Nixon and Reagan enjoyed in their reelection campaigns, he would have been on track to win a much larger share of the popular and electoral vote than he actually did. Even before the debate fiasco, Biden seemed likely to lose.[67] After the debate, "likely" became "certain." Through the Republican convention, the Trump team had been supremely confident of victory and looked forward to trampling the elderly incumbent along the way back to the White House. At one point, the PredictIt betting market reported that a contract for a Trump victory cost $0.67, suggesting that he had a 67 percent chance of winning. Biden traded at $0.27.[68]

By not pulling out later than he did, Biden enabled Harris to lock up the nomination weeks before the party convention. (Chapter 4 will explore her quick victory in greater detail.) Journalist J. V. Last expressed hope that bypassing the primary route would benefit Harris and her party: "One of Harris's many advantages in this particular moment is that she doesn't need to manage a startup this time. She has been given the keys to a mature business. Meaning that she is freed to leverage her strengths."[69] Even at the start of the campaign, however, there were signs of tension and discord within the hybrid organization. After the election, Harris loyalists and Biden loyalists blamed each other for mistakes, and some Democrats suggested that Biden's withdrawal gave the Democrats an opportunity that they squandered by picking Harris.

And by not pulling out sooner—say, in mid-2023—Biden prevented Democrats from using the regular nominating process. Since 1972, every previous party nominee had come through the primaries and caucuses. A Biden withdrawal in 2023 would have triggered a multicandidate primary contest, which could have been divisive and expensive. Harris might not have survived it at all: her 2020 presidential campaign was an ill-managed mess that ended before the first primary. Democrats might have ended up with a candidate who would have won—or would have lost by a bigger margin.

In any event, the late switch caught the Trump campaign by surprise. For years, it had been planning to run against an elderly incumbent. Now, it had to run against an energetic vice president who was 18 years younger than Trump. Once Harris was in the race and doing well in the polls, Trump recognized his problem with Biden's withdrawal: "You know he wanted to debate," Trump said during an August 9 speech in Montana. "If we didn't have a debate, he'd still be there. Can you imagine? Why the hell did I debate him?"[70]

Harris's abrupt elevation seemed to elated Democrats to be a game-changer, but she was far from a sure winner. Very little was sure about the election.

AN ELECTION UNLIKE ANY OTHER

In hindsight, it might seem obvious that the fundamentals of the election doomed Harris's candidacy right from the start. Americans disapproved of the incumbent president's performance and overwhelmingly believed that the country was on the wrong track. By fall, Republicans had pulled ahead of Democrats in Gallup's measure of party identification.[71] Yet right until Election Day, many astute American political observers thought the race was a toss-up. A close look at the returns shows that this belief was hardly far-fetched. As noted at the beginning of this chapter, the aggregate national vote was quite close. Trump carried the battleground states of Pennsylvania, Michigan, Wisconsin, and Georgia by less than 3 percent. A relatively small shift—within he polling margin of error—would have changed the outcome.

There was good reason to be uncertain about polling data. Under the best conditions, any survey has a statistical margin of error (MOE), but the 2024 election did not present the best conditions. For decades, pollsters could get reasonably good samples via telephone using random-digit dialing. With the rise of smartphones and call screening, fewer and fewer Americans answered when pollsters called. By 2023, response rates had plummeted to low single digits.[72] Survey researchers tried to compensate by using online surveys, which involved severe challenges in reaching representative samples. (Not everybody is online all the time.) Surveys remained helpful in getting a broad sense of public opinion, but they were increasingly prob-lematic as a way of figuring out what would happen in a tightly contested election. On social media, Harry Enten of CNN posted this frank assessment of election polls in 2024: "I'm not being too revolutionary here. . . . The true margin of error is wider than I fear a lot of folks think it is. . . . It's much wider than the reported MOE given that only covers certain types of error. Anything from a very clear Trump to a very clear Harris win is on the table."[73]

Journalists, scholars, and pundits have sought to find historical patterns in presidential elections, but aside from the closeness of 21st-century contests, it was not clear how these patterns would work out in 2024. In several ways, this election was like no other.

The incumbent party's record looms large in most analyses, but what happens when the challenger was the incumbent just four years earlier? That situation had happened only twice. In 1892, Democratic Grover Cleveland reclaimed the White House from Republican Benjamin Harrison, who had won the electoral vote (though not the aggregated popular vote) in 1888. (Trump supporters took heart from the Cleveland comparison, but skeptics noted an important difference: whereas Cleveland had won the popular vote twice before his third try, Trump had lost it twice.) In 1912, Theodore Roosevelt ran as a Progressive against his Republican successor, William Howard Taft. Democrat Woodrow Wilson benefited from the party split and came out on top. These races happened long before modern public opinion polls, in circumstances radically different from the 2024 election. In neither case was there a global pandemic that spanned both administrations and killed a million Americans.

The idea of incumbency is even murkier when the nominee is the sitting vice president, who inherits much of the president's support and opposition but has no independent power to make policy. Over the previous hundred years, there had been only four such cases. Richard Nixon (1960) and Hubert Humphrey (1968) both lost, albeit by tight margins in the aggregated popular vote. George H. W. Bush (1988) won healthy majorities in both columns. Al Gore (2000) narrowly lost the electoral vote while winning a thin popular vote plurality. And Biden's publicly cordial (albeit reluctant) handoff to Vice President Harris was unique in the modern era. Not since Rutherford B. Hayes declined to run in 1880 had an elected president stepped aside after serving only four years.[74]

Accordingly, Harris and Trump each ran as the candidate of "change" against "more of the same." Harris promised to bring "a new way forward, and turn the page on the last decade of what I believe has been contrary to where the spirit of our country really lies."[75] Trump posted at his social media site: "Kamala and her 'handlers' are trying to make it sound like I am the Incumbent President, so that they can blame me for the failure of the past four years. No, it was their failure! It is one of the worst Presidencies in History, and she is definitely the Worst Vice President."[76] One problem for Trump was that his surrogates routinely referred to him as "the president," without the word *former.* He also tried to take maximum advantage of his quasi-incumbency during the Republican primaries before shifting gears.

Nevertheless, as we shall see, Trump's record—especially his handling of the pandemic—did not weigh heavily on the voters' minds.

In the past half-century, presidential aspirants had typically announced their candidacy at least a year in advance. That schedule gave them ample time to develop policy agendas and define themselves in front of the national electorate. That opportunity was particularly important for incumbent vice presidents Bush and Gore, who needed to demonstrate that they were more than extensions of their predecessors. Kamala Harris had exactly 107 days between her announcement and Election Day. The unusually short runway was both an asset and a liability for Harris. On the one hand, it prevented GOP opposition researchers from doing a more thorough dissection of the Harris record. Republicans worried that the short campaign would allow her to make it to Election Day without undergoing full scrutiny. On the other hand, it did not give her sufficient time to separate herself from the unpopular Biden. A sympathetic host on a television show asked her whether she would have "done something differently" than Biden. "There is not a thing that comes to mind," she said.[77] The remarks went viral. One should not ascribe too much significance to a single remark, but her failure to give a better answer was a sign of her inability to shake Biden's bad mojo. A more extended campaign would have given her time to develop talking points that stressed her independence without alienating Biden loyalists.

In previous presidential elections, voters did not have to ponder a candidate's rap sheet. In 2024, one candidate's record included a civil judgment of fraud, civil verdicts of sexual abuse and defamation, two impeachments, four criminal indictments, and a criminal conviction. Years earlier, one would have assumed such things to be disadvantages. In the 1988 campaign, Senator Gary Hart had to withdraw from the Democratic nomination contest merely because of a consensual affair with a grown woman. In 2000, George W. Bush lost his edge in the popular vote after the revelation of an old drunk-driving arrest. In 2024, Trump used his legal woes as a badge of honor and a fundraising tool. Republicans rallied behind him because they saw the charges as politically motivated and because they thought the alternative was worse.

By the end of July 2024, the alternative was a woman of Black and Asian ancestry. Race and gender do have some impact on vote choice, but once again, the number of cases is too small for generalizations. Barack Obama was the only other Black nominee, and Hillary Clinton was the only woman. There had never previously been a nominee with roots in India. Obama and Clinton both won the aggregated popular vote, and Gallup data shows that most Americans say they are willing to vote for a Black or female candidate.[78] But Gallup did not ask about voting for an Asian candidate, much less someone with all three identities. There was no track record to show how her unique background would affect voter support.

And to top it off, there had never been a presidential race in which a major-party nominee survived assassination attempts so close to the election. The nearest analogue is the October 1912 shooting of Theodore Roosevelt, running as the Progressive Party candidate. (His wound was not life-threatening, and he proceeded to deliver his scheduled speech.) Luck was with Trump the first time, as the bullet merely grazed his ear and a photographer caught him defiantly raising his clenched fist. Would the incidents affect public perceptions of Trump? Anxious Democratic operatives thought back to 1981, when Reagan's near-death experience at the hands of a would-be assassin measurably bolstered his standing with the public. After the Trump shooting, polls showed only a slight increase in his favorability ratings. Perhaps more important, however, 51 percent of Republicans said that Biden and Democrats were very responsible for the shooting and 49 percent said the same about left-leaning media.[79] The assassination attempt did not transform Trump's public image, but it deepened existing partisan divisions.

Abortion was another question mark. Most of the time, Americans know little about specific decisions of the Supreme Court. *Roe v. Wade* was different. In an open-ended question, a 2022 survey asked Americans if they could name a Supreme Court decision. With 40 percent, the most common answer was *Roe*. In second place, with just 6 percent, was *Brown v. Board of Education*.[80] Ever since the decision, Americans had been ambivalent about abortion policy. On the one hand, they were deeply troubled by abortion and favored certain restrictions and regulations. On the other hand, most supported the decision and opposed a blanket ban on abortion.[81] Under Ronald Reagan, George H. W. Bush, and George W. Bush, Democrats warned that the end of *Roe* was nigh. As the decades passed and the precedent survived, the warnings seemed to have limited effect. An informed voter could assume that the pro-lifers could not go further than curbing abortion at the margins. As for pro-life rhetoric about reversing *Roe* and banning abortion, pro-choice voters could shrug it off as performative rhetoric for the GOP base—the equivalent of shooting blanks on a movie set.

But after *Dobbs*, the gun was loaded.

As we shall see in chapter 6, the issue helped Democrats in the 2022 midterm election, even though they lost their narrow majority in the House. In the year after the midterm, the issue continued to work in their favor. When a 2023 KFF poll asked respondents which party best represents their views of abortion, Democrats came out ahead, 42–26 percent.[82] In November 2023, 57 percent of Ohio voters approved a ballot measure establishing a state constitutional right to "make and carry out one's own reproductive decisions," including decisions about abortion. It was striking that the measure passed by such a large margin in a state that Trump had won in 2020 with 53 percent of the vote. It was not the only straw in the wind. Ever since the *Dobbs* decision, voters in California, Kansas, Kentucky, Michigan, Montana, and Vermont either supported measures to secure abortion access or blocked attempts to curb it.[83] Democrats hoped the issue would have a significant impact in 2024, especially with a woman at the top of the ticket. In the end, though, *Dobbs* did not push Harris across the finish line.

In the chapters ahead, we shall discuss these policy issues and political uncertainties. The 2024 election will have profound consequences for American history, and the story of how the Republicans triumphed deserves detailed attention. And there is more to that story than the price of eggs.

Chapter 2

Biden, Harris, and the Democrats

When President Biden announced his withdrawal from the race, many commentators compared him to Lyndon Johnson in 1968. But the two cases were quite different, illustrating the evolution of American politics in the intervening 56 years. LBJ did not "quit" the race, because he did not join it in the first place. Although the political community assumed he would run, he neither declared his candidacy nor formed a reelection committee. He did not even file in the New Hampshire primary. Write-in votes gave him a victory in the state, but Senator Eugene McCarthy's unexpectedly strong showing convinced him that he would have to fight for the nomination. Exhausted from the Vietnam War and worried that his health would fail, he did not have the stomach for such a fight, especially after his longtime nemesis Robert F. Kennedy got into the race.

Kennedy made his announcement on March 16, 1968. In the 21st century, it would be nearly impossible for a major candidate to enter primaries that late. Changes in the nomination process and the immense increase in the cost of campaigning meant that candidates now had to build their organizations and raise their money years in advance. Biden formally announced his reelection bid on April 25, 2023, and had been informally building toward it long before.

Like Vice President Kamala Harris, Vice President Hubert Humphrey became the Democratic Party's nominee after the incumbent president stepped aside. In 1968, relatively few states had primaries or open caucuses; elsewhere, state and local party leaders chose the delegates. Most of those leaders lined up behind Humphrey, guaranteeing him the party's nomination even though he did not enter any primaries. Nevertheless, Humphrey had a rough ride. McCarthy and Kennedy continued to campaign, and after the latter's assassination, Senator George McGovern served as a stand-in candidate for Kennedy delegates. Disorder erupted inside and outside the convention. Protesters objected both to Humphrey's support of the Vietnam War and the purportedly undemocratic means by which he secured the nomination. Humphrey began his campaign by proclaiming "the politics of joy," a phrase that sounded discordant during a year of assassinations, riots, and mounting war deaths.

Though Harris, too, won the nomination despite having entered and won no primaries, she had an easier time. Biden's abrupt withdrawal came as a huge relief to Democrats who were fearing a Trump rout. Harris's candidacy threw them a lifeline, and they did not want to wait for a better rescuer. Accordingly, Harris enjoyed overwhelming support from Democratic office-holders and voters.[1] More generally, the electorate had dreaded a rerun election between two old men, one stumbling and one snarling. Many welcomed the option of voting for a woman who was younger (albeit nearing age 60) and exuberant. As in 1968, the Democratic convention was in Chicago, but there were no major riots in the city's streets.

In one way, the 1968 race did foreshadow the future of the Democratic Party. Humphrey represented the party's past, the old New Deal coalition of big-city organizations and industrial labor unions. His opponents for the nomination represented what the party would become. Kennedy appealed to Black and Hispanic voters, though neither yet had the numbers or influence they would gain over the next several decades. McCarthy was the candidate of white college-educated professionals who lived in cities and suburbs. This group would also loom larger over the years. In 1968, only about 10 percent of Americans over age 25 had a college degree, a population share that would nearly quadruple by 2020.[2]

That year, Biden made himself acceptable to the Democratic coalition of the 21st century. But why did he run again four years later?

WHY BIDEN RAN

Did President Biden think that he could convince voters that he could serve effectively until age 86? Though Biden seemed humble in comparison with Donald Trump, he did have a big ego. After all, no one runs for president three times over 32 years without immense self-confidence. He also had a long record of defying expectations. In 1972, when he was 29, he defeated an incumbent United States senator. In 2020, after he lost the Iowa caucuses and the New Hampshire primary, most of the political community wrote him off as an aging has-been. As we described in *Divided We Stand*, he then scored an astounding comeback in South Carolina and swept to the nomination in a matter of weeks. He was proud that he beat Trump that year and believed he

been in the game
for a long time

was the only one who could do it in 2024. At a Massachusetts campaign stop, he said: "Folks, this is a big deal, this election. We've got to get it done—not because of me, and I mean that. If Trump wasn't running, I'm not sure I'd be running. But we cannot let him win, for the sake of the country."[3]

Despite all the dangers besetting Biden, one warning light did not turn red: a significant intraparty challenge. Since the 1960s, every incumbent president who faced a serious primary opponent either opted out of the race (Johnson in 1968) or lost the general election (Ford in 1976, Carter in 1980, Bush in 1992). In 2024, Robert F. Kennedy Jr. briefly mounted a primary challenge. Mostly because of his famous name, he attracted national attention and got about 19 percent support in early surveys of Democrats.[4] That share was also his ceiling. His strange beliefs kept him from expanding his base of support in the party. (Among other things, he said: "COVID-19 is targeted to attack Caucasians and black people. The people who are most immune are Ashkenazi Jews and Chinese."[5]) As we shall note in chapter 5, he dropped out of the primary campaign to pursue an independent candidacy. He later ended that effort and endorsed Trump.

Marianne Williamson, often described as a "new age guru," ran for the second election in a row, with no better luck. Businessman Jason Palmer also ran, gaining a smattering of votes here and there and winning the low-turnout Democratic caucuses in American Samoa (with 51 total votes to Biden's 40).

Biden's nearest rival was Representative Dean Phillips (D-MN), whose quixotic campaign ended in early March after netting four delegates. Despite posing little threat to Biden, Phillips did expose some warning signs for the president. The obscure Minnesotan won nearly 20 percent of the vote in New Hampshire, where Biden ran a write-in campaign, and 13 percent in Ohio. After Phillips withdrew on March 6, Democratic primary voters in 14 states had the option of voting for uncommitted delegates. On average, 1 in 10 of them did so. In four primaries (New Hampshire, Maine, New York, and West Virginia), more than 10 percent voted for a variety of other options that were on the ballot. Nevertheless, whatever discontent might have been simmering below the surface, no major Democratic figure arose to channel it.

Biden's free ride is a bit of a puzzle. Political weakness typically draws the attention of ambitious rivals, and Biden was undoubtedly vulnerable. In late 2023, a CBS poll found that 39 percent of Democrats thought he should not run for reelection.[6] Starting with his age, the incumbent had a chum bucket full of problems, so why were there no sharks in the Democratic waters?

None of his rivals from 2020 were in a good position to challenge him in 2024. Biden had named Kamala Harris as his running mate and Pete Buttigieg as Secretary of Transportation. It would have been strange for either one to turn on their patron. Senators Cory Booker, Elizabeth Warren, and Amy Klobuchar saw their 2020 campaigns fizzle without any primary victories.

The same was true of former New York mayor Michael Bloomberg, whose lavishly financed effort only went to show that money cannot always buy voter love.[7] Tulsi Gabbard left the party and became a commentator on Fox News—the ultimate bridge-burning for a onetime progressive. The last man standing in 2020 was Vermont senator Bernie Sanders, who was a year older than Biden—and looked it. The final debate between the two was a low-key, civil exchange, and after winning the presidency, Biden made a point of strengthening his relationship with his former Senate colleague. In 2023, Sanders announced that he would support Biden, arguing that Democratic disunity could lead to a Trump victory. He told AP: "The last thing this country needs is a Donald Trump or some other right-wing demagogue who is going to try to undermine American democracy or take away a woman's right to choose, or not address the crisis of gun violence, or racism, sexism or homophobia."[8]

Aside from Democratic fears of Trump and the personal characteristics of potential candidates, there was another reason why Biden got a pass. The candidates who mounted significant challenges all had major policy differences with the incumbent:

- In 1968, Eugene McCarthy and Robert Kennedy opposed Lyndon Johnson over the Vietnam War.
- In 1976, Ronald Reagan broke with Gerald Ford over Cold War policy and the Panama Canal treaty.
- In 1980, Edward Kennedy fought with Jimmy Carter over various domestic policies, especially national health insurance.
- In 1992, Pat Buchanan ran on an "America First" platform, attacking George H. W. Bush over trade, immigration, and foreign policy.

It would be hard to identify many top-ranking Democratic figures who had such stark differences with Biden. Governors Gavin Newsom of California and Gretchen Whitmer of Michigan, who had often come up as future contenders, were vocal defenders of the incumbent. Among Democratic senators, all but one voted with Biden at least 94 percent of the time in 2023.[9] The one outlier was Joe Manchin of West Virginia, who supported Biden's position 87 percent of the time and announced his retirement a year ahead of the election.

Some left-wing House members did disagree with Biden on important issues, especially the Middle East. Their chamber is a poor launching pad for a presidential race: the last member to succeed was James A. Garfield in 1880. House members usually have a lower national profile than senators or governors and thus have a harder time raising the money necessary for a national campaign. In the Internet age, a handful have achieved attention, but usually for scandal or outlandish behavior. One exception might have caused problems for Biden: Alexandria Ocasio-Cortez (D-NY). She was young (barely meeting the constitutional age requirement of 35 in October 2024), telegenic, and passionate in her commitment to democratic socialism. Most of all, she had a national base: in 2024, she had 13 million followers on X/ Twitter and was the tenth most popular Democrat in a YouGov survey.[10] Like her mentor Bernie Sanders, however, she endorsed Biden, worried that a fight over the nomination would guarantee Trump's election. She said, "this question is larger than any policy differences. This is truly about having a strong front against fascism in the United States."[11]

Dean Phillips, who had no major policy disagreements with Biden, tried to raise the age issue. He told Axios: "At that stage of life, it is impossible ultimately to conduct, to prosecute the office of the American presidency in the way that this country in the world needs right now. That is an absolute truth."[12] In early 2024, that message struck no sparks with primary electorates. Democratic politicians and voters worried about Biden's age and reelection prospects, but he remained their default option. The story of how he got there—and why Kamala Harris was in the wings to take his place—is about the evolution of the Democratic Party.

RACE, ETHNICITY, AND GENDER

On Fox News in 2006, Chris Wallace asked Biden about his candidacy for the 2008 Democratic presidential nomination: "Thirty seconds or less, what kind of a chance would a Northeastern liberal like Joe Biden stand in the South if you were running in Democratic primaries against Southerners like Mark Warner and John Edwards?" Biden answered: "Better than anybody else. You don't know my state. My state was a slave state. My state is a border state. My state has the eighth-largest black population in the country. My state is anything from a Northeast liberal state."[13]

On the one hand, the remarks illustrated Biden's penchant for gaffes: by the 21st century, it was odd for Democratic politicians to boast that they came from a slave state. On the other hand, it also was a sign of his party's complicated history with race and the South. From Reconstruction until the middle of the 20th century, the South was the cornerstone of the Democratic coalition. With near-total control of the region's state governments and congressional seats, white Southern Democrats had disproportionate influence over their party's national policies, especially on civil rights. Despite Democratic majorities in Congress and personal sympathy for the plight of Black Americans, Franklin Roosevelt faced severe political constraints on what he could do for them. Harry Truman desegregated the armed forces but could not get civil rights legislation through Congress. Then things changed. Both as Senate majority leader in the 1950s and president in the 1960s, Lyndon Johnson successfully challenged the power of his fellow Southern Democrats and won enactment of laws that did much to end segregation and secure political rights.

The Voting Rights Act of 1965 enlarged the Black electorate and started decades of transition for the party. Some segregationist Democrats, such as Senator Robert Byrd of West Virginia, changed their position. Over time, others stepped down, and newer generations of Democratic lawmakers put the party's segregationist legacy behind them.

Amid this transition came Senator Biden. As a mainstream liberal with national ambitions, he generally supported civil rights. But as a lawmaker from a border state where many white voters favored a "go slow" approach, he opposed racial-balance busing for public schools. By the early years of the 21st century, court decisions had ended busing, and Biden was in tune with the party's civil rights positions. In 2008, he became Barack Obama's running mate, which cemented his bond with Black voters. "Among older African American voters, Biden's loyalty to the country's first black president is a key factor in their support," said NPR reporter Asma Khalid. "And it's why there's such a willingness to forgive and defend him."[14]

Support from Black Democrats was crucial to his victory in the 2020 primaries. Between 1992 and 2016, the Democratic presidential nominee had always been the candidate who got a majority of the Black vote in the primaries.[15] After Biden lost badly in Iowa and New Hampshire, many observers thought he was a goner. But he won the crucial endorsement of Representative James Clyburn, a civil rights icon in South Carolina. That endorsement enabled him to triumph in the state's primary, where most Democratic voters were Black. It was the first time he had ever won a primary in his three presidential campaigns. The dynamics of the nomination race abruptly changed, and he swept most of the remaining contests.

The Black vote was also crucial in the general election, as Biden stressed in a 2024 post on X: "Folks, if anyone is wondering whether your vote matters, remember this. Because Black Americans voted, I am president, Kamala Harris is a historic vice president, and Donald Trump is a loser."[16] Whites voted for Trump 58–41 percent. Biden won the overall popular vote with overwhelming majorities among Black, Hispanic, and Asian voters.[17] That result fit the pattern of the 21st century: in every election since 2000, white voters had supported the Republican candidate by double-digit margins.[18] Although Hillary Clinton won the popular vote in 2016, key states saw a decline in Black turnout, contributing to her defeat in the electoral vote.[19]

Like other national Democrats, Biden was acutely aware of his political debt to Black voters. During a South Carolina debate in the 2020 campaign, he made a pledge that helped him win Clyburn's support: "We talked about the Supreme Court. I'm looking forward to making sure there's a Black woman on the Supreme Court, to make sure we in fact get every representation."[20] As president, he kept that promise by nominating Ketanji Brown Jackson to succeed Justice Stephen Breyer. Even more important, he chose Kamala Harris as his running mate. Early in 2024, the White House published a long list of policy initiatives and accomplishments for Black Americans.[21]

A midyear Ipsos survey asked Black registered voters whom they would "definitely" or "probably" vote for.[22] For Biden, the good news was that he led Trump 74–14 percent. The bad news was that, compared with the same period in the 2020 campaign, there was a drop-off in the number of respondents who planned to vote. The decline was especially significant among younger Black voters, who disapproved of his job performance. A Pew poll suggested an explanation: more Black voters placed their priority on education and the economy than race-specific matters.[23] Apparently, post-COVID-19 problems with inflation and learning loss were weighing down Black voter enthusiasm. Moreover, the 2020 election had shown a noticeable shift to the GOP.[24] A significant share of Black voters held conservative views on immigration, crime, and other domestic issues. Democratic rhetoric about the civil rights era had a diminishing impact on Black voters born after the 1960s.

Among other demographic groups, policy positions aiming to benefit Black Americans potentially entailed a political cost. In June 2023, Biden denounced a Supreme Court decision against affirmative action in college admissions: "Today, the Court once again walked away from decades of precedent and by making our schools less diverse, this ruling will harm the educational experience for all students. . . . I strongly—strongly disagree with the Court's decision."[25] In an unusual move for a vice president, Harris issued her own statement: "By making our schools less diverse, this ruling will harm the educational experience for all students."[26] A Gallup survey found that most American adults thought the decision was "mostly a good thing," including 72 percent of whites, 68 percent of Hispanics, and 63 percent of Asians.[27] Black respondents were about evenly divided. Biden suggested that he would try to achieve affirmative action goals by other means. Survey analyst Eli Yokley cautioned: "But elevating the issue is not without electoral risks in 2024 given that roughly half of the electorate (51%)—including 52% of white voters and more Black voters than not (45% to 38%)—believe that race-conscious affirmative action is unfair to a majority of students."[28]

A similar dilemma stemmed from Biden's approach to Hispanic voters, who had supported him 65–32 percent in 2020.[29] Even as some Democrats started to get cold feet after the debate with Trump, the campaign arm of the Congressional Hispanic Caucus endorsed Biden. Hispanic voters were less eager. Though they tended to favor less stringent immigration policies than other groups, a majority still thought that the government was doing a poor job at the border.[30] In any case, Democratic strategists were erring if they thought that immigration was the dominant issue for Hispanic citizens. When a survey for UnidosUS and Mi Familia Vota asked Hispanic voters to name the most important issues elected officials should address, the top answers were inflation, the economy, health care, crime, and housing. Immigration ranked *sixth*.[31]

"Democrats cannot conceive that non-white voters are anything other than civil rights voters," political consultant Mike Madrid told Axios. "In their mind, all Latinos need to be talked to like farmworkers or the undocumented."[32] More than 70 percent of Hispanic Americans are proficient in English.[33] Among eligible Hispanic voters, U.S.-born citizens outnumber naturalized citizens by three to one.[34] Hispanic voters have diverse backgrounds and perspectives, and a growing number are making economic gains and leaning rightward. A 2023 survey found that 33 percent identified as conservative, up from 28 percent 10 years earlier.[35] And they are far from monolithic on border issues. Pew found an even split on whether making it harder for asylum seekers to gain temporary legal status would make the situation better (29%) or worse (27%).[36]

In 2024, Asian Americans accounted for a smaller share of the electorate (about 6 percent) than Blacks or Hispanics. Most voted Democratic, but in the past, the national party had not placed a high priority on Asian outreach. Most Asian American voters lived in California, New York, Texas, Hawaii, and New Jersey, none of which was a swing state.[37] As a result of the 2020 election, however, the Asian vote got a closer look. Biden carried Georgia by just under 12,000 votes, and strong support from the state's fast-growing Asian population might have provided him with his winning margin. In Georgia's 2022 Senate runoff election, Senator Raphael Warnock's campaign worked hard for Asian American votes, releasing digital ads in Vietnamese, Mandarin, and Korean.[38] An exit poll showed that Warnock carried 78 percent of the Asian vote, contributing to his narrow win over Herschel Walker.[39]

In 2024, Democrats maintained a strong party-identification advantage among Asian Americans, but as with Blacks and Hispanics, there were potential signs of vulnerability. As mentioned earlier, most Asian Americans part company with Democratic leaders by disapproving of affirmative action in college admissions (likely, at least in part because statistics showed that Asian American applicants were disadvantaged by affirmative action policies more than whites).[40] In major cities, perceptions of rising crime nudged some Asian American voters in the GOP's direction.[41] Democrats sought to shore up support by foregrounding Vice President Harris, whose mother was an immigrant from India. Recognizing that Asian Americans could be pivotal in swing states again, she kicked off her Asian outreach efforts in Pennsylvania and Nevada.[42]

In addition to being the first Black and first Asian American vice president, Harris was also the first woman in that role. She served as a leading spokesperson for the administration's message on abortion, hoping to rally women who opposed the *Dobbs* decision. That issue worked to the Democrats' benefit in 2022, but it was hardly the only issue women cared about. Just as Hispanic voters did not put immigration at the top of their concerns, women voters put other issues ahead of abortion. A midyear KFF poll found that only 10 percent of woman said that abortion was the key issue determining their vote behind immigration and threats to democracy. The most frequently mentioned issue, with 40 percent of women respondents, was the one that vexed Democratic politicians the most: inflation.[43]

COLLEGE AND METRO AMERICA

Through the mid-1960s, most political observers assumed that educated and affluent people voted Republican. In his book on the 1968 campaign, however, journalist Theodore H. White wrote of "a new type of affluent American . . . an educated, technically trained elite" that voted differently from gray-flannel men of the 1950s. "Sensitized by the influence media, protected from violence by the suburban belt, aware of a larger world abroad and a crescent scientific world a-borning, they vote as their conditioned intelligence tells them."[44]

What political scientist Ruy Teixeira calls "the Brahmin left"—affluent, educated, liberal, and metropolitan—gradually became a core element of the Democratic Party.[45] In 2020, Biden won a majority of college-educated voters and 62 percent of voters with graduate degrees.[46] While rural voters overwhelmingly supported Trump and suburban voters split about evenly, urban voters broke for Biden 60–38 percent.[47] Of the 10 wealthiest House districts in the 118th Congress, nine elected Democratic representatives.[48] The Democratic leaders of both chambers were from New York City: Senator Charles Schumer (undergraduate and law degrees from Harvard) and Representative Hakeem Jeffries (MPP from Georgetown and law degree from NYU). And much of the party's financial support has come from educated professionals and "knowledge economy" that revolves around technology and intellectual property.[49] Between 2018 and 2022, total contributions to Democratic House and Senate candidates far exceeded those for Republicans.

In the past, a counterweight to this wing would have consisted of union members working in construction and manufacturing. But in 2023, only 10 percent of workers belonged to unions, and nearly half of those were in public-sector jobs. The highest unionization rate (32.7 percent) was among workers in education, training, and library occupations.[50] Of union members in 2021, 46.5 percent had college degrees or more, and their share was growing.[51] In other words, unions spanned the diploma divide.

Lacking a prestigious degree and coming from a border state without big cities, Biden was an outlier among 21st-century Democratic leaders. But as he did with racial minorities and women, Biden strove to appeal to the party's emergent wing of educated professionals. The most obvious (some would say "blatant") example was student debt relief: through various executive actions, the administration sought to cancel billions in loan debt, though the courts struck down one attempt and paused further efforts in the summer of 2024. College-educated Democrats tend to take progressive positions on social and cultural issues, not just those engaging their direct material interest. Biden sought to accommodate these positions as well.[52] Among the diverse provisions of his "Inflation Reduction Act" were a $35-per-month cap on insulin prices, tax breaks to reduce carbon emissions, an extension of Affordable Care Act subsidies, a 15 percent minimum corporate tax, and expanded IRS enforcement. Other liberal initiatives included:

- Setting aggressive goals to reduce emissions of greenhouse gases;
- Signing the first significant gun-control legislation in 30 years;
- Reversing the ban on transgender service members in the military;
- Issuing executive orders to protect access to abortion and contraception;
- Pardoning all prior federal offenses for simple marijuana possession.[53]

Despite misgivings about the administration's support for Israel and its backtracking on immigration, party progressives generally backed Biden until the final days of his candidacy. During those final days, he stepped up his progressive outreach, calling for a ban on assault weapons and proposing legislation to limit rent increases.[54]

Appealing to the educated professionals meant risking support elsewhere in the electorate. One poll found that Biden's student debt policies drew more opposition than support, with about 4 in 10 adults saying it was extremely or very important for the federal government to provide student debt relief, with a similar share saying it was not too important or not important at all.[55] It is easy to see why. Most adults do not have such debt or have already paid it off. Leaving aside the propriety of the president assuming the power of the purse, opponents could cast debt forgiveness as making farmers and bricklayers pay for the education of future doctors and lawyers.

Educated professionals tend to congregate in cities and suburbs, creating physical as well as social distance from rural areas.[56] In recent decades, rural Americans have developed a sense that the Brahmin Democrats treat them as untouchables. To some extent, this perception stemmed from changes in the makeup of national Democratic leadership. Harry Truman, Lyndon Johnson, Jimmy Carter, and Bill Clinton all played up their rural roots. Obama was the first Democratic president of the postwar era, except for JFK, who did not grow up in a rural area. [57] Obama's 2008 campaign hit a rough patch when he spoke of people in declining small towns: "And it's not surprising then they get bitter, they cling to guns or religion or antipathy to people who aren't like them or anti-immigrant sentiment or antitrade sentiment as a way to explain their frustrations."[58] Hillary Clinton and Joe Biden also struggled with rural voters, who saw them as suburbanites.

A similar shift occurred on Capitol Hill. In contrast to the distinctly urban character of recent Democratic leaders, House Speaker Tom Foley (1989–1995) came from rural Washington State, and Senator Tom Daschle (who served as Senate Majority Leader or Minority Leader from 1995 to 2005) represented South Dakota. "Democrats are increasingly perceived as elite and focused almost exclusively on urban matters," Daschle told *The New York Times*. "Rarely do national Democratic candidates spend time in rural America, and that 'flyover' perception continues to increase the perception of this divide."[59]

Much of the problem, however, involves policy. Moving away from fossil fuels is simply common sense to Democratic environmentalists, but it threatens the livelihoods of people who must drive long distances to the nearest town, who work in mining or drilling, or whose job involves diesel-powered equipment. Likewise, Brahmin Democrats tend to see gun control as incontestable and scoff at the idea that firearms provide self-defense. If the nearest sheriff's station is an hour away, however, a handgun can come in handy.

The toxicity of Brahmin Democrats in rural America is a nagging problem for the party. True, Democratic presidential candidates are unlikely to carry Kansas or North Dakota, but party strategists sometimes forget that large industrial states such as Michigan and Pennsylvania have sprawling rural areas. And their residents did believe that the Democrats had forgotten them. In February 2023, a freight train derailment in rural East Palestine, Ohio, caused massive environmental damage. Soon afterward, Trump visited the disaster site with Senator J. D. Vance. Biden did not set foot in East Palestine until a year later. By contrast, it took him only a week to show up at the site of a bridge collapse in Baltimore.

THE RISE OF KAMALA HARRIS

Kamala Harris's path to the 2024 Democratic nomination resulted from circumstance, luck, and skill. In several ways, she embodied the 21st-century

Democratic Party. She was a Black and Asian woman whose parents both had PhDs. (Conservative commentators said that her estranged father was a Marxist economist.[60]) She had built her political base in the San Francisco Bay area—the world capital of the knowledge economy.

Harris started her career as a prosecutor, first in Alameda County, then in San Francisco. Meanwhile, a personal relationship with legendary Assembly Speaker Willie Brown (who was married but separated from his wife at the time) opened doors to future political allies and contributors. Even after their romance ended, he remained a friend and mentor. His help would be valuable during her first campaign, in 2003. Unhappy with incumbent district attorney Terence Hallinan, she switched to the city attorney's office, and then planned to run against her former boss. Brown, now the mayor, quietly persuaded donors to support her, even some who had previously backed Hallinan.[61] Despite Brown's efforts, Harris had a steep climb. She recalled that Hallinan "had a reputation as a fighter; in fact, his nickname was Kayo (as in K.O.)—a tribute to the many knockouts he scored in his boxing youth."[62] In the first round of voting, she edged out another opponent and placed second to Hallinan. She proved to be a remarkably effective candidate in the runoff. She appealed to moderate voters by attacking the liberal incumbent for his low conviction rate and failure to prosecute domestic violence. In an endorsement titled "Harris, For Law and Order," *The San Francisco Chronicle* editorial board wrote: "Harris is qualified, dedicated to law enforcement and willing to try new approaches to address the root causes of crime. We were impressed with her potential to build coalitions."[63]

She also showed a tough side. A union leader recalled a conversation: "[S]he came up to me and she put her finger in my chest and she said, 'You better endorse me, you better endorse me. You get it?'"—suggesting that she was going to win and that it was in the union's best interest to side with her. "I never forgot it," he added. "She's an intelligent person. She is a—let's see, I better pick this world carefully: Ruthless."[64]

She won the runoff 56–44 percent, gaining more votes than any other candidate in the city, including the incoming mayor, Gavin Newsom. For decades, Harris and Newsom would be frenemies: alternately rivals within the Democratic Party and allies in general elections. The 2003 campaign would have other repercussions in the future. Newsom's wife publicly alleged that Harris had once tried to block her from regaining her job as a prosecutor in the district attorney's office.[65] The wife, Kimberly Guilfoyle, would later divorce Newsom and go on to national notoriety as the long-time fiancée of Donald Trump Jr. and as a surrogate in Trump presidential campaigns. Another public figure who was displeased with Harris's victory was House Minority Leader Nancy Pelosi. Long a power in San Francisco politics, Pelosi had strongly supported Hallinan—and she did not like to lose. From then on, her attitude toward Harris would lack enthusiasm.

During her campaign, Harris promised not to seek the death penalty in criminal cases. Soon after becoming district attorney, she kept her promise in a case involving a cop killer. The police union attacked the decision, and Senator Dianne Feinstein publicly disagreed with it. But even though California voters generally supported capital punishment, attitudes were different in progressive San Francisco, and she survived the controversy. It would come up again in future races.

Both Harris and Newsom pleased City voters during their first term in office and easily won reelection in 2007. Harris was unopposed and Newsom faced only token challengers. Both then set their sights on Sacramento. Newsom launched a campaign for governor but soon withdrew because of overwhelming Democratic support for former governor Jerry Brown. (Their relationship would thenceforth be civil but cool.) Newsom instead ran for lieutenant governor, and would wait eight years for his chance at the top job. Harris ran for state attorney general.

In 2010, California Democrats took every statewide race and kept large majorities in the state legislature. Whereas Brown and Newsom scored double-digit victories, Harris had a close contest. Her opponent was Steve Cooley, a Republican who had won three terms as district attorney in strongly Democratic Los Angeles County. (Cooley's main opponent in the Republican primary was John Eastman, who would later face serious legal trouble for his efforts to overturn electoral votes in the 2020 presidential election.) National Republicans spent huge sums supporting Cooley, seeing him as their best chance to gain a statewide office that could be a base for a future gubernatorial race. There was also another motive for Republican interest, as journalist Dan Morain reported at the time:

Republicans believe Harris would become a formidable candidate for higher office in California, and perhaps nationally, if she is elected attorney general on Nov. 2. A defeat would not fit with such ambitious plans. "If that is a byproduct of defeating her, we're perfectly happy with that," said Adam Temple, spokesman for the Virginia-based group Republican State Leadership Committee.[66]

Cooley effectively attacked Harris on the death penalty and seemed ahead in the race. Then he made a big mistake. During their one debate, a reporter asked if he would accept his county pension while taking a salary as attorney general. Cooley said that he would, arguing that the attorney general's pay (which was just short of $150,000 at the time) was too low and that he had earned his pension. It was a foolish comment in a state still suffering severely from the Great Recession. "Go for it, Steve," Harris laughed. "You've earned it, no question."[67] Harris quickly used Cooley's admission in attack ads. The encounter showed that Harris was a skillful debater who could exploit an opponent's vulnerability. She would again display this skill in 2024.

Cooley nevertheless led on election night, and he declared victory even though many mail ballots were left to count. That was another mistake, albeit an understandable one. In the past, mail ballots had favored Republicans: they tipped the close 1990 race for attorney general from Democrat Arlo Smith to Republican Dan Lungren. But by 2010, voting by mail was more common—accounting for nearly half the tally—and Democrats now had an edge. Moreover, Cooley assumed he would do well in his home turf, Los Angeles County. He neglected to consider that his three previous victories there had taken place in nonpartisan elections. In 2010, he was running as a Republican just as the party brand had become box-office poison in California. So as the slow count dragged on, Cooley's lead shrank day by day. Three weeks after election night, Harris pulled ahead, and Cooley conceded. (In 2020, commentators would refer to the GOP's illusory election-night advantage as "the red mirage.")

Her record as attorney general eludes a single label. On the one hand, she declined to defend a state ballot measure that banned same-sex marriage, saying that it violated the Constitution.[68] On the other hand, she sought to reverse a lower-court ruling that the death penalty was unconstitutional, arguing that it rested on flawed legal reasoning.[69] (Her position prevailed in the Ninth Circuit.) In 2014, she declined to take a public position on a ballot measure to reduce penalties for certain drug and theft offenses. The measure passed, and critics later blamed it for spikes in property crimes. (In 2024, a measure to repeal the law was on the state ballot, and she again declined to state a position.) Conservatives said that her record was too liberal. Some on the left said it was not liberal enough. Professor Lara Bazelon wrote: "Time after time, when progressives urged her to embrace criminal justice reforms as a district attorney and then the state's attorney general, Ms. Harris opposed them or stayed silent. Most troubling, Ms. Harris fought tooth and nail to uphold wrongful convictions that had been secured through official misconduct that included evidence tampering, false testimony and the suppression of crucial information by prosecutors."[70]

One aspect of her work as attorney general would prove to be an asset in the 2024 campaign. During her first year in office, she made an official trip to the U.S.-Mexico border to discuss strategies for fighting cross-border crime. She coordinated state and local investigations of transnational gangs engaged in drug smuggling and human trafficking.[71] She later pointed to these efforts to cast herself as tough on border security.

With her progressive—but not *too* progressive—record, she coasted to reelection in 2014. In January 2015, Senator Barbara Boxer announced that she would not seek another term, and just days later, Harris declared her candidacy for the seat. She immediately started raising money and collecting endorsements, an aggressive approach that struck some Democrats as unseemly. She brushed off these misgivings. "I have always entered races early and run hard, and that's what I've done in this race," she told Seema Mehta of the *Los Angeles Times*. "I make no apologies for it."[72] Unseemly or not, her fast-break strategy deterred most Democratic competitors. Her only significant opponent was Representative Loretta Sanchez of Orange County. Under the state's top-two primary system, which had gone into effect a few years earlier, the top two vote-getters in the primary would proceed to the general election, regardless of party. By 2014, the California GOP was so weak that none of its candidates made the cut. Sanchez placed second, meaning she would face Harris again in November.

Sanchez should have been a strong candidate. She was Hispanic, had a relatively moderate voting record, and had raised substantial sums in her House campaigns. Under the top-two system, she might have had a chance to build a winning coalition of Republicans, moderate independents, and Hispanic Democrats. Fortunately for Harris, Sanchez was prone to strange, unforced errors. Discussing Native Americans at a Democratic convention, she tapped her hand over her mouth in a cringeworthy imitation of a war cry. And during her one debate with Harris, she finished an answer with a dance move called "the dab." A top Democratic operative said: "One could call her actions eccentric, or courageously charting her own path, or bad political judgment. But they're not actions that enhance someone's ability to run a credible Senate campaign."[73] Harris won 62–38 percent.

In the Senate, she had a consistently liberal voting record.[74] With Trump as president and Mitch McConnell as the majority leader, she had little chance to get major liberal legislation onto the books. Instead, she developed a national following through intense questioning of Republican witnesses and nominees during televised hearings. She was well-prepared and ready to create memorable video clips. One example that would later become part of her advertising was a question she posed to Supreme Court nominee Brett Kavanaugh. After he declined to take a clear position on *Roe v. Wade*, she asked: "Can you think of any laws that give the government the power to make decisions about the male body?"[75] His stumbling admission that he could not think of any was a moment of triumph for the Democrats, even though he won confirmation.[76]

By this point, she had shown that she was tough and telegenic. She was also very ambitious. In January 2019, just two years after taking her seat in the Senate, she announced that she was running for president. She got off to a strong start, with promising poll numbers and impressive fundraising hauls. During an early debate, she attracted attention for a sharp exchange with

Biden, in which she criticized his past opposition to racial-balance busing. The Harris surge was fleeting. By the end of the year, with contributions and polls sagging badly, she pulled the plug on the campaign. What happened?

First, her messaging did her little good.[77] She supported a ban on fracking, a fossil-fuel-extraction technique that alarmed environmentalists. She introduced legislation that would have forced the auto industry to make a rapid transition to electric and hydrogen vehicles. And she favored decriminalizing border crossings. The idea of the leftward shift was to appeal to party progressives, but it was hard to win their hearts and minds when her competition included Bernie Sanders and Elizabeth Warren. She made things worse by waffling on issues such as Medicare for all, first endorsing the abolition of private insurance, then proposing a complex plan that included private insurance.[78] In a debate, Tulsi Gabbard echoed Lara Bazelon's criticisms, attacking Harris's credentials as a progressive prosecutor. She tried to transcend divisive issues by saying that she would "prosecute the case" against Trump but the theme fell flat since everybody else was attacking Trump, too. (In 2024, she tried to put her 2020 agenda behind her, but opposition researchers had been taking notes.)

Second, her campaign was disorganized. Her sister Maya Harris served as campaign chair, but a ramshackle set of advisers shared authority, with headquarters both in San Francisco and Baltimore.[79] Her kludge of a campaign failed to solve her message problem, and it faltered at basic organizational tasks such as budgeting. Short on money and averaging 3.4 percent support in national polls, she dropped out of the race before the primaries and caucuses.[80]

Harris returned to work in the Senate, and by mid-March, Biden wrapped up the nomination with his astonishing comeback. The identity of his running mate was the next big question. In the past, nominees had sometimes tapped their primary competitors as a way of unifying their party: Reagan chose George H. W. Bush in 1980, and Obama went with Biden in 2008. Harris may have seemed a long shot initially, but her odds improved on March 15, when Biden promised that the vice presidential candidate would be a woman. In April, a group of 200 Black women, including celebrities, published a letter urging him to pick a Black woman.[81] Although Representative James Clyburn did not publicly disclose it then, he later revealed that he also urged a Black female running mate.[82] Then the death of George Floyd in Minneapolis at the end of May triggered a national focus on race that worked to further push Biden in that direction.

Harris was the logical choice: she had won statewide races, had executive experience, and could claim a working knowledge of national security issues through her service on the Senate Intelligence Committee. And with adequate preparation, she was an effective communicator on television. Her shortcomings as a candidate for the nomination were largely irrelevant. She now did not have to develop her own issue agenda: she only had to advocate Biden's. And the management problems of her campaign did not matter since the Biden organization would oversee her schedule.

It would be hard to claim that her presence on the ticket tipped any states in Biden's direction. With the possible exception of LBJ in 1960, no vice presidential candidate had done so in the modern era. The critical thing is that she did no harm.

VEEP

The example of LBJ also illustrates the constraints of the vice presidency. The power of the office depends almost entirely on what the president chooses to delegate to its occupant. Johnson had been the master of the Senate, but the Kennedy White House gave him little to do, and staffers laughed at him behind his back.[83] There has often been a certain degree of coolness between presidents and vice presidents. During the 1980s, Reagan's circle was wary of George H. W. Bush, and Mrs. Reagan scorned him. Obama was often annoyed with Biden's tendency to say the wrong things at the wrong time. (A Biden hot mic moment made "BFD" a social media abbreviation.)

On the other hand, vice presidents since Harry Truman in 1945 have attained some stature that was previously unknown to the office. Over time, they gained staff and office space in the White House complex. Post-war presidents have also often assigned vice presidents a project of some domestic policy importance (such as the space program for Lyndon Johnson, deregulation for Dan Quayle, or reinventing government for Al Gore), made them a channel to an important constituency (organized labor and congressional liberals for Walter Mondale, evangelicals for Mike Pence), or sent them on nontrivial diplomatic missions (Richard Nixon and George H. W. Bush). In turn, vice presidents since World War II have become viable presidential aspirants in a way that was nearly unheard of in the 19th- and early 20th-century party systems.

One particularly notable departure from the earlier vice presidential pattern was Dick Cheney, who wielded significant influence during George W. Bush's first term, mainly because he had far more Washington experience than the president. By contrast, Kamala Harris had only served part of one Senate term before she assumed office under a chief executive who had served 36 years as a senator and eight as vice president. She was also not a favorite among Biden's close circle of highly protective advisers, who remembered she had opposed him in the primaries. Just as Nancy Reagan seethed for years about George H. W. Bush's criticism of "voodoo economic policy," First Lady Jill

Biden resented Harris's 2020 debate attack on her husband's past opposition to racial balance busing. Shortly after that comment, Mrs. Biden reportedly blew up on a conference call: "With what he cares about, what he fights for, what he's committed to, you get up there and call him a racist without basis? Go f— yourself."[84]

Vice presidents preside over the Senate but lack real power over its day-to-day operations. They cannot give speeches in the chamber without permission and cannot vote except to break ties. They cast tiebreakers in accordance with the president's agenda, not their own, so it is not really a "power" in the everyday sense of the word. In fact, it is an unwelcome chore because it sometimes requires vice presidents to stay in the Capitol when they would rather be doing other things. Whether she liked it or not, Harris secured a footnote in congressional history. Because of the close partisan division in the Senate, she had cast a record 33 tiebreaking votes by the time she announced for president in 2024.[85] (As vice president, Biden had cast none.) Two of those were particularly notable (and potentially damaging to her prospects): Kamala Harris's tiebreaking vote was decisive in the passage of the American Rescue Act and the Inflation Reduction Act, two expensive pieces of legislation that critics often pointed to as fuel for the inflationary fire.

Like several other postwar vice presidents, Harris was also assigned a diplomatic role by the president—in her case, the job of engaging Mexico and Central American countries that served as the source of much of the surge of illegal immigration. Harris's staff privately grumbled that she had been given a no-win task, and her defenders later contended that the label "Border Czar" had been an exaggeration. One way or another, her efforts, such as they were, made no noticeable dent in the problem, and her reputation suffered. She was also occasionally the recipient of unfavorable press reports that claimed that she was an abusive boss whose nastiness led to 90 percent staff turnover in three years.[86] And she became a frequent target of memes ridiculing her "word salads." Examples included a call for Americans to become "unburdened by what has been" and a declaration that "You exist in the context of all in which you live and what came before you."[87]

After *Dobbs*, Harris did take a leading role in advocating the administration's position on abortion, where she was on stronger ground politically. For the most part, though, like most vice presidents, she was not independently at the forefront of public attention. She was, for better or worse, tethered to the president, or so it seemed. In March 2021, the White House communications office instructed federal agencies to refer to the "Biden-Harris Administration," and both Biden and Harris declared that she would be the last person in the room when Biden made important decisions.[88] Accordingly, her poll numbers largely tracked with Biden's.[89] By June 2024, that linkage to Biden meant her polls looked grim.[90]

Chapter 3

Trump Reprise

The Comeback Begins

During his presidency, Donald Trump had struggled politically. According to the RealClearPolitics average of job approval ratings, Trump never topped about 47 percent approval, spent all but the first week "underwater," with more disapproving than approving, and spent long periods of time in the low 40 percent range. Likewise, his personal favorability ratings hovered around 41 percent for his entire presidency.[1] In 2018, under his leadership, Republicans lost the House majority they had gained in Barack Obama's first midterm election in 2010; their loss of 40 seats was the third worst suffered by a president's party since 1974.[2] Then, in January 2021, Trump had arguably cost Republicans the Senate, as well, when his anger over his presidential defeat in Georgia spilled over into a grievance-filled runoff election campaign that ended with both GOP Senate candidates in Georgia losing narrowly to their Democratic challengers.[3]

In an earlier era—say, 2008—Trump's political future would have consisted of a comfortable retirement, plenty of time to play golf and write memoirs, and perhaps (or perhaps not) an invitation to speak at the next national convention. For Donald Trump to make a comeback that would return him to the White House, he first had to effect an historically improbable comeback within his own party. Indeed, the last repeat nomination for a losing candidate was the Democratic nomination of Adlai Stevenson in 1956. Before that, Thomas Dewey (1944 and 1948) and William Jennings Bryan (1896, 1900, and 1908) had repeated, but none had been a repudiated president. In the entire history of the United States, only Grover Cleveland in the late 1800s had served as president, been defeated, then come back to be nominated by his party again and win a second (though nonconsecutive) term.

Yet, by July 2024, Trump had won his third Republican nomination in a row and was clearly in command of his party. Indeed, in certain respects, it had become the Trump Party, an outsized manifestation of the modern era's tendency to subordinate the party to presidential personalism. How this occurred is one of the essential stories of the 2024 election.

 **TRUMP'S REPUBLICAN PARTY**

Trump had changed the center of gravity in the party. The traditional conservatives were overwhelmed and the Tea Party contingent either co-opted or marginalized (though a handful obstinately persisted in the House Freedom Caucus). In some respects, the changes were years in the making, and Trump merely identified the trend, attached himself to it, and accelerated it.[4] In other cases, he was the pathbreaker. Trump was sometimes cause, sometimes effect, but always in the middle of the change.

Many of these changes revolved around the U.S. relationship with the world. Prior to Trump's ascent, Republicans had long been more committed to free trade than Democrats. Under the heavy influence of the unions, Democrats such as Congressman Richard Gephardt of Missouri promoted varying forms of trade protectionism. To be sure, Republican Ronald Reagan sometimes nodded in that direction, and Democrat Bill Clinton consummated the North American Free Trade Agreement. But it was no accident that when Clinton won passage of NAFTA in 1993, more House Republicans voted for it than Democrats. A string of GOP presidents, including Reagan, George H. W. Bush, and George Bush, made freer trade a major part of their economic programs. Trump plowed a different field, seeded by H. Ross Perot and Patrick Buchanan, more skeptical of trade and less inclined to see it in a strategic or humanitarian light.[5] By 2024, Republicans had largely joined Trump, supporting higher tariffs against imported goods.

Similarly, Republican military interventionism peaked under George W. Bush, then receded. The Iraq War provided a hard lesson for many in the limits of U.S. power, particularly America's limited capacity to drag third-world societies into the world of advanced democracies. Trump became a symbol for those who blamed neoconservatives and other assorted hawks for America's "forever wars." Although Trump had initiated modest U.S. military aid to Ukraine while he was president, he became critical of Biden's expanded aid and attracted support from incipient isolationists such as Tucker Carlson.[6] Regarding international engagement, whether through trade or military intervention, Trump revived the pre–World War II Republican tradition. "America First" was originally the name of Charles Lindbergh's isolationist committee prior to Pearl Harbor (and was later the name of Patrick Buchanan's 1992 presidential campaign committee).

Immigration was a more complicated matter, as Trump's restrictionist position has long had a following among Republicans in Congress and at the state and local level. Republican presidents, most recently George W. Bush, pushed for "comprehensive immigration reform" including a "pathway to citizenship" for those in the United States illegally. Trump's embrace of restrictionism was novel insofar as he adopted that view at the presidential level and made it as a central part of his appeal.[7]

What all three issues had in common was that Trump's position had always been more popular among ordinary voters than presidents of either party. As a self-conscious outsider, or "populist," Trump seemed instinctively skilled at identifying those voters and appealing to them.

On the domestic front, Trump subtracted from traditional Republican doctrine a commitment—honored sometimes in the breach but rarely foresworn altogether—to some degree of fiscal restraint and responsibility. Even when George W. Bush had made feints in the direction of unrestrained spending, Republicans in Congress resisted. Each major Republican electoral surge of recent times—1980, 1994, and 2010—revolved substantially around themes of limited government and slowed domestic spending. Trump not only did not embrace such themes, he positively disdained them, consigning erstwhile entitlement reformer Paul Ryan to the outer darkness and promising never to touch Social Security and Medicare despite their impending insolvency.[8]

Finally, in the wake of the *Dobbs* decision overturning *Roe v. Wade*, Trump gradually executed a shift on abortion that culminated in a new Republican platform position on the issue for the first time since Republicans officially came to support a constitutional amendment banning most abortions in 1980. First, Trump intimated that Florida's ban on abortion after six weeks gestation had gone too far. Then he argued that it had been right to allow each state to make its own abortion policy. Finally, his supporters rewrote the platform to remove the commitment to a human life amendment to the Constitution as well as language calling abortion into moral question. Instead, Republicans declared themselves in favor of life, family, and state-level decision-making, and opposed to late-term abortion. Some pro-life activists noted the party's transformation with alarm, but most Republicans, focused on immigration and 2020, seemed to shrug.[9] Trump had spent most of his presidency from 2017 to 2021 doing conventional Republican things with a few embellishments. By 2024, he had redesigned Republican fiscal and economic policy, social policy, and foreign policy.

At the least, he had undone traditional Republican policy in those areas, leaving somewhat uncertain what was to come. Trump was always clearer about what he was against than what he was for. Was there even such a thing as Trumpism, separate from Trump's personality?[10] This indeterminacy may have been an advantage, allowing him to focus on emotive themes and

ʒ voters to project onto him varying (and sometimes incompatible)
. Nevertheless, some in the politico-intellectual world sought to fashion
an iueology that would lend greater coherence to Trumpism. Hence was born
"National Conservatism," which had its own conferences and its own manifesto. Released in 2021 and signed by mostly pro-Trump conservative thinkers,
the manifesto extolled national sovereignty, gave two (but not three) cheers
to the free market, and warned against the dangers of globalism.[11] National
conservatism provided a framework for Trump's intellectual supporters to
rally around—and perhaps a mechanism that they could use to try to fashion a
Trump more to their liking—but it struck many as an attempt to lasso a tornado.

National conservatism aside, Republicans in early 2024 were not the same
as in 2016 or 2012. They were relatively more "working class," though at
that point perhaps more by subtraction than addition. Trump's two previous
elections had seen him attract no more working-class support than George W.
Bush in 2004, but considerably less support by white-collar professionals, a
trend that continued past 2020. Indeed, for the eight years of the Trump era,
Republicans had bled college-educated voters and suburbanites. An exhaus-
tive voting study conducted by the Democracy Fund based on the 2016 election had identified five types of Trump voters:[12]

Is there a Dmzy of sort suma of who could get these voters how?

1. Preservationists, relatively low-income, low-information voters pri-
   oritizing limits on immigration, representing 20 percent of Trump's
   general election voters;
2. Staunch conservatives, combining fiscal conservatism, moral tradition-
   alism, and moderate skepticism toward immigration, who constituted
   31 percent of Trump's support;
3. Anti-elites, middle-class, a bit younger, and more economically liberal,
   with 19 percent of Trump's voters;
4. Free Marketeers, small-government fiscal conservatives with higher-
   education and incomes who tended to support Ted Cruz in the 2016
   primaries, who were 25 percent of Trump's fall voters; and
5. The Disengaged, younger and substantially alienated from both parties
   (5 percent of Trump's general election voters).

Some, particularly Anti-Elites and Disengaged, did not predominantly
identify as Republicans. Among the Republican groups, the eight years from
2016 to 2024 undoubtedly saw a shift in the center of gravity away from Free
Marketeers and toward Preservationists. At the same time, what it meant to be
a Staunch Conservative underwent significant revision. These trends confirm
the argument by political scientists Hiram and Verlan Lewis that ideology
in American politics is more a matter of tribal affiliation than a consistent
philosophical framework.[13]

A Pew Research study released a year after the 2020 election used a different typology. In the Pew study, among Republican leaners, 23 percent were identified as "Faith and Flag Conservatives," toughest on immigration and most socially conservative. Another 15 percent were "Committed Conservatives," generally conservative and most pro–free market. The least free-market oriented were the 23 percent in the "Populist Right," the most unambiguously pro-Trump group in the GOP coalition. Another 18 percent were found in the "Ambivalent Right," which, along with the "Committed Conservatives," viewed Ronald Reagan as the best president of the last 40 years. Finally, 15 percent of the Republican coalition (and 13 percent of the Democratic coalition) consisted of the "Stressed Sideliners," who lean slightly liberal on economics and slightly conservative on social issues.[14]

FIVE OBSTACLES, FIVE SOLUTIONS

The transformation of the Republican Party since 2016 gave Trump an edge in 2024, but did not assure his renomination. Five notable obstacles stood in the way of Trump's recovery and renomination. In some cases, the efforts of Trump and his supporters were paramount in overcoming those obstacles, but more often than not, he received invaluable assistance from Joe Biden and the Democrats. ⎰⎱⎰

Defeat. A serious barrier to all defeated presidents was, well, their defeats. Even Grover Cleveland, the only president to overcome it, had the advantage of having actually outpolled his 1888 opponent in the nationally aggregated popular vote. Whether nominating decisions were made by party bosses or by primary voters, parties have historically wanted to win.[15] After their incumbents have lost, they have typically fixed on a fresh face, someone who can recalibrate and try a new appeal. If we want to win, bosses and voters alike have reasoned, why would we give our precious nomination to someone who had just lost? The bias against renominating a losing incumbent has been so strong that most losing presidents have not even tried to throw their hats back in the ring.

On paper, this obstacle seemed even greater for Donald Trump than for most defeated incumbents. The win that brought him into the White House in 2016 was unimpressive by historical standards. He won in the Electoral College by squeaking by in a few key states as he trailed the nationally-aggregated popular vote by three million votes to Hillary Clinton, possibly the most widely disliked Democratic nominee of the modern era. Trump entered the presidency with Republicans in control of the White House, the Senate, and the House of Representatives, and left the presidency with Democrats in charge of all three. Trump then suffered another political blow in 2022, when Republicans lost several seemingly winnable U.S. Senate races with candidates Trump had endorsed in the primaries.[16] Biden and Democrats saw Trump as enough of a Republican liability that they made considerable efforts—including a nationally televised presidential speech in front of Independence Hall in Philadelphia—to make the midterm elections about the threat to democracy posed by Trump and "MAGA extremists."[17] Exit polls of voters indicated that the desire to stop Trump essentially canceled out the desire to hold Biden accountable for poor performance: 32 percent said they cast their vote to oppose Biden to 19 percent who said they were aiming to support Biden (a net effect of –13), while 28 percent cast their votes to oppose Trump and 16 percent to support him (–12).[18] Not since 1974 had a midterm swung as heavily as a referendum on someone who was not president any longer. It was little wonder that many analysts held that Trump had steered his party toward another defeat.

The disappointing (for Republicans) 2022 results did lead to a brief reassessment by Republican voters of Trump's value as a candidate. Florida governor Ron DeSantis vaulted into a position as a viable challenger to Trump when DeSantis won a huge gubernatorial victory in Florida, long a swing state (DeSantis had won his first race in 2018 by less than a 1 percent margin). DeSantis soared in the polls while Trump slumped. For a moment it appeared that political gravity was reasserting itself—defeated incumbent presidents simply do not persuade their parties to double down on a losing experience. That moment, however, did not last.

One factor that helps to explain Trump's rise and renomination is the post-1972 shift in the presidential nomination system and the associated rise in "amateurs" relative to "professionals" within the parties. Those changes favored personalistic and charismatic outsiders unconnected to a preexisting organized movement.[19] Trump would almost certainly never have been nominated in an earlier system under greater influence by party officeholders and other insiders. Nevertheless, studies tended to show that party primary voters in recent decades had hardly thrown electability overboard as a criterion when assessing candidates for nomination.

More than the benefit of an outsider-oriented nominating system was needed, and it took the form of a concerted effort by Trump and his supporters, launched in the wee hours of election night 2020 and sustained all the way through the 2024 convention, to convince Republicans that Trump had not actually lost. Trump himself took a lead role in this play, repeatedly referring to the RIGGED election and the STOLEN election that robbed him of his LANDSLIDE. Trump had been telegraphing this line of argument for months. Referring to the pandemic change in voting procedures, he tweeted in June: "RIGGED 2020 ELECTION: MILLIONS OF MAIL-IN BALLOTS WILL BE PRINTED BY FOREIGN COUNTRIES, AND OTHERS."[20] The weekend before the 2020 election, the news site Axios reported that sources inside the White House were saying that Trump was already planning to claim fraud if the vote totals started trending against him; as if on cue, in the early morning hours of November 5, Trump appeared on national television asserting that "This is a fraud on the American public."[21] He proceeded to run a "Stop the Steal" campaign that culminated in the ill-fated rally in the Ellipse on January 6.

For the entirety of the Biden presidency, Trump beat the same drum, assailing both the Democrats and those Republicans he deemed insufficiently supportive of the Stolen Election narrative, such as Vice President Mike Pence, Senate Republican leader Mitch McConnell, and Georgia's governor Brian Kemp and secretary of state Brad Raffensperger. As late as August 2023, Trump had scheduled a press conference to release what he described as a 100-page report detailing massive voter fraud in Georgia; just before the appointed day, he canceled the press conference, saying he would be putting the evidence into court filings instead.[22] Trump's unending campaign against the "Stolen Election" was reminiscent of Andrew Jackson's four-year-long crusade against "King Caucus" and the "Corrupt Bargain" that he claimed cost him the 1824 election.

Trump was aided by others. In mid-2022, for example, conservative activist Dinesh D'Souza produced a film titled *2000 Mules* (also published as a book) that purported to show that in 2020 around 200,000 mail ballot votes— and possibly as many as 800,000 votes—were illegally deposited into unsupervised ballot boxes by "mules," left-wing activists engaged in mass "ballot harvesting."[23] Two years later, a survey conducted by Rasmussen and the Heartland Institute found that 21 percent of 2020 mail ballot voters recalled having cast their ballots illegally.[24]

The D'Souza film had serious shortcomings, including great leaps of logic. Conservative commentator Ben Shapiro contended that "The conclusions of the film are not justified by the premises of the film itself. There are a bunch of dots that need to be connected. Maybe they will be connected, but they haven't been connected in the film."[25] Ultimately, the filmmakers had to withdraw distribution of the film and issue an apology to a Georgia man who had been alleged in the film to be engaged in illegal ballot harvesting when an official investigation by the State of Georgia found that he had been delivering ballots for his family quite legally.[26] The film's creator, Dinesh D'Souza, admitted in December 2024 that "We recently learned that surveillance videos used in the film may not have actually been correlated with the geolocation data" of individuals dropping off ballots, though the supposed correlation was the very basis of the film.[27] Likewise, the survey was hardly dispositive proof of a "stolen election." Voters have notoriously bad recollection of their behavior a few months after the election, not to mention a few years after. Moreover, the activities admitted to by voters did not involve casting invented votes but rather things like filling out ballots for friends and family members. In any case, the survey also found that these irregularities were roughly evenly shared between Republicans and Democrats, canceling out any effects on the election outcome.[28]

Other analyses supported the general tenor of Trump's claim without alleging mass fraud. For example, Mollie Hemingway's 2022 book *Rigged: How the Media, Big Tech, and the Democrats Seized Our Elections* did not dilate on Trump's more extravagant fraud assertions. Rather, she argued more plausibly, the media was heavily stacked against Trump, rules changes probably harmful to Trump were imposed in mid-campaign through lawsuits, and leftist activist organizations influenced local government voter turnout operations in Democratic-leaning areas by way of Mark Zuckerberg's $400 million grant program.[29]

The great problem with the "Stolen Election" thesis, aside from a shortage of evidence, was that the election had never been Trump's to lose. The RealClearPolitics website collected 230 head-to-head matchups between Trump and Biden from the summer of 2019 through the weekend before Election Day 2020, surveyed by polling firms across the political spectrum. Biden led in 225 of the 230, including all but one after February 2020. The site's estimate of electoral votes, based on statewide polls, likewise showed Biden in the lead consistently. And in what turned out to be the six most crucial battleground states—Arizona, Georgia, Michigan, Nevada, Pennsylvania, and Wisconsin—Biden had established a small but steady lead in the months before the election in all but Georgia, where the two had traded small leads and the state was a genuine toss-up.[30] The officially certified result of the 2020 election was what one should have expected under the circumstances. No extraordinary explanation was necessary.

Nevertheless, people generally believe what they want to believe, a fact that most politicians and all demagogues instinctively understand. Most Republicans wanted to believe that Trump had been robbed of his rightful victory in 2020. And there were enough unusual developments during that election to feed the myth. In the November 2022 midterm election exit polls, about a third of the electorate said that Biden did not legitimately win the 2020 presidential election.[31] By late 2023, when the primary campaign was in full swing, polls indicated that about 70 percent of Republicans in the United States believed 2020 had been a stolen election.[32] And if Trump did not really lose in 2020, why not nominate him again?

The focus on 2020 had another benefit for Trump. If Republicans were focused on 2020, they would not be focused on 2018, when they lost the House, 2021, when they lost the Senate, or 2022, when they lost a chance to reclaim the Senate, all of which could plausibly be laid at Trump's doorstep.

Too old

Age: If elected again in 2024, Trump would be 78 when inaugurated for his second term. Prior to 2020, no president had been elected at an age greater than 69 (Ronald Reagan in 1980) or 70 (Trump himself in 2016) or reelected at an age greater than 73 (Reagan in 1984). Although the American population had been aging and more Americans were living vigorous lives past the age of 80, the presidency is an extremely demanding job, both physically and mentally. Even if the former president appeared to be in the best condition, his advanced age would likely raise questions of fitness. Indeed, some commentators pointed to certain signs of Trump's deterioration.[33] Moreover, Republicans had struggled with young voters since Barack Obama appeared on the scene in 2008, and critics argued that nominating a superannuated version of Donald Trump seemed an unlikely route to mitigating that shortcoming.

Fortunately for Trump, the man who beat him in 2020 was Joe Biden, the oldest person to be elected president in the history of the United States. Biden would be 82 by the time voters went to the polls in 2024. Even better luck for Trump was that the difference in capacity between Trump and Biden seemed to many Americans to be greater than the four years difference in chronological age. The obvious mental and physical deterioration of Biden over the course of his term in office is detailed in chapter 4, but here it is enough to know that Biden's condition often made Trump seem vigorous by comparison. In an Associated Press–National Opinion Research Center poll taken in August 2023, nearly a year before Biden abruptly dropped his presidential bid, 77 percent of Americans (including 89 percent of Republicans and 69 percent of Democrats) said they viewed Biden as too old to serve effectively as president for another four years; 51 percent who said the same thing about Trump.[34]

The disparity between the two had initially been obscured by Biden's basement campaign in 2020, but had grown more obvious over time. It had been a Trump theme even in their first contest—the Trump campaign had demanded that Biden take a drug test before their first debate in September 2020, on the grounds that Biden could only compete with Trump if he benefited from pharmaceutical stimulation.[35] Once Biden was sworn in, his physical and verbal miscues became regular fodder for Trump and Republicans. One popular conservative blog (PowerlineBlog.com) ran a regular feature highlighting these mishaps titled "I have half a mind to be president." Trump's focus on this issue served two purposes. One was to directly undermine Biden. The other was to deflect attention from the fact that Trump was nearly as old.

Conduct: A third obstacle to Trump's recovery was the widespread perception that his conduct in office was unbecoming a president. Indeed, 2020 exit polls showed that Trump had won a slight plurality of voters who said that a candidate's stand on issues was the primary factor in their vote, while

Biden prevailed by a 2–1 margin among those who said personal qualities were most important.[36] And that was before Trump's postelection meltdown, which culminated in the January 6 occupation of the Capitol by Trump supporters. Trump became the first president ever impeached by the House twice.

Concerns about Trump's conduct were bolstered by a number of memoirs by members of Trump's administration, including Mike Pence and Attorney General William Barr. Barr, for example, offered a detailed account of Trump's desperate attempt to overturn his electoral defeat and criticized Trump for his actions, saying Trump had become "detached from reality."[37] When he announced his own candidacy for the 2024 Republican presidential nomination, Pence declared that Trump "demanded I choose between him and the Constitution. I believe that anyone who puts themselves over the Constitution should never be president of the United States. And anyone who asks someone else to put them over the Constitution should never be president of the United States again,"[38]

Here Democrats and Republicans combined to reduce the negative effect on Trump's chances. Republicans achieved this by downplaying and trivializing January 6, Democrats by weaponizing it and overplaying their hand.

Almost immediately, Democrats and their allies began using January 6 to tar Republicans in general and to justify what amounted to social media censorship. Twitter and Facebook kicked Trump off their platforms, citing the assault on the Capitol. Over 1,400 individuals faced federal charges, of whom nearly 900 were sentenced by mid-2024 (about one-third were convicted of felonies, about two-thirds of misdemeanors).[39] Democrats described the event as an "insurrection," a term that was not unjustified however much Republicans may have chafed at it. The rioters had attempted to use force and intimidation to prevent Congress and the vice president from carrying out their constitutional duty to execute the peaceful transfer of power in keeping with the legally certified results of the elections in 50 states and the District of Columbia. Moreover, violence was used, and 174 police officers suffered injuries, 40 of whom required hospitalization.[40] Some of the estimated 2,000 to 2,500 invaders also engaged in looting and vandalism.

Trump's defenders saw a double standard. During his second impeachment trial, his attorney Michael van der Veen said: "For months, our Federal courthouse in Portland was placed under siege by violent anarchists who attacked law enforcement officers daily and repeatedly and tried to set fire to the building. Speaker Pelosi did not call the violent siege of the Federal building an insurrection. She called the Federal agents protecting the courthouse 'stormtroopers.'"[41] Republicans cited other examples from the summer of 2020, including a siege of the White House, attacks on police stations, and short-lived creation of an "autonomous zone" in Seattle that purported to have seceded from the United States—altogether, rioting that caused approximately $2 billion of damage and perhaps 19 deaths.[42] To many Americans, Democrats' refusal to call out insurrectionary behavior by left-wing forces put their condemnation of Trumpist insurrection into the realm of partisan hype. Insurrection for me, but not for thee, seemed to them to be the Democratic order of the day.

For their part, after a brief moment of genuine shock and apparent revulsion, Republicans went about the task of sanitizing and trivializing January 6. Apologists fixed on several main arguments.[43]

For an insurrection, there was a very light death toll. Indeed, only one person died in the violence—Ashli Babbitt, who was shot to death by Capitol Police. Capitol Police officer Brian Sicknick, often cited as a casualty by Democrats (including Joe Biden), actually died of natural causes a day later, though the medical examiner contended the circumstances of January 6 contributed to his stroke This minimization of the violence was often linked to another claim, that the rioters were unarmed. In actuality, though, at least 75 arrests were made on weapons charges, and rioters were found in possession of loaded guns, stun guns, knives, batons, axes, baseball bats, and chemical spray. Oath Keepers leader Stewart Rhodes acquired approximately $10,000 worth of firearms, which were stored in the group's Alexandria, Virginia, hotel for use by the group's "Quick Reaction Force" if necessary;[44] Lonnie Coffman not only brought a loaded pistol onto Capitol grounds but parked a truck a few blocks away containing more loaded guns, Molotov cocktails, and other weapons.[45]

Arrested protesters were nonviolent political prisoners simply exercising their First Amendment rights. In fact, some defendants remained in jail for lengthy periods awaiting trial, and a few convictions were overturned or charges reduced to misdemeanors by judges.[46] However, most defendants were released within a few days. Those who weren't were generally ordered held by judges who concluded they were violent or posed a flight risk. The longest sentence—22 years for Seditious Conspiracy—was handed out to Enrique Tarrio, founder of the Proud Boys group, who organized and led his group in a well-planned breach of the Capitol.

Rioters were invited into the building by Capitol Police. In actuality, police engaged in full-scale battles to block as many entrances as they could—hence the 174 injured police officers—and most rioters forced their way through defended doorways or entered through broken windows. In a few cases, outnumbered police were more accommodating and attempted to deescalate by allowing entry.

The entire event may have been a "false flag" operation. From an early date, Trump and some of his media supporters suggested that left-wing groups such as Antifa or Black Lives Matter had staged the riot to discredit the president. However, investigation uncovered only one participant with any history of BLM involvement. On the other hand, the contingent of rioters was shot through with members of a variety of far-right groups and, more than anything else, sincere Trump supporters who believed in the Stolen Election narrative. The FBI later acknowledged that a "handful" of FBI confidential sources were among the rioters, leading some sympathetic to Trump to question whether provocateurs had been planted with the intention of creating a disturbance. In early 2024, one national survey found that 25 percent of U.S. adults said it was "probably" or "definitely" true that "FBI operatives organized and encouraged" the January 6 Capitol riot. However, there is no evidence they played a part in driving the event, and it would be surprising, if not disconcerting, if the FBI did not have some informants among the groups who led the charge at the Capitol.[47]

A key moment came in early 2023 when conservative commentator Tucker Carlson obtained security footage from the Capitol on January 6, 2021, and devoted a lengthy segment of his television program to showing selectively edited clips that emphasized the ridiculous or harmless moments of the occupation of the Capitol while omitting the violent and dangerous. "These were not insurrectionists," Carlson contended, "they were sightseers."[48]

The intersection of Republican minimization and Democratic maximization of January 6 came in the congressional hearings held by the special House committee on January 6 appointed by Speaker Nancy Pelosi. The committee, stacked 7–2 with Democrats and with zero voices sympathetic to the former president, was almost guaranteed to approve a report highly critical of Trump, but for that very reason was unlikely to have any effect on the thinking of most Republicans.

As its proceedings wore on, the J6 committee occasionally received enlightening testimony, but often overplayed its hand. For example, White House aide Cassidy Hutchinson claimed that Trump had been so angry that he could not go to the Capitol in the midst of the riot that he put his hands around the throat of a Secret Service agent transporting him back to the White House after the Save America rally. However, she admitted she was relating the incident secondhand and her testimony was soon tempered by other sources that agreed that Trump and the agent had a heated exchange but that the president had kept his hands to himself. Moreover, the sensational but questionable tale overshadowed Hutchinson's more solid and equally disturbing firsthand account of the president in the White House watching the riot unfold on television and waiting hours to say anything at all to try to control it. The committee's final report was damning, but landed with a thud because most Republicans saw the inquiry as fixed to begin with.[49] Altogether, one news analysis would contend that, although many factors contributed to Trump's comeback, not least was "how effectively he and his loyalists have laundered the history of Jan. 6, turning a political nightmare intro asset."[50]

Character: Concerns about Trump's conduct in office were fus broader concern dating back to his first presidential campaign, that he lacked the character necessary to be fit for the presidency. He seemed to manifest a shortage of self-control of all sorts, and was impulsive, narcissistic, and undisciplined in both his public life and his private life, where had been married three times, divorced twice, and had engaged in multiple extramarital affairs. He was frequently mendacious, delighting in mocking and insulting his opponents and more generally saying things others found offensive. To be charitable, his relationship with the truth was frequently strained.[51] Not least, critics argued that he had a habit, throughout both his business career and his political life, of seeing the rules established by law or custom as no more binding on him than mere suggestions. Prior to the 1990s, a public profile of this sort would have disqualified one from the presidency in both parties.

There was both a long-term, underlying reason and a short-term, more focused, reason that Trump's renomination did not fall victim to his character flaws. The longer-term reason was that, quite simply, the day had passed when problematic character was disqualifying. Here the Bill Clinton era was decisive. By the end of the 1990s, Clinton had survived a 1992 primary battle in which numerous scandals came to light, survived a 1996 reelection campaign in which he was still battling the scandals hanging over his head four years earlier as well as new revelations prior to the election that his campaign had engaged in significant campaign finance violations, and then survived another crisis when he was impeached by the House for perjury and obstruction of justice in yet another sex scandal. Throughout his reelection and impeachment battles, the country was subjected to constant spin and was implored by Clinton's supporters to look past his suboptimal character because, in essence, the economy was doing well. Republicans spent a large part of the 1990s raging against this formula—the president's character is important, dammit! Having ultimately turned against their own president when Richard Nixon's deep character flaws were exposed, they had expected Democrats to do the same. Democrats' decision instead to circle the wagons and defend Clinton to the death—and their ability to bring the country along with them—was momentous, establishing a new set of political rules. Republicans ultimately internalized and then turned to their own advantage the new rules of the game.

The more immediate reason character was not the obstacle to Trump's reascent that many people expected was that Democrats again overplayed a strong hand. Once out of the White House, Trump was besieged by legal difficulties, both civil and criminal.[52]

Civil cases included a suit brought by author E. Jean Carroll who claimed Trump had defamed her when he denied her charge that he had sexually assaulted her in a department store dressing room. The jury concluded Trump had indeed assaulted and defamed Carroll, and awarded her almost $90 million. Another civil suit claimed that Trump's business empire in New York had committed financial fraud. When he lost that suit, he was charged a $355 million penalty plus interest, and his company was barred from doing business in New York for three years.

Greater attention focused on four criminal cases. Two were federal, brought by special counsel Jack Smith on behalf of the Justice Department. Two were brought at the state level, one in New York and one in Georgia. Trump was in sufficient legal peril that some critics would suggest that he was running for election to stay out of prison, and he promised to fire Smith (who ultimately resigned days before Trump took office.)

Arguably the strongest case of the four was the federal case charging Trump with 37 felonies for improper handling of classified documents after leaving office. Trump as much as admitted guilt, arguing that his offense was excusable because the president could classify or reclassify whatever he wanted. There was strong evidence that Trump had improperly retained documents, stored them haphazardly, refused to return them despite repeated government requests, and lied about it through his attorney. The conservative publication *National Review* called the indictment "damning," and noted that "Just as paranoiacs sometimes have enemies, people obsessively pursued for alleged violations of the law by their political opponents sometimes commit criminal offenses."[53] Even here, though, Trump gained support within the GOP when the FBI conducted a highly publicized raid of his Mar-a-Lago estate to search for evidence.[54] Republicans said it was a case of selective prosecution. They noted that Special Counsel Robert Hur did not charge President Biden even though Hur acknowledged uncovering "evidence that President Biden willfully retained and disclosed classified materials after his vice presidency when he was a private citizen." But part of Hur's reasoning was very damaging to Biden: "at trial, Mr. Biden would likely present himself to a jury, as he did during our interview of him, as a sympathetic, well-meaning, elderly man with a poor memory."[55]

The other federal case and the Georgia case involved Trump's post-election activities, alleging conspiracies by Trump to tamper with election results, including (in the federal case) promoting the January 6 riots. In Georgia, prosecutor Fani Willis wove Trump into a racketeering case charging the former president and 18 others with conspiring to overturn the state's election results. In Washington, DC, Jack Smith charged Trump alone with four election-subversion felonies. Both cases were complicated cases, requiring evidence for coordination between multiple individuals beyond Trump and/or depending upon unprecedented and creative application—critics said unreasonable stretching—of the statutes in question.

The most questionable case was the New York case, brought by Brooklyn District Attorney Alvin Bragg, who had campaigned for election on a promise to get Trump. Bragg's claim was that Trump had violated federal election law by authorizing a payment of hush money to Stormy Daniels in 2016 because Trump had funneled the payments, which Bragg alleged were designed to affect the outcome of the election, through his personal attorney rather than through his campaign fund. Under New York state law, because the misreporting was designed to facilitate another crime (the campaign finance violation), it elevated the misreporting instances from misdemeanors into felonies.

Ther four criminal cases were charged in quick succession: Bragg's in March 2023, the documents case in June 2023, and the two election subversion cases in August 2023. Ultimately, only the Bragg case came to trial before Election Day. The other cases faced difficulties. The documents case was dismissed when Judge Aileen Cannon ruled that Jack Smith's appointment had been unconstitutional. In the Georgia case, three charges were dismissed as outside state jurisdiction, and the rest languished pending a determination of whether Willis, who was accused of improprieties, would remain on the case. And the federal election subversion case was put on hold while Jack Smith wrestled with the implications of the July 1 Supreme Court ruling requiring a determination of which of Trump's actions were in his official capacity as president (and hence immune from prosecution) and which were not.

Critics of the Bragg case, many of whom were not fans of Donald Trump, found it disturbing that Bragg had apparently targeted Trump even before being elected DA and then cast about for whatever way he could find to bring the former president down. They also complained that the statute of limitations on the misdemeanors that served as the foundation of the felonies had expired, then been extended by the New York legislature, and that the judge's guidance to the jury instructed them to convict Trump even if they could not agree on exactly what law had been broken. When the jury returned a guilty verdict on all 34 counts, Democrats from Biden down rushed to condemn Trump the Felon, but some commentators worried about abuse of prosecutorial power to punish political opponents. As former federal judge Michael W. McConnell argued in the pages of the *Wall Street Journal*, "Using the criminal-justice system to handicap the opposing political party is a deep-dyed violation of democratic norms—something we expect from authoritarian regimes, not in a mature, well-functioning democracy."[56]

Indeed, many Republicans saw this "lawfare," as they called it, indicative of a coordinated Democratic plan to attack Trump. The Justice Department, which brought two of the four cases, was headed by an Attorney General (Merrick Garland) answerable to the president, while the other half of cases were brought by elected Democratic prosecutors. This picture was complicated by the fact that Smith was an independent who has worked under Republicans and Democrats, and who had investigated officials of both parties. Some of the more conspiratorially minded speculated that Democrats had not only coordinated their attack but that, seeing Trump as their weakest opponent, had anticipated that persecuting him was likely to lead otherwise reluctant Republicans to rally around him.

That the prosecutions were rooted in an unspoken common desire by local Democratic prosecutors and the Biden Justice Department to visit partisan vengeance on Trump was not hard for Republicans to believe, but it took another leap to believe all the cases were tied together in some vast left-wing conspiracy. Indeed, the weakness of Bragg's case made it a poor case to lead with, if one were devising a coordinated legal strategy.[57] Rather, the cases appeared to be a hodgepodge of the serious, the plausible but contentious, and the problematic, developing independently in rather random order.

However one judges the merits of the cases, it seems clear that Trump benefited from them politically in his quest for renomination. One conservative commentator asked, "How has a president out of office for four years and under constant attack from Democrats and the Left not simply retained his high daunting support but continued growing it? For an answer, his opponents should begin by looking at themselves. Rather than eviscerating Trump, have they exonerated him to a growing number of Americans?"[58] Republicans noted that no former president of the United States had ever been subjected to prosecution before. Both parties had long refrained from endorsing or carrying out prosecution of former presidents out of fear that such prosecutions would taint the judicial system in the eyes of half the country and would open the door to an endless cycle of partisan payback. Now prosecutors at varying levels were not just opening that door, they were kicking it in. For their part, Democrats argued that no former president had been prosecuted before because no former president been as contemptuous of the law as Trump.

Perceived performance in office: A final obstacle facing Trump as he hoped for renomination was the widespread perception of his presidency at the time. To be sure, most Republicans and many independents cheered aspects of Trump's presidency. Prior to COVID-19, jobs and incomes were up. The United States attained energy independence, becoming a net exporter of energy. The president took a stand against doctrines such as critical race theory that many saw as deliberately divisive. Trump also took a stand against illegal immigration, beginning construction of his vaunted "beautiful wall." Abroad, his administration brokered a peace agreement between Israel and many of its erstwhile Arab foes, building a coalition to contain Iran. And after nearly three years of investigation by Special Prosecutor Robert Mueller into the worst charges against Trump during his presidency, that he colluded with Russia to tip the 2016 election in his favor, Mueller declined to make a recommendation and the Democratic House dropped the matter.

At the same time, though, most Americans according to polls saw fewer pluses than minuses. Trump's 2017 tax cuts, one of his few legislative accomplishments, were never very popular. The border crackdown led to a backlash against family separation and other policies widely seen as draconian (though Barack Obama had employed some of them, too). Trump's administration was something of a wreck, with high rates of turnover and many key positions left open for months or years. Fiscal policy was undisciplined, as Trump resisted any serious spending restraint and deficits soared toward $1 trillion a year. Then came 2020, a toxic brew of pandemic, short-term economic collapse driven largely by anti-COVID-19 policies, and destructive riots in the wake of the death of George Floyd in Minneapolis in May. By the time he left office, about 400,000 had died with COVID-19 (though how many died *of* COVID-19 was another, unanswered, question).[59] Overall, every day seemed to bring a new drama, excited by Trump himself. As noted before, Trump's average RealClearPolitics approval rating never exceeded 47 percent, and was typically found in the low 40s. In November 2020, when the decisive electoral verdict was handed down by Americans, roughly two-thirds declared the country to be on the "wrong track."[60] So how did Trump overcome this disability?

Trump's apparent predicament was limited by the polarization gripping the nation, for his mediocre overall approval was an average between exceptionally low ratings among Democrats and exceptionally high ratings among Republicans, i.e. the voters who would decide whether he would receive another GOP nomination. Trump was fortunate that Joe Biden's presidency managed to make many Americans either forget his own or remember it more fondly. The biggest burst of inflation in 30 years and associated decline in real incomes, a near-total collapse of the Southern border, an ignominious retreat from Afghanistan, Iran and Russia back on the prowl, trillions of dollars in additional spending and debt, and controversial social policies on transgenderism and other issues, all coupled with Biden's visible deterioration, produced approval ratings for Biden that were comparable to or worse than Trump's four years earlier.[61] Even COVID-19, which had helped propel Biden into the White House, ceased to work for him. First, less than a year after Biden took office, COVID-19 deaths under Biden surpassed those under Trump, then the issue itself faded away as the disease mutated and became less deadly.[62]

2024 PRIMARIES

Against the ever-present backdrop of Trump versus himself, the former president also faced a number of challengers in the Republican primaries, who calculated that his vulnerabilities left an opening for a new contender. These included:

- Doug Burgum, successful businessman and governor of North Dakota, whose primary accomplishment was turning his state into an energy powerhouse.
- Tim Scott, junior senator from South Carolina, who in 2012 had become the first African American senator from his state.
- Chris Christie, former governor of New Jersey and former ally of Trump who had since turned bitter critic.
- Tech entrepreneur Vivek Ramaswamy, at 37 when he announced his candidacy the youngest of the lot, with an evident determination to be Trumpier than Trump.
- Mike Pence, Trump's vice president, who sought to weave a path between embracing most of Trump's policies while rejecting his character flaws and his postelection conduct—not least what Pence saw as his incitement of the January 6 riot that featured a crowd shouting "Hang Pence!"
- Nikki Haley, former South Carolina governor and ambassador to the United Nations during the Trump administration.
- Ron DeSantis, in his second term as governor of Florida, fresh off a blowout reelection in what is normally a close state.

Despite the apparent opportunity. the challengers struggled to gain traction. Except for Christie and Pence, they eschewed a strategy of frontally attacking Trump. In this, they repeated the strategic decision of most Republican candidates in 2016 to refrain from hitting Trump hard in hopes that he would fall of his own weight, or perhaps would fall from the blows of others. The end result was also the same.

Scott, despite stirring some initial interest, never caught on, his sunny optimism seemingly at odds with the tenor of the party. He dropped out on November 12, 2023. Burgum made no impression and left the race on December 4. Ramaswamy, who referred to Trump as "the best president of the 21st century,"[63] offered no compelling rationale for superseding the very stable genius, and was, on top of it, seen by some as arrogant and obnoxious (though others saw him as refreshing and authentic). Christie and Pence faced stiff headwinds in a party still smarting over Trump's loss, and still in the grip of his enthusiasts. Languishing in the polls, Christie dropped out five days before Iowa. Pence had already left the race by the end of October.

Pence's failure was more notable than it was noted. To many analysts, he already seemed like yesterday's news. But he was, arguably, the member of the 2024 Republican field most emblematic of the three-legged stool of the traditional conservative movement: a genuine fiscal conservative and free-marketeer, a strong social conservative on issues important to the religious right, and a vigorous supporter of national defense together with enthusiastic engagement with the allies who make up what was once called the Free World. That he fell so short was a sign of the changes that had taken place in the Republican Party since 2016, all the more so because he started the race as a recent vice president.

Through World War II, the vice presidency had been a dead-end job unless the president himself met a dead end. Since then, the position had become a launching pad for presidential aspirations. Since 1960, seven vice presidents had sought their party's presidential nomination. Six had succeeded—Nixon in both 1960 and 1968, Humphrey in 1968, Mondale in 1984, Bush in 1988, Gore in 2000, and Biden in 2016. Only Dan Quayle, running eight years after leaving the vice presidency, failed to secure a nomination. Until Pence. Then again, only Pence had to run for the nomination against the president under whom he had served.

In the end, only two candidates posed a real challenge to Trump: DeSantis and Haley, in that order.

DeSantis appeared first on the horizon in the wake of his gubernatorial win in the 2022 midterm elections. He was the politically successful and administratively competent governor of a large, important state. Like Trump, he was prone to picking fights on cultural issues; unlike Trump, he picked his fights carefully, and usually won. Like Trump, he professed his opposition to "globalism" and left-wing social fads. "Florida," DeSantis proclaimed, "is where woke goes to die." Promising Trumpism without Trump and his baggage, DeSantis had narrowed the gap with Trump to 10 percentage points (45 percent to 35 percent) at the beginning of January 2023.[64] Trump was concerned enough that he gifted the Florida governor a Trump-trademark nickname: Ron DeSanctimonious.

But then the Florida governor's progress stalled. Some observers sensed that he let his momentum stagnate, waiting too long to announce. When he made his campaign official in an online announcement event, the site crashed. Although his campaign could argue that the technical failure was a good sign, evidence of massive interest, it was not a good look for a candidate claiming to have an edge on competence. Once he began campaigning in earnest, he often came across as dry and technocratic—Trumpism without Trump's baggage, but also without his roguish charm. As two Republican consultants later dissected his campaign, it "should have defined their candidate as Trump-plus, something like the former president but better. Instead of merely trying to imitate Trump, they needed to add something of value, casting DeSantis' own vision for how Republicans can win the future. Instead, they offered the voters Trump-minus. DeSantis pretended to be just like Trump but in a less bombastic and less entertaining package."[65]

Moreover, just as DeSantis was poised to challenge Trump, Trump was indicted, indicted again, and indicted yet again. The backlash set in. Republican voters rallied around Trump, and his lead over DeSantis rebounded—to that extent, not a reflection on DeSantis, but on Republican voters' judgement against Trump's accusers. By January 1, 2024, a month before the Iowa caucuses, Trump averaged 61 percent nationally to DeSantis's 12 percent.[66]

While the Trump-DeSantis contest played out, Nikki Haley was moving up on DeSantis as the main alternative to Trump. Her plan was similar to Marco Rubio's strategic concept in 2016: finish in the top three in Iowa, win or come close in New Hampshire, then capitalize on her home-state status to win South Carolina, often seen as the gateway to the South. At this stage, Haley seldom criticized Trump frontally, but invited audiences to move past Trump and his drama. She appealed as a fresh, young face, fluent in both domestic and international affairs. Whichever party ditched its 80-year-old candidate first, she contended, would win. She also noted polls showing her defeating Joe Biden handily, unlike Trump, who seemed no better than a 50–50 gamble. By January 15, the day of the Iowa caucuses, Haley had surpassed DeSantis in the national polls.[67]

Trump eventually noticed Haley, too. He complained that she had promised him she wouldn't run against him, and gave Haley her own nickname—"Birdbrain"—leading some to ask why he had made her ambassador to the United Nations.[68] Haley was one of the few candidates who stepped into the minefield of entitlement spending, suggesting that the Social Security retirement age might need to be increased. Trump hammered her for betraying Grandma. For her views supporting continued U.S. aid to Ukraine, Haley was pilloried by some of Trump's supporters, who labeled her a "warmonger" and a RINO (Republican In Name Only), even though only a few years before Republicans as a whole were harshly criticizing Barack Obama as an appeaser for *not* providing military aid to Ukraine.

For the most part, though, Trump ignored his Republican opponents, clearly preferring to be treated as an incumbent. Like any heavily favored incumbent, he did not deign to debate his rivals, instead leaving them to fight among themselves on the crowded debate stage. Some tried to make the case that Trump owed his party a chance to see him and the other contenders side by side—and perhaps even a chance to hear him explain, under hostile questioning, why he should get another chance. Trump, of course, did not see the point, and no one could make him. So an incumbent he was, skipping the debates and traveling in the next best thing to Air Force One with a retinue befitting a president.

Until votes started coming in, at which point his campaign—and most of the major media—began acting as if he was just one challenger among equals. In the Iowa caucuses, traditional starting point to the delegate selection season, Trump prevailed with 51 percent of the vote to DeSantis's 21 percent and Haley's 19 percent. Not only did Trump win by an impressive margin, but his campaign bragged that he had broken the 50 percent mark, which no non-incumbent Republican candidate had ever done in a contested Iowa caucus race.[69] An incumbent held to 51 percent was a very different story, but few heard it. Seeing no way forward, DeSantis dropped out, along with Vivek Ramaswamy, who had garnered around 8 percent of the Iowa vote. Haley retained hope that she might win a breakthrough in New Hampshire, a state known for its political independence and its open primary. She was caught in a bind, though. To win, she would have to maximize her support among the state's crossover voters. But if she appealed too openly to Democrats and Independents, New Hampshire's Republicans would embrace Trump more tightly.

After Iowa, Haley's national standing improved—but so did Trump's, as he benefited from DeSantis's withdrawal. Eight days later, Trump won New Hampshire with 54 percent to Haley's 43 percent. Again, a solid win for Trump—if he was not compared to other incumbents. When incumbents such as Lyndon Johnson in 1968, Jimmy Carter in 1980, or George H. W. Bush in 1992 won the first-in-the-nation primary by a margin in that neighborhood, it had been widely seen as a sign of serious trouble for the winner—a vulnerable front-runner and a divided party caught up in an uncertain race.

When the contest moved to South Carolina, Trump beat Haley in her own backyard, 60 percent to 40 percent, and Haley's best opportunity to change the direction of the race was gone. She remained an active candidate through Super Tuesday on March 5, winning primaries in Vermont and the District of Columbia and averaging 27 percent, but she never again really threatened Trump. She was widely seen as more "moderate" than Trump, but it might be more accurate to say that she was closer to the traditional Republican, esteeming fiscal sobriety and international engagement in ways Trump did not. Unfortunately for her, the traditional Republican Party was swamped by MAGA. Haley's position on abortion—that states should decide the issue, and that good policy should make certain popular exceptions—was essentially Trump's position, too. As the campaign wore on, Haley also grew more sharply critical of her former boss, in mid-February calling him "diminished" and "unhinged."[70]

As the last serious holdout, Haley became the vehicle for the expression of residual dissatisfaction or concern about Trump among Republican primary voters. She dropped out on March 6, but for the remainder of the primary season she frequently won 15–20 percent of the vote even as a noncandidate.

Trump had accomplished the nearly unprecedented—winning renomination after having lost reelection—and did so without much difficulty. Two facts highlighted his conquest of the Republican Party apparatus. One was his ability within days of his Super Tuesday blowout to install his handpicked team at the head of the Republican National Committee—Michael Whatley as chair and his own daughter-in-law Lara Trump as co-chair. The Trump family takeover spoke for itself.[71] The second was Trump's performance in party caucuses. This act took place in the darker corners of the nominating process, in the few states that still used caucuses to select national convention delegates. The caucuses, which typically have low turnout, have always been more favorable ground for candidates who either dominate the party machinery or have the support of well-organized movements.[72] In 2016, Ted Cruz and Bernie Sanders were the big caucus winners in their respective parties. In 2024, though, Donald Trump dominated the Republican caucuses after Iowa, winning 100 percent in Missouri, 99 percent in Nevada, 98 percent in Michigan, 97 percent in Hawaii, 85 percent in Idaho, and 84 percent in North Dakota—typical of an incumbent president in control of his party.

But it would not be quite right to say that Trump's conquest of the Republican Party was absolute. A significant minority of Republicans were still willing, if not eager, to vote for someone else, even when no other candidates were campaigning. Whether these holdouts would vote for Trump in November remained a question until November.

Chapter 4

The Summer of the Switch

For good reason, many commentators have described Donald Trump as a divisive figure. But in an odd, 2024 kind of way, he was also a unifying figure. As we have seen, he managed to unify the Republican Party behind him, winning support from voters and party elites. He also unified the other side, too. Democrats saw the prospect of a second Trump as so frightening that they shied away from divisive challenges to Joe Biden. And when it was clear that Biden could not carry on effectively, they dispensed with a contentious fight about his successor and instantly rallied around Kamala Harris.

The summer of 2024 gave the nation a wild ride. Between June 27 and August 22, the election was seemingly turned on its head. At the same time, as the French say, the more things changed, the more they stayed the same.

An influential 2008 book titled *The Party Decides* argued that party elites continued to wield enormous influence over presidential nominations even in the age of primaries and caucuses.[1] These elites include elected officials, party officers, major contributors, interest group leaders, and other influencers. During the Trump era, the book's thesis no longer applied to the Republican Party: even though few party leaders supported him at the start of the 2016 campaign, he bulldozed his way to the nomination and eventually remade the GOP in his image. Nevertheless, the book's analysis continued to work on the Democratic side. As we explained in *Divided We Stand*, Biden clinched the 2020 nomination when his victory in the South Carolina primary triggered an outpouring of support from the Democratic establishment.

The establishment giveth and the establishment taketh away.

THE DEBATE THAT UPENDED THE RACE

On June 27, President Joe Biden and former president Donald Trump met in their first debate since October 2020. Biden, who had fallen behind Trump by 1.5 percent in the RealClearPolitics polling average and was suffering from ongoing questions about his age, challenged Trump to the debate three months before debates usually begin and before either had been officially nominated by their parties. The news network CNN was the host, and the rules adopted by the network were designed to curb intervention by the moderators and to foster a more civil discussion than the two men had shared four years before. To discourage interruptions, microphones would be turned off while the other candidate had a turn.

From the beginning of the debate, Trump seemed in command. Biden, on the other hand, seemed old, confused, tired, and even at times dazed. The debate, as usual, ranged over a variety of issues, but it was Biden's evident deterioration, rather than any issue, that was decisive. The Reuters news agency reported "The early going favored Trump, 78, who appeared forceful and energetic when compared to the 81-year-old Biden, who spoke in a hoarse, halting voice and offered sometimes meandering replies or trailed off during his answers to several questions."[2] In contrast to the 2020 presidential debates, Trump showed more discipline, rarely talking over Biden. As Reuters described one exchange over the national debt,

Biden seemed to lose his train of thought . . . his voice trailing off several times, Biden first referred to "billionaires" as "trillionaires" before correcting himself. Then, while arguing that the wealthy should pay more tax, he seemed unable to complete his sentence, pausing for an extended awkward moment, before ending his thought in a way that sounded nonsensical. Tax reform would create money to help "strengthen our healthcare system, making sure that we're able to make every single solitary person eligible for what I was able to do with the, with the COVID, excuse me, with dealing with everything we had to do with," Biden said before pausing. "We finally beat Medicare," Biden said, likely referring to COVID-19.

Before the June 27 debate, Democratic elites publicly said little about Biden's frailty. He had shown alertness and vigor often enough so they could publicly rationalize his senior moments as occasional missteps that anybody could make. Weeks before, the *Wall Street Journal* had published an explosive report based on inside sources that claimed Biden had been failing for months.[3] The reaction from the Democratic establishment and Democratic-leaning media was ferocious. The *Washington Post* editorial page, CNN's Oliver Darcy, and others dismissed the report as Republican propaganda,[4] and Vice President Harris continued vouching for Biden's soundness, as she had for months.[5]

But now, Biden had faltered at a high-stakes event for which he had plenty of time to prepare. Almost immediately, establishment figures started backing away. When a reporter asked if Biden were the party's most effective messenger, House Democratic Leader Hakeem Jeffries (D-NY) said: "I'm looking forward to hearing from President Biden. And until he articulates a way forward in terms of his vision for America at this moment, I'm going to reserve comment about anything relative to where we are at this moment, other than to say I stand behind the ticket." Under normal circumstances, the correct answer would have been "yes." Jeffries's convoluted prose suggested "no."[6]

In the following weeks, Biden faltered in media interviews that were intended to show that June 27 was an aberration. Trump's modest lead grew and some Democratic lawmakers publicly said Biden should withdraw from the race.[7] Many others said so privately. In a television interview, Nancy Pelosi did not call on him to pull out, but she sent an implicit message by declining to say that he should stay in. "It's up to the president to decide if he is going to run," she said. "We're all encouraging him to make that decision. Because time is running short."[8] Biden had insisted that he would keep running, so encouraging him to "make that decision" was tantamount to urging his withdrawal. Pelosi had stepped down from party leadership, but her opinion carried weight among Democratic elites. Major donors got the message, and Biden's fundraising plunged.

So did his support among rank-and-file Democrats. A couple of weeks after the debate, an AP-NORC poll found that most members of his party thought he should withdraw.[9] Journalist Jonathan Alter explained that "the common experience of gently taking the car keys away from elderly parents helped lead two thirds of Democrats to the conclusion that Biden was too old to run again."[10]

Democratic officeholders and candidates worried Biden would falter again, lose badly to Trump, and take many downballot Democrats with him. His persistence put them in a bind. If they called for his withdrawal, they would anger his loyalists within the party. If they said that he should stay in, Republicans would attack them for covering up his incapacity. Even if they were in no danger of losing their seats, such attacks could undermine their credibility with constituents. At the *New York Times*, Carl Hulse reported on a closed-door meeting of Senate Democrats: "Sheldon Whitehouse of Rhode Island said that if Mr. Biden continued to insist on running, he would be a loyal soldier and keep saying that the president was in good shape. But if Mr. Biden were to have another breakdown, that would make a liar of him, and his constituents would never believe him again. The argument resonated strongly with his colleagues."[11] Senate Majority Leader Schumer directly told Biden that he should drop out.

According to Bob Woodward, Secretary of State Anthony Blinken raised the question with Biden, framing it sympathetically. "Anyone who is written about gets one sentence," Blinken said. It would be fine if a decision to stay in the race ended in victory, but if it ended in defeat, "that's the sentence." Blinken also alluded to the reality that Biden would be 86 at the end of a second term. "Can you see yourself doing it for another four years? You've got to answer that question. And that's different than saying I'm doing the job at the moment. And that's what I'm concerned about."[12] Even after that discussion with his longtime friend, Biden leaned toward staying in.

BUOYANT REPUBLICANS

In the face of Biden's travails, Republicans, who had been cautiously optimistic, became veritably buoyant. Uncharacteristically, Trump became quiet, allowing the public to focus on the Democrats wallowing in their dilemma without distraction. (As Napoleon was reported to have said, never interfere with the enemy when he is in the process of destroying himself.) After a couple of weeks, Trump rejoined the campaign in earnest in the countdown to the Republican National Convention.

Then, at a campaign rally in Butler, Pennsylvania, on July 13, Trump was nearly killed by an assassin's bullet. As a he turned his head to point to a large chart on illegal immigration projected to a nearby screen, a bullet whizzed by his head, nicking his ear. Other bullets followed. Secret Service agents scrambled to cover him, and then moved him to a vehicle for a quick exit to the hospital. As he stood up to leave the stage with blood trickling down his ear, he pumped his fist and mouthed "Fight! Fight! Fight!" to the crowd. An alert photographer, Associated Press photojournalist Evan Vucci, caught pictures of Trump which immediately became iconic.

The 20-year-old attempted assassin, Thomas Matthew Crooks, had scouted the field in advance, had climbed onto a nearby roof, and had taken his shots from about 150 yards away, He failed to kill Trump, but did kill a project engineer and volunteer fireman sitting behind the former president, Corey Comperatore. He was then killed by a Secret Service sniper. He left behind no manifesto and few clues about his motivation. He also left behind serious worries about the competence of the Secret Service. A well-trained marksman would almost certainly have made a shot from that distance.

Politics in America being what they are in 2024, some on the right wondered whether the Secret Service had allowed the attempt to go forward. Some on the left suggested it was faked or that Trump's ear had not actually been wounded, while others expressed dismay on social media that the bullet had missed its mark. President Biden spoke to the nation from the White

House, saying "An assassination attempt is contrary to everything we stand for as a nation. Everything, Unity is the most elusive goal of all, but nothing is more important than that right now—unity."[13]

The assassin had come perilously close to succeeding. Had Trump not turned his head at the last second, the bullet that hit his ear would likely have hit his head and killed him.

The Republican convention opened in Milwaukee two days later in an atmosphere of near-euphoria. Not only was Joe Biden looking increasingly like a loser, but Donald Trump's narrow survival had injected a feeling of destiny into Trump's enterprise. The first day of the convention also saw Trump announce his choice for vice presidential running mate.

Speculation about the Republican veepstakes had been growing since Trump wrapped up his nomination in March. A wide variety of names had been floated by Trump or others—the *New York Intelligencer* published a list of 18[14]—but by early July, the field had reportedly narrowed to Governor Doug Burgum, Senator Tim Scott, Senator Marco Rubio, and Senator J. D. Vance. Rubio had the most experience in the Senate and might have extra appeal for Hispanic voters, but he had run against Trump for the Republican nomination in 2016. He also hailed from Florida, Trump's home state since 2019, and electors from Florida could not vote for both. In a close election won by Trump, the vice presidential selection might be thrown into the Senate, with an outcome impossible to know in July 2024. Scott, like Rubio, had crossed Trump in a nomination contest (in his case, 2024). On one hand, his challenge to Trump had been less serious than Rubio's; he had dropped out of the race before any votes were cast, and he had spent the intervening months smoothing things over with the former president. On the other hand, his solidly Republican home state of South Carolina was never going to be in play, and he showed none of the modest national appeal Rubio had demonstrated in 2016. Burgum was nondescript enough to never upstage Trump and his background in energy could be a mild plus, but it was not clear that he would really bring anything to the ticket.

J. D. Vance of Ohio was the one contender left standing, and Trump announced his selection on the opening day of the convention. Vance was young (39), smart (Yale law degree), and articulate. He had rocketed to national prominence as the author of *Hillbilly Elegy*, a 2016 memoir of his hardscrabble upbringing. In 2022, he had won an open U.S. Senate seat in Ohio by a solid margin (though he trailed governor Mike DeWine's reelection percentage by a significant margin). Traditional Republicans were wary, but MAGA loved the choice. Vance was, in some ways, Trumpier than Trump. Trump was an outsider, but had served as president four years; Vance had not even completed two years of his first Senate term. Trump had used tariffs as a weapon to advance better trade deals; Vance was more thoroughly protectionist. Trump expressed skepticism toward aid for Ukraine; Vance had revealed a deep hostility to Ukraine's cause, declaring during his Senate campaign that "I don't really care what happens to Ukraine one way or another,"[15] and proceeding in the Senate to act as if he meant it. Trump was a practical politician, where Vance seemed more like an ideologue, though the contours of his ideology were still developing. At times, he attached himself to set of thinkers who called themselves "post-liberal"—liberal in the classical sense, as in John Locke and the Declaration of Independence. What was perhaps more important to Trump, Vance had pledged the former president his absolute fealty, proclaiming that he would have done on January 6 what Trump unsuccessfully implored Mike Pence to do: refuse to count electoral votes from Biden states that Trump had contested, an act that would have thrown the United States into a constitutional crisis with no obvious endpoint.[16] Aside from all of this, Vance was the first candidate on a major party ticket since Benjamin Harrison in 1892 to sport a beard. On the Wednesday of the convention, Vance delivered his acceptance speech, introducing his Indian American wife and calling for an American patriotism based less on love of abstract American ideals than on love of hearth and home.[17]

The rest of the Republican convention was a Trump-fest, punctuated by speaking slots for several members of Trump's family, an appearance by longtime professional wrestler Hulk Hogan, and finally Trump himself, who spoke for 92 minutes to accept his nomination. The former president spent the first half hour of his speech reflecting on the recent assassination attempt, promising a gentler approach to politics, and embracing Corey Comperatore's volunteer fire uniform, which was draped over a mannequin on stage. The remaining hour, concluding after midnight Eastern Time, was spent in Trump's familiar meandering style—what he called his "weave"—extolling his first presidential administration and attacking Joe Biden and other assorted liberals.[18] Throughout, Trump assumed the mantle of someone who had been spared by divine intervention to accomplish a great destiny. Most Republicans at the convention seemed to agree.

Republicans left Milwaukee in good spirits, expecting to do battle for the next three months with an enfeebled Joe Biden and a dispirited Democratic Party. Three days after the end of the convention, Trump had a national lead of 47.8 to 44.8 in the RealClearPolitics polling average. However, some observers such as Keith Naughton complained that Trump's speech was "a momentum-killer and a stupendously lost opportunity."[19] Trump had gained ground in the polls since the debate, but not as much as one might expect given Biden's situation. The so-called "double-haters," voters who didn't much like either Trump or Biden, still seemed to be in the driver's seat. Then the picture changed abruptly.

DEMOCRATS COME BACK

In the most literal sense, the elites could not force Biden out. He had the support of nearly all the delegates to the Democratic convention. Most of them had gotten to be delegates because they were strong Biden supporters, so it was unlikely he could lose the nomination if he pressed on. But would the nomination be worth having? Donor reluctance would hobble his campaign in the fall, and Democratic calls for withdrawal would weaken his public support even further. The last straw was internal polling that showed he was not only behind in swing states but was hemorrhaging voter support in states he had counted on.[20] On July 21, he decided to withdraw.

During the party's weeks of indecision, some Democrats wondered whether Harris would be a good replacement candidate. They worried about her low poll ratings, the disorganization of her 2020 campaign, and her frequent word salads, which Republicans had gleefully turned into snarky videos. Nancy Pelosi, who had been Harris-skeptical since the 2003 district attorney race in San Francisco, floated the idea of an open convention to choose a Democratic standard-bearer.[21] The idea was impractical. The party had not had an open convention in more than 60 years, and nobody knew how it would work.

Despite some trepidations within her party, Harris was an obvious successor. The Democratic bench was not deep, probably limited to a handful of potential contenders such as Arizona senator Mark Kelly and governors Josh Shapiro of Pennsylvania, Gavin Newsom of California, and Gretchen Whitmer of Michigan. Unlike most of the rumored candidates, Harris had undergone a thorough vetting, first as a candidate for the nomination in 2020, then as Biden's running mate. Only she would have unfettered access to Biden's campaign funds because she was already on the filing statements as a candidate with Biden.[22] And because of the power of the Black vote, it would have been difficult for the Democratic Party to pass over the first Black vice president. Just before Biden announced his withdrawal, he consulted with James Clyburn, to whom he owed the 2020 nomination. In an interview with reporter Jasmine Wright, Clyburn recalled: "When Joe Biden called me that morning, read me his statement, I said to him at the time, 'There's something missing in this statement.' And he knew what I meant. And he said to me at the time, 'I will be issuing a second statement within the hour.' And that was the statement endorsing her."[23]

Initially, Pelosi held her endorsement, as did Barack and Michelle Obama. After the November election, Pelosi complained that Biden's late exit and quick endorsement of Harris short-circuited the option of another candidate, saying "And because the president endorsed Kamala Harris immediately, that really made it almost impossible to have a primary at that time. If it had been much earlier, it would have been different."[24] Less diplomatically,

Democratic campaign surrogate Lindy Li told Fox News that "I actually think President Biden, the whole endorsing her 30 minutes after he dropped out, I think that was a big, F you to the party. 'If you don't want me, here's somebody you may not like, deal with it.'"[25]

Whatever machinations were taking place behind the scenes, the party united behind Harris with astonishing speed. Within a couple of days, she won support from most Democratic governors, senators, and House members—including Nancy Pelosi.[26] Nearly every leading Democrat bowed out of consideration, and Harris got commitments from enough convention delegates to clinch the nomination.[27] Meanwhile, more than $100 million poured into the Harris campaign (immediately rebranded from Biden-Harris), the Democratic National Committee, and joint fundraising committees.[28]

The clock was one reason for the hasty unification. Because of legal questions surrounding Ohio's deadline for certifying general election candidates, the Democrats had decided to make the nomination official through a virtual roll call in early August.[29] Another reason was the drive and ambition that Harris had displayed in previous campaigns. Biden gave her the news shortly before he went public. She assembled her advisers and was ready to start working the phones one minute after Biden announced his decision. By the end of the day, she had called 100 Democratic leaders to lock down their support.[30] She also launched a whip operation to wrangle delegates.

Perhaps most of all, it was the sudden release from the threat of an electoral wipeout. Exhilaration flowed through the ranks as anxious Democratic politicians learned they now had a fighting chance after all. They did not want to blow it by toying with unvetted alternatives or a divisive convention. Democratic voters agreed: 79 percent expressed satisfaction with Harris.[31]

CAPTURE THE FLAG

Harris won 99 percent in the virtual roll call that decided the nomination, so the convention would instead feature a made-for-television "celebratory roll call." The choice of the vice presidential candidate was the only actual decision ahead. With the convention starting on August 19, she had to act quickly. Former Attorney General Eric Holder led the accelerated vetting process, which appraised the advantages and disadvantages of various potential candidates. The choice came down to Senator Mark Kelly of Arizona, Governor Josh Shapiro of Pennsylvania, and Governor Tim Walz of Minnesota. Kelly was a veteran, a former astronaut, and the devoted husband of former representative Gabby Giffords, who had suffered disabling wounds from a shooting. Though his story was inspiring, his speaking skills were not, and he was the first of the three to drop from consideration. Shapiro, by contrast, was a gifted orator and the popular governor of a crucial swing state. Many commentators suggested his presence on the ticket would enhance Harris's chances of winning Pennsylvania. On the other hand, the media reported various considerations that weighed against him: in particular, his strenuous support for Israel in the Gaza war had purportedly made him unacceptable to hardcore progressives.[32] Some commentators, such as the famous attorney Alan Dershowitz, even suggested that progressive antisemitism was working against the Jewish Shapiro.[33] Whatever her reasons for rejecting Shapiro, Harris picked Walz.

Progressives applauded Walz for his liberal record as governor. He also had potential appeal to mainstream voters. His longtime service in the National Guard seemed likely to give him credibility among veterans, though critics noted inconsistencies in how he had described his military record. He had been a teacher and coach, two professions Americans tend to admire. His "regular guy" demeanor was a counterweight to the pretentious image of the Brahmin wing. And whereas Harris's life and career had unfolded chiefly in big cities, Walz had grown up in rural Nebraska and had spent most of his adult life in Mankato, Minnesota, the soybean-crushing capital of the world. His selection showed that Harris took the party's rural voter deficit seriously, or so Democrats hoped.[34] (He would still have to defend a record that placed him firmly on the left, including support for a Minnesota bill that required schools to provide menstrual products to "transmale" students.[35])

For all the buzz surrounding the choice, it was unlikely to drive a statistically significant share of the vote. As suggested earlier, neither Biden nor Harris had singlehandedly tipped any states into the Democratic column when they were vice presidential nominees. But in an election that could hinge on tiny margins in a few states, even a small difference could make a big difference.

Although political conventions no longer command the same share of the television audience as in the pre-cable area, they still give parties a chance to reshape their public image. In Chicago, the Democrats sought to claim the mantle of patriotism with abundant flags, numerous speeches by military veterans, and repeated chants of "USA! USA!" Harris's acceptance speech went further, not only proclaiming her own patriotism, but questioning Trump's. Alluding to the January 6 attack on the Capitol, she said: "You can always trust me to put country above party and self; to hold sacred America's fundamental principles, from the rule of law to free and fair elections to the peaceful transfer of power." [36] She added that a reelected Trump would do the opposite: "he would use the immense powers of the presidency of the United States not to improve your life, not to strengthen our national security, but to serve the only client he has ever had: himself."

In an election that could come down to a sliver of moderate voters in a few swing states, Harris positioned herself as a bipartisan centrist. On the fraught issue of immigration, she said: "Last year, Joe and I brought together Democrats and conservative Republicans to write the strongest border bill in decades. The Border Patrol endorsed it. But Donald Trump believes a border deal would hurt his campaign, so he ordered his allies in Congress to kill the deal." Whereas Trump had literally called her a communist, Harris proposed "access to capital for small-business owners and entrepreneurs and founders." She summed up her domestic policy by calling for an "opportunity economy"—a variation on "opportunity society," a favorite phrase of Ronald Reagan.[37]

That was not her only pitch to the center-right. On national security, she sounded downright hawkish: "As commander in chief, I will ensure America always has the strongest, most lethal fighting force in the world. . . . And as president, I will stand strong with Ukraine and our NATO allies." She drew a contrast with her opponent: "Trump, on the other hand, threatened to abandon NATO. He encouraged Putin to invade our allies. Said Russia could, quote, 'do whatever the hell they want.'" These remarks also showed how far the Democrats had come since the 2012 campaign, when Barack Obama ridiculed Mitt Romney's prescient assertion that Russia was our number one geopolitical foe.

Like Republicans in Milwaukee, Democrats left Chicago joyful. The party seemed unified. Outside the convention center, there were protests against American policy in the Gaza war, but the much-feared repeat of the 1968 riots did not materialize. Money was coming in, and volunteers were signing up. But in the back of their minds, Democrats also had memories of 2016, when they were confident of victory until the night of the election. It also remained to be seen whether Harris's abrupt transformation from a California progressive into a centrist would seem plausible to enough voters to win the day.

The day after the Democratic convention ended, it had been 57 days since the momentous debate between Trump and Biden. In that period, the nation had witnessed a politically fatal debate, the first withdrawal of a sitting president from his reelection effort since 1968, a barely failed assassination attempt, and two party conventions, including one that nominated a candidate who had not competed in any primaries for the first time in the modern era. Heads were spinning, and one could be forgiven for thinking that everything had changed. Underneath it all, though, the more things changed, the more they stayed the same.

Chapter 5

General Election

The Comeback Completed

When Joe Biden left the race, it quickly reset to what it seemed to be roughly a year earlier. By the by time the Democratic national convention ended, the public opinion polls said that Trump's national lead over Biden had been supplanted by a Harris lead of 1.5 percentage points.[1] Estimates of the electoral vote lagged a bit, but RealClearPolitics showed Harris moving into the lead on August 29 if no states were considered toss-ups and on September 12 if toss-ups were taken into account. [2] Moreover, Harris had undergone a transformation of public perception. On July 24, 39 percent saw her favorably and 52 percent unfavorably. By August 24, her favorables had risen to 47 percent, nearly even with her unfavorables; after another month, she was in net positive territory.[3] To many Democrats, Harris's lead was a natural result of Trump now facing a fully sentient opponent and could be expected to be sustained through Election Day. To Republicans, it was a "sugar high" that would naturally subside as public dissatisfaction with the Biden administration reasserted itself and Harris's own shortcomings came into clearer view. They could both be wrong, but they could not both be right.

STATE OF PLAY

Regardless of candidates, campaigns, and unpredictable events—what one might call the contingencies—every presidential election is bounded by what one might call the fundamentals. There are a number of factors, sometimes reinforcing, that political scientists have focused on to try to explain or even predict presidential election results. Most pointed in the direction of a win by a Republican candidate in 2024 (who happened to be Trump, in the actual instance).

71

The economy: Many measures of economic health, such as GDP growth and unemployment, were relatively strong. The problem for Democrats was that the worst economic indicator since January 2021, inflation, was the one that had the nation's attention. Overall prices measured by the Consumer Price Index rose by nearly 21 percent from January 2021 to November 2024. In contrast, overall prices rose by about one-third as much during Trump's presidency between January 2017 and November 2020.[4] Unlike unemployment, which can be painful but usually affects a limited portion of the population, almost everyone feels the effects of rising prices. As a result, large majorities in the fall of 2024 said the economic condition of the country was not good, though those majorities were even larger in the late spring.[5]

Right track/wrong track: Undoubtedly related to public perceptions of the economy, most Americans were telling pollsters that the country was on the wrong track, not the right track. On August 21, the RCP average was showing that nearly two-thirds (64.8 percent) agreed with the wrong-track assessment, only about a quarter (25.5 percent) with the right-track view.[6] Though there had been some ups and downs over the years, those numbers had been fairly consistent for a decade and a half, and were not far off from the right track/wrong track responses in every presidential election from 2008 on. In only one of those elections did the incumbent party return to office (2012).

Presidential approval: Another underlying "fundamental" reflecting the election environment is the incumbent president's approval rating. This factor is important even when there is no incumbent running because, metaphorically speaking, the incumbent is always on the ballot. No matter what names appear, there is always some degree to which the election will serve as a referendum on the incumbent party. Throughout 2024, there was an open question about whether Trump would fully be able to run as the challenger, but there was no question that Biden would be a drag on the Democratic candidate. On August 24, Biden's average approval rating according to RealClearPolitics was 40.8 percent, and it would barely budge through Election Day.[7]

Vice Presidents: Generally speaking, although vice presidents in the modern era have had the inside track when seeking their party's presidential nomination, it is difficult for a sitting vice president to win the general election. Indeed, since the rise of the stable two-party system in the 1830s, only two vice presidents have managed it: Martin van Buren in 1836 and George H. W. Bush in 1988. Since World War II, three others had tried it but lost, including Richard Nixon in 1960, Hubert Humphrey in 1968, and Al Gore in 2000. (Gore did win the aggregated popular vote, however.) The individuals may change, but the dilemma is always the same. Vice presidents running for president must show they are independent-minded and untainted by the President's failings without appearing disloyal.[8] The Monday after the Democratic convention, Kamala Harris got a foretaste of this challenge when she insisted that Biden's handling of the Afghan withdrawal was "courageous and right."[9]

The state of the parties: Underlying any election is the state of the parties at that moment. It is a reasonable question whether this factor should be seen as fixed or variable, a question that frequently bedevils pollsters. By the autumn campaign, however, there is little room for movement. In September, Gallup found that Democratic and Republican party identifiers were essentially even (30 percent Democrat, 29 percent Republican). Including "leaners" who initially claim to be independent but later admit to leaning toward a major party, Republicans held a 50–45 percent lead.[10]

At the same time, a flurry of third-party activity had raised the question of whether an upsurge in dissatisfaction by the "double-haters" might leave an opening for third-party contestants. Possible spoilers included Libertarians, Greens, No Labels moderates, pro-Palestinians represented by Cornel West, and Robert F. Kennedy Jr. In April, No Labels gave up trying to find a candidate, leaving Kennedy as the strongest third-party option.[11]

Robert F. Kennedy Jr., son of the late senator and scion of the first family of Democratic politics, started as an environmental lawyer—a suitable occupation for a Kennedy. In the early 2000s, however, he embraced the discredited notion that vaccines cause autism. He published a 2005 article on the subject in *Rolling Stone* and *Salon*, and it was so badly flawed that both publications later retracted it. In 2007, he founded a nonprofit that spread inaccurate information about fluoridation as well as vaccines. The COVID-19 pandemic turbocharged fringe theories, and Kennedy began reaching a larger audience.

He initially entered the 2024 race as a candidate for the Democratic nomination. Despite some respectable showings in the polls, he switched to running as an independent. Because of the Kennedy name alone, Democratic operatives feared that he would act as a spoiler, drawing votes from Biden. Adding to their concern was the disclosure that a major GOP donor was bankrolling a pro-Kennedy super PAC. In April, 15 members of the Kennedy family pushed back against the spoiler threat by publicly rejecting their relative and endorsing Biden. The following month, a survey suggested that he would draw support mostly from Democrats who would otherwise defect to Trump. Apparently, his anti-vaccine stand appealed to this group, making him a spoiler for Trump instead of Biden. The day after the Democratic convention ended, Kennedy withdrew from the race and endorsed Trump.[12] Overall, the two-party balance slightly favored Republicans, and the possibility of a third party shaking up that equation greatly diminished. Advantage: Trump.

Longevity of party control: Finally, one structural factor seemingly worked in favor of Kamala Harris. An incumbent party seldom loses after holding the White House for only one term. In the 10 presidential elections since World

War II that saw a party switch in control of the presidency, only two came after one term. One case was Jimmy Carter, the other was Donald Trump himself. That fact, however, could cut two ways. On one hand, Trump had already lost when most similarly situated candidates had won, so Harris supporters could optimistically expect that he would lose again when in his new, less structurally favorable, situation. On the other hand, since he had already recently served one term himself, perhaps Harris's advantage here would be mitigated.

Altogether, the fundamentals weighed against Harris. At any rate, they pointed to a couple of imperatives for the Harris campaign: it would have to try to refocus Americans' attention away from rising prices and toward more favorable economic news, and it would have to find some separation from the unpopular Biden. Those tasks would prove as difficult as they were important. Political campaigns are seldom capable of convincing Americans that they should be less concerned with their economic problems or that the vice president is not really part of the administration. The second task was further complicated by Kamala Harris herself at varying points.

THE FALL CAMPAIGN

Regardless of the setting, campaigns invariably involve decisions about what themes to emphasize and where to employ resources—money, volunteers, and the time of the presidential and vice presidential candidates.

The "where" part was mostly obvious. In 2016, Trump prevailed in the electoral vote by winning some close large states that had been trending Republican (Ohio and Florida), holding on to some midsize states that had long been Republican-leaning but were getting closer (Georgia, Arizona, and North Carolina), and squeaking by in the so-called "Blue Wall" of long-standing Democratic states in the Rust Belt (Pennsylvania, Wisconsin, and Michigan).[13] In 2020, Trump won Ohio, Florida, and North Carolina, but lost the rest—both the Blue Wall states and Georgia and Arizona.[14] In both years, Democrats won Nevada by small margins. By 2024, not much had changed in the prospective outlook. Ohio and Florida had gone out of reach for Democrats, leaving seven obvious "swing states" that could seemingly go either way—Georgia and North Carolina in the Southeast, Pennsylvania, Michigan, and Wisconsin in the Rust Belt, and Arizona and Nevada in the Southwest.

Throughout the fall, other states would occasionally appear targets. At various points, Trump strategists thought New Hampshire, Virginia, or even Minnesota, Tim Walz's home state, could be in play. Democrats briefly dreamed of Texas, Florida, or, on the last weekend before Election Day, Iowa. But the seven top targets remained constant, and Pennsylvania was first among equals.

If the geography was easy, messaging was harder. To be sure, some themes pursued by each candidate were obvious. Trump would hammer at inflation, asking voters if they were better off than they were four years before, and would claim "tariff" was "the most beautiful word in the dictionary."[15] As he had done all year, he would also hammer at the collapse of the southern border and would connect the influx of illegal immigrants to crime and other quality-of-life issues. Trump also struck hard at cultural issues, focusing on a facet of "wokeness" that struck many Americans as extreme: Harris's apparent devotion to transgender ideology. Using as a wedge her 2019 campaign statement that she would provide federal funding for sex-change operations for federal prison inmates, a widely aired Trump campaign ad emphasized Trump's opposition to biological males participating in girls' sports with the tagline "She's for they/them. President Trump is for you." Analysts across the party spectrum claimed the ad was unusually effective, and some studies agreed (for example, one study by Future Forward claimed the ad shifted voters who saw it against Harris by 2.7 percent).[16] Above all, Trump labeled Harris too liberal and sought to connect her to Biden, as one would expect any challenger to do when facing the vice president of an unpopular president.

Harris tried to dodge that blow by claiming the mantle of change for herself, saying it was "time to turn the page" and touting the slogan "A new way forward." In that light, she adopted a hopeful appearance as she moved to become the very personification of "joy." She even adopted some of the signature elements of Barack Obama's 2008 campaign, such as the Obama-style portrait emblazoned with the word "Joy" where Obama's "Hope" had been. Harris promised an "opportunity economy," but it largely amounted to a $5 trillion tax increase, including a widely panned tax on unrealized capital gains, and price controls.

With two-thirds of Americans believing the country was on the wrong track, joy would not be enough. Complementing joy were two crosscutting themes, not only different from Joy/Change but in tension with it. One was abortion. The Democratic campaign thought that focusing on the loss of abortion rights in the *Dobbs* case would mobilize women and the young enough to carry the day. The other was democracy. Biden had gotten some purchase in 2022 with his midterm election argument that defeating Trump-affiliated MAGA Republicans was necessary to protect democracy, and Harris hoped a similar argument would bear fruit in 2024. The juxtaposition of democracy and abortion was not entirely coherent—after all, the overturning of *Roe v. Wade* put abortion back in the hands of voters and elected officials, arguably a move toward greater democracy. Nevertheless, the issues had in common a dark fear of extinguished freedom that did not necessarily mesh with joy. And the defense of democracy, an argument contending that only Harris and

Democrats could forestall malign change, also did not quite fit with Harris as agent of change. Was she conservative or progressive?

One serious issue did not get serious attention from either candidate. That was the federal deficit of approximately $1.8 trillion in fiscal year 2024 and the accumulated national debt of around $36 trillion. The mind-boggling numbers posed a serious threat to national well-being, but the most either candidate could muster was a charge by Harris that Trump was secretly planning to cut Social Security, which Trump denied. Otherwise, both candidates were quickly sunk in a pander-fest. Harris promised more student loan forgiveness and free money for house down payments, Trump free IVF treatments and tax-free Social Security and tips (later copied by Harris).[17]

Nor was there much specificity about foreign policy. Harris hardly discussed it at all, except to berate Trump for his bromances with foreign dictators during his first term. Trump referred to foreign policy more often, but only by way of noting the disorder that had overtaken the world during Biden's stewardship. Democrats were deeply divided over Gaza, Republicans over Ukraine, and both candidates had an incentive to paper over their internal differences.

The events of the fall proceeded apace, but the standing of the candidates appeared to change very little. There were a handful of moments of note.

1. Presidential debate. After Harris was confirmed as the Democratic nominee, the two campaigns agreed to a debate on September 10 hosted by ABC News. Harris was on the offensive for most of the debate, and was judged by most viewers to have "won." Throughout, she goaded Trump into focusing on his grievances, and he went down a rabbit hole when he claimed Haitian immigrants in Springfield, Ohio were eating other people's pets, a story subsequently denied by the town's mayor and the governor of Ohio. A CNN flash poll showed that viewers of the debate thought Harris did better by almost a 2–1 margin.[18] It was not clear how much difference it made. On September 10, the day of the debate, RCP showed Harris leading the national vote 48.4 to 47.3 percent. On September 18, Harris peaked at 49.4 to Trump's 47.4 percent.[19] Essentially, Trump had held steady, and Harris had gained a point—potentially important in a close race, but hardly a game changer. And then even that meager effect faded. At the time, Democrats in the know such as David Plouffe intimated that their own internal polling was not consistent with a big Harris lead; after the election, Plouffe said the campaign's own polls never showed Harris ahead.[20]

    Moreover, some focus groups of undecided voters showed a more mixed verdict. Some of Trump's arguments had scored.[21] He may also have benefited from a perception of media unfairness. ABC had announced before the debate that the moderators would not engage in any "fact-checking" during the debate. They did anyway, frequently correcting Trump but never correcting Harris, even when she made clear misstatements.[22] Some conservative commentators described the debate as a three-on-one contest—Harris and the two moderators against Trump.

In the wake of the debate, Trump announced he would consider no second debate with Harris. Democrats said Trump's refusal was evidence that he had lost the debate and did not want to tangle with the prosecutor Harris again. Republicans argued that Trump's refusal meant that he concluded that he won the debate, was winning the election, and did not want to give Harris another chance.

2. Vice presidential debate. As has become customary, the vice presidential candidates also debated. On October 1, J. D. Vance and Tim Walz met in New York City. The result was different from the Trump-Harris debate in two respects. First, the debate was more civil and substantive, leading some commentators to express regret that Walz and Vance were not at the top of their party's tickets.[23] Second, Vance pretty clearly got the better of Walz, who was reduced at one point to acknowledging "I'm a knucklehead" when confronted with the fact that he had not, as he had claimed, been in China at the time of the Tiananmen massacre.[24] Walz landed a blow late in the debate when he asked Vance who won the 2020 election and the Ohio senator would not answer, but the general view of analysts was that Vance had won.[25] A week later, almost nothing had changed in the polls, but Trump then began a steady upward climb. At a minimum, Vance seems to have significantly enhanced his own public standing. Exit polls would show that Vance was the only candidate of the four on the major party tickets with a net positive favorability rating.[26] There would be no further debates, presidential or vice presidential.

3. Smith filing. Of the four criminal cases against Trump, three remained. The federal documents case was dismissed when the judge held that the appointment of the prosecutor was unconstitutional. The Fulton County election racketeering case was still on hold pending review of ethical questions surrounding the prosecutor. The Jack Smith January 6 case charging Trump with conspiracy to overthrow the election results was also on hold as Smith sorted through the complicated implications of the Supreme Court's presidential immunity decision. Although Smith could not proceed to trial, he could continue to prepare his argument. On October 2, with the permission of District Court Judge Tanya Chutkan, Smith released to the public 1,800 pages of detailed evidence behind the charges and a 165-page summary. For those who read it,

the document put Trump in an even worse light regarding the January 6 riots.[27] Most Americans, however, did not read it. At most, they read about it, and what they read was a mixed bag. Smith outlined his case more strongly than ever, but Smith's unorthodox reveal was widely interpreted as an attempt to interfere in the election; even the *Washington Post* called the timing "dubious."[28] In the end, the filing confirmed the views of Democrats that Trump was unfit, confirmed the views of Republicans that Trump was sore oppressed, and seemed to have little effect on those in the middle, who had probably already priced in Trump's legal problems.

4. The Harris interviews. By mid-September, Harris was coming under increasing criticism from friend and foe alike for avoiding live interviews and talk shows since becoming the de facto Democratic nominee six weeks earlier. She responded by embarking on a series of interviews. These interviews frequently reminded voters of Harris's propensity for word salads and reluctance to provide specifics. At one point, asked what she would do about inflation, Harris provoked ridicule by falling back on a long, winding, and frequently repeated disquisition about her childhood. "I grew up a middle-class kid. . . . I grew up in a neighborhood of folks who were very proud of their lawn."[29]

It was an appearance on *The View* on October 8 that was most harmful, though. Asked by Sunny Hostin what she would have done differently from Joe Biden as president—a question she should have both expected and hoped for as an opportunity to achieve some distance from the president—she answered, "There is not a thing that comes to mind. . . . I've been a part of most of the decisions that have had impact."[30] Later in the interview, she offered something, though it was largely symbolic; unlike her boss, she would have appointed a Republican to a cabinet post. But the damage was done, and she essentially repeated her initial answer in subsequent interviews. Harris's battle to establish an independent persona, so critical to any vice president of a president widely seen as unsuccessful, was over, and she had lost.

"There is not a thing that comes to mind" became the mantra of Trump ads flooding the airwaves. If Vance's debate performance may have made a marginal timed-release contribution to Trump's rise, Harris's gaffe was more clearly connected. Harris appeared on *The View* on October 8, and Trump's poll rise began almost immediately after. The fundamentals place constraints on election outcomes, but they may need to be activated somehow to have their full effect. The interconnected cascade of inflation, wrong-track numbers, presidential (dis)approval, and vice presidential disadvantage may have been more fully activated by Harris's positive self-connection to Biden.

5. Trump surges. For the remainder of October, Trump gradually closed the gap, eventually overtaking Harris. On October 15. Harris led national polls by 1.7 percentage points, on October 22 she led by .9, and by October 30 Trump led by .4 in the RCP polling average, though some other polling aggregators still showed Harris ahead by a bit.[31] It began to appear that Trump might win the nationally aggregated popular vote, which no Republican had done since 2004. For a longer time, it had been clear that Trump held the advantage in the electoral vote. Leaving aside states so close that they were considered toss-ups, Trump had led narrowly (219 to 215) since September 23. On October 30, that score became 219–211 when New Hampshire moved from the "leans Democrat" to "toss-up" category.[32] When assigning every state to the leading candidate, no matter how narrow the margin, Trump had surged into a lead as early as September 29, when Pennsylvania flipped for the umpteenth time. By October 17, when Wisconsin flipped to Trump, Trump appeared to have a 312–226 lead in the Electoral College.[33] Consequently, until late October, it was widely expected that Trump might win the electoral vote—and hence the presidency—while again trailing in the aggregated popular vote. Betting odds had shifted dramatically in Trump's favor. After leading there most of the time since August 8, the last day that Harris led in the betting odds was October 5. On October 6, Trump edged ahead, and by October 29, betting markets estimated Trump had a 63.9 percent probability of winning.[34]

Harris continued stumbling through interviews, and Trump continued attacking her for the failures of the Biden-Harris administration. One of the biggest events of October was the annual Al Smith charity dinner held by New York Catholics. Traditionally, presidential candidates come, joke gently with each other and at themselves, and demonstrate their commitment to common civility. At the October 18 dinner, neither candidate crowned themselves in glory. As he did in 2016, Trump delivered remarks that were widely seen as mean-spirited and inappropriate to the event though, uncharacteristically, he apologized for one joke that he acknowledged was too nasty. The only thing that saved his night was that Harris did not show up at all, sending a widely-panned videotaped message.[35]

Trump had the momentum. He was also in a stronger position in 2024 than he had been in 2016 (when he won) and 2020 (when he nearly won).[36] All eyes, of course, were on the seven key swing states. In late October, according to RealClearPolitics, Trump led in all seven, if only narrowly.[37]

6. The end game: Dumpster Fire. All of this set up a denouement that raised the question "who was going to make the last and worst mistake?" On the other hand, the last two weeks also offered up some of the best political entertainment since Richard Nixon appeared on *Laugh-In*.

On the Republican side, Donald Trump leveraged his instincts and experience as an entertainer, trolling Harris when he served French fries at the drive-through window of a Philadelphia-area McDonald's. (Harris had claimed she worked at a McDonald's as a teenager, but had difficulty verifying it.) The joy had officially migrated from Harris to Trump.

Trump also increasingly ventured deep into Democratic territory. Having gone to Coachella for a Southern California rally, he scheduled a rally for Madison Square Garden in New York City on October 27. The rally was, as usual, boisterous. It was also, in the view of many observers, indicative of a familiar lack of discipline that seemed to return to Trump after a period of somewhat greater campaign discipline under campaign manager Susie Wiles. Trump himself spoke for 80 minutes, again calling the left "the enemy within." A line of Trump supporters led off, emitting a variety of obscenities. And then there was comedian Tony Hinchcliffe, whose joke that Puerto Rico was a "floating island of garbage" became the focus of critics' ire.[38] Although the joke was anchored in real struggles the island had experienced for years with issues of trash disposal, it was seen by many (including several Republican elected officials with large Puerto Rican constituencies) as an insult to Puerto Ricans.[39] At the very least, the furor around the joke was a distraction at an inopportune time, and Trump's campaign had to disavow it.

Just as Trump was put on his back foot, Joe Biden did him a favor. Three days after the rally, Biden told a Latino voting group, "The only garbage I see floating out there is his supporters," igniting a new firestorm.[40] Harris felt obliged to disavow the comment, and Biden later claimed he really meant to say that the comedian was garbage. Then there was additional scandal when the Associated Press reported that the White House press office had violated protocol and released an altered transcript supporting Biden's "clarification" over the objections of the White House stenographer.[41]

At almost the exact hour that Biden was making his contribution to the politics of garbage, Harris held a rally at the Ellipse in Washington to deliver her "closing argument." The argument, that Trump was a threat to national unity, that it was time to turn the page on Trump's enemies lists and the divisiveness of an earlier era, was largely drowned out by Biden calling half the country "garbage."[42] Biden's insult opened the door for Trump to engage in a second high-profile show in 10 days. In Green Bay on October 30, Trump donned an orange work vest and drove a garbage truck decorated with a Trump 2024 sign and Trump-Vance flags.[43]

At the same time Biden was giving Trump his opportunity, Democrats were attacking the Madison Square Garden rally from another overheated and counterproductive angle. The Garden, as it is called in New York, is a venerable site for major events. For decades, it has been the site for home games of the New York Knicks (NBA) and New York Rangers (NHL). It also hosted the 1976 and 1980 Democratic national conventions and 2004 Republican national convention, and serves as the location for annual graduation ceremonies of the New York Police Academy, Yeshiva University, and Baruch College. It turns out that a different building with the same name was the site of an infamous 1939 rally by the German-American Bund, a pro-Nazi organization. Newsreels of the event at the time revealed to shocked Americans scenes of Bund members in German stormtrooper uniforms beating up Jewish bystanders as if they were in Munich rather than Manhattan.

Harris had already escalated her rhetoric on democracy, and in her speech at the Ellipse she called Trump a "petty tyrant" and "wannabe dictator" who is "unstable, obsessed with revenge, consumed with grievance, and out for unchecked power."[44] To this end, she had also campaigned with Liz Cheney, the former Republican congresswoman who was one of two Republicans on the January 6 committee in the House. Others added their views that Trump had fascistic tendencies, including John Kelly, Trump's former chief of staff, who said Trump would fall into the "general definition of a fascist, for sure."[45] When White House Press Secretary Karine Jean-Pierre was asked if President Biden agreed with the characterization of Trump as a fascist, her answer: "Yes."[46] Now, Trump's rally at the Garden became the target of Democrats who drew a straight line between Trump's rally and the 1939 German-American Bund rally. Among others, Hillary Clinton and Tim Walz both compared the two events at the Garden.[47]

The problem was that Trump as run-of-the-mill authoritarian, with his outsized ego and demonstrated record of subordinating the Constitution to his own political needs, was much more plausible than Trump as Hitler, the author of genocide and the most destructive war in human history. The Trump-as-Hitler argument was also undermined when Democratic senators Bob Casey of Pennsylvania and Tammy Baldwin of Wisconsin, both caught in difficult reelection campaigns, began running ads touting their agreement with Trump on various issues.

Finally, the closing phase of the campaign brought to the fore old media and new media, and both worked against Harris. Important parts of the old media, clearly in her corner since August, abandoned her. On opposite coasts, the *Los Angeles Times* and *Washington Post*, two pillars of the liberal media, declined to endorse Harris. It was the first time in 36 years that the *Post* had failed to endorse the Democratic candidate for president, and the first time in 20 years that the *LA Times* had failed to do so. In both cases, reports indicated that their well-heeled publishers put a stop to planned endorsements of Harris. They explained that they hoped to reestablish their newspapers as trustworthy and unbiased purveyors of news, though they may also have feared retribution by Trump in the increasingly likely event that he won.[48] In both cases the backlash was fierce.[49] The *Times* lost a large part of its editorial staff and the *Post* lost a quarter of a million subscriptions in a week.[50] The two big papers did not endorse Trump, but their non-endorsements spoke loudly.

Not only did the old media turn its back on Harris, but she did not fully take advantage of alternative media. She did go on some podcasts directed primarily to female audiences, but she neglected a giant in the new media environment: the podcast hosted by Joe Rogan, former wrestler who delighted in poking the bear with controversial "politically-incorrect" topics, with an audience up to 15 million people, many of them young men. Rogan invited both Harris and Trump for a three-hour conversation on his podcast. Trump accepted and spoke at length with Rogan, part of the effort to reach the "Manosphere" reportedly brought to his attention by his son, Barron.[51] The Harris campaign reportedly attempted to set a variety of conditions, including no discussion of marijuana legalization. Rogan would accept no conditions, and Harris's appearance was off. It was later reported that Harris was also afraid of the reaction of her young, progressive staffers if she were to go on Rogan.[52] Given an opportunity to reach 15 million listeners more-or-less unfiltered, Harris declined. Though he remained uncommitted until the end, Rogan endorsed Trump the day before the election.[53]

The effect of this jumble was uncertain. On one hand, there were some indications that Harris had stopped Trump's momentum. On Election Day, the RCP national average had Harris back up by one-tenth of a percentage point; if including third-party candidates, Trump led the average by the same slender amount, essentially a statistical tie.[54] There were indications that inside the Trump campaign, confidence was collapsing, as fears mounted that Trump's undisciplined final act might prove costly.[55] But Democrats were also increasingly nervous, and exit polls later showed that Trump decisively won voters who made up their minds in the last week.[56] Trump continued to lead Electoral College estimates; though Harris had regained a slim lead in Michigan and Wisconsin, Trump was seemingly ahead in five of the seven key states. All seven looked close, and the final RCP estimate was 219 Trump, 211 Harris, the rest toss-ups.[57] In general terms, this left the race approximately where it was in 2016 and 2020—no one went into Election Day with enough electoral votes locked up to guarantee victory. It could make for a very long several days of vote-counting, or one candidate could catch a breeze, sweep all the close states, and end the night early. Betting markets were still calculating that Trump had a 60 percent probability of winning.[58] Nate Silver's model showed Trump winning, as well, though less certain of leading the aggregated popular vote.

Uncertainty led to concern over potential unrest. In 2016, left-wing riots erupted in numerous cities when Trump won. In 2020, Trump supporters invaded the Capitol when he lost and claimed fraud. In 2024, Trump had already begun making claims of fraud in Pennsylvania before Election Day, undoubtedly laying the groundwork for challenging the election results if he lost again.[59] On Election Day, 7 of 10 voters reported being concerned about the potential for violence.[60]

ELECTION RESULTS

What?

All of the polls and all of the models become footnotes when the actual vote comes in. The result was a Trump sweep of the swing states, a solid 312–226 Trump win in the Electoral College, and a narrow Trump lead in the nationally aggregated popular vote, where the former and future president ended with 49.7 percent to Harris's 48.3 percent. In every respect, it was Trump's strongest election of his three.

The third-party contenders made no splash. Green Party candidate Jill E. Stein received a total of .56 percent of the vote, while Libertarian Chase R. Oliver got .42 percent. Robert F. Kennedy Jr. netted just shy of half a percent from votes received in the states where he remained on the ballot despite exiting the race. Around a quarter of a percent of voters submitted a write-in vote for president, many of them for Nikki Haley, who endorsed Trump.

It was apparent early on election night that Harris could be in trouble. Trump jumped out to a lead in Virginia and was still leading with over half of the vote counted. Harris wound up winning, as expected, but her 5 percentage point margin was half of Biden's four years earlier. New Hampshire also looked good for Trump early, before Harris pulled ahead by less than

3 percent. Democratic hopes for a surprise in Florida crumbled early. The state's hyperefficient vote-counting system produced a result within a couple of hours. In contrast to four years before, when he won by 3.4 percent, Trump beat Harris by 13 this time. More decisively to the presidential result, Trump pulled ahead in Georgia, North Carolina, and Pennsylvania, and held his lead, winning by 2.2, 3.3, and 1.7 percentage points—hardly blowouts, but better than 2020, when he lost two of the three, and beyond the reach of recounts. Georgia had looked good for Trump for weeks. North Carolina had been a question mark ever since Hurricane Helene laid waste to the heavily Republican western part of the state, but in the end the result was not much different from four or eight years before. Pennsylvania was Ground Zero in the campaign—the focus of substantial campaign resources, stage for Trump's McDonald's stunt, and site of the nearly successful assassination attempt in Butler in July. More than one analyst had described Pennsylvania as the state both candidates had to win. Trump won it, but it turned out that he didn't need to.

As the race turned to the rest of the Rust Belt, Trump locked down Michigan and Wisconsin, reversing his 2020 losses by 1.4 percentage point in Michigan and .9 in the Badger State. Wisconsin is always hard-fought. Michigan was a real test of whether Harris could hold on to the substantial Arab American vote in Dearborn, one of America's largest Muslim enclaves. Among many of those voters, anger over Biden's Gaza policy was enough to outweigh Trump's pro-Israel stance and Jewish son-in-law, and he scored some important local endorsements late.[61] It also could not have helped Harris when CNN reported that her campaign was running more pro-Palestinian commercials in Michigan at the same time as relatively pro-Israel ads in New Jersey, home to a large Jewish population.[62]

By the time polls closed in Arizona and Nevada, the two outstanding swing states, they were moot. Nevertheless, it was notable that Trump broke through in Arizona, winning by 5.5 percentage points in a state he had lost by a sliver in 2020. Nevada was the last to be determined, and was the only state Trump won in 2024 that he did not win in 2016. Nevada went to the Republican by 3.1 percentage points. It was hardly a coincidence that the two swing states with the biggest turnarounds for Trump were on or near the Mexican border and contained the largest proportion of Hispanic voters. Trump's total vote margin in the seven closest states was more than twice as great as the accumulated margins in the seven closest states in each of the elections going back to 2000.[63] (See table 5.1.)

Overall, Trump's national popular vote lead was modest, but was politically significant. Pursuit of that lead—constitutionally meaningless but a powerful symbol of democratic legitimacy—may explain why Trump held rallies in California and New York late in the game. He was not going to win

Table 5.1. Trump Margins in Seven Key States, 2016–2024 (in percentage points)

State	2016	2020	2024
Arizona	+3.5	−0.3	+5.5
Georgia	+5.1	−0.2	+2.7
Michigan	+0.2	−2.7	+1.4
Nevada	−2.4	−2.4	+3.1
North Carolina	+2.7	+1.3	+3.3
Pennsylvania	+0.7	−1.2	+1.7
Wisconsin	+0.7	−0.6	+0.9

Source: Dave Leip's Election Atlas, uselectionatlas.org.

those states, but he would have to reduce his margins of defeat there if he were to have any chance of leading the aggregated popular vote. Another reason may have been to boost Republican turnout in some local House races in New York and California that would help determine whether the GOP could continue to hold on to its House majority. In either case, Trump's campaign was putting more importance on long-term strategic thinking.

Trump's popular vote plurality, though shallow, was broad. He gained vote share in every state that he lost in both 2020 and 2024, usually by a significant amount. In all but two such jurisdictions, he cut his losing margin by more than 10 percent. In four states, he reduced his margin by 11 to 20 percent, in another five by 21–30 percent, in four by 31 to 40 percent. In Virginia, New Mexico, and New York, Trump reduced his losing margins by close to half. New Jersey and New Hampshire saw Trump slice his 2020 margins by around two-thirds.

Trump also improved his margins in every state that he won in both 2020 and 2024, making the biggest gains in Florida and Texas. Altogether, he was the first presidential candidate in 40 years to gain vote share in every state in the union from one election to the next.

The battle of interpretations began immediately. Exactly how substantial was Donald Trump's victory? Naturally, his supporters made big claims. The terms "blowout" and "landslide" were frequently heard, starting with Trump himself and his aides and supporters. Trump called the election "the biggest mandate in 129 years."[64] His opponents were more divided on the question. Though many were reluctant to cede to Trump the glory of a blowout victory, others were more willing, especially if they were dissatisfied with the current course of the Democratic Party and hoped to nudge it in a different direction. Much of the media, though hostile to Trump, also adopted the language of 2024 as a "resounding" victory.[65]

There is no official, objective definition of a presidential landslide. Historically, though, the term has tended to apply when the winning candidate led the popular vote by around 10 percentage points or more and won at least 400 electoral votes. In such elections, the winning candidate also often carried a significant number of co-partisans into Congress at the same time. Some classic landslide winners in the past century have included Franklin Roosevelt in 1932 and 1936, Dwight Eisenhower in 1952 and 1956, Lyndon Johnson in 1964, and Ronald Reagan in 1980. (In 1972 and 1984, Richard Nixon and Reagan each carried 49 states but had very short coattails.) By these standards, the most recent near landslide was George H. W. Bush's win in 1988, though that was slightly short of the 10 percent margin and featured nonexistent congressional coattails. Trump's 2024 win is not in the same ballpark. (See table 5.2.)

Table 5.2. Trump 2024 versus Historic Landslides

Election	Popular Vote	Margin	Electoral Vote	House Seats	Senate Seats
Trump 2024	49.7%	1.4	312	−1	+4
Bush 1988	53.4%	7.7	426	−2	0
Reagan 1984	58.7%	18.2	525	+14	−2
Reagan 1980	50.8%	9.8	489	+34	+12
Nixon 1972	60.7%	23.2	520	+12	−2
Johnson 1964	61.1%	22.6	486	+37	+1
Eisenhower 1956	57.4%	15.4	457	−2	−1
Eisenhower 1952	55.1%	10.7	442	+22	+1
Roosevelt 1936	60.8%	24.3	523	+12	+7
Roosevelt 1932	57.4%	17.7	472	+90	+9

Sources: Dave Leip's Election Atlas, uselectionatlas.org; Gerhard Peters, "Seats in Congress Gained or Lost by the President's Party in Presidential Election Years," The American Presidency Project, ed. John T. Woolley and Gerhard Peters. Santa Barbara: University of California, 1999–2025.

Table 5.3. Trump 2024 versus Presidential Elections, 1992–2020

Election	Popular Vote	Margin	Electoral Vote	House Seats	Senate Seats
Trump 2024	49.7%	1.4	312	−1	+4
Biden 2020	51.3%	4.5	306	−13	+3
Trump 2016	45.9%	−2.1	304	−6	−2
Obama 2012	51.0%	3.8	332	+8	+1
Obama 2008	52.9%	7.3	365	+23	+8
Bush 2004	50.7%	2.4	286	+3	+4
Bush 2000	47.9%	−.5	271	−3	−4
Clinton 1996	49.2%	8.5	379	+9	−2
Clinton 1992	43.0%	5.5	372	−10	0

Sources: Dave Leip's Election Atlas, uselectionatlas.org; Gerhard Peters, "Seats in Congress Gained or Lost by the President's Party in Presidential Election Years," The American Presidency Project, ed. John T. Woolley and Gerhard Peters. Santa Barbara: University of California, 1999–2025.

Since then, only one candidate (Barack Obama in 2008) has exceeded about 51 percent of the vote, and no one has won more than the 379 electoral votes that Bill Clinton garnered in 1996. (See table 5.3.)

Some have suggested that the new era of presidential election parity may justify a new conception of the landslide. Surely, 51 percent of the vote is more impressive now than it used to be. Even within this more competitive recent period, Trump's 2024 win was middling. Within the period from 1992 to 2024, Trump in 2024 represented both the median popular vote percentage and the median electoral vote total (fifth highest out of nine). His loss of one House seat was also the median in this period. His popular vote margin was seventh out of nine, and the smallest positive margin of any (the two winners below him—one of whom was also him—won despite a negative margin in the popular vote), though the Republican gain of four Senate seats was tied for second best.

Still, it is no small thing in this era that Trump took a lead in the popular vote, as Bush in 2000 and he himself in 2016 did not; that he won more electoral votes than Bush in 2000 and 2004 or Biden in the last election; that he swept every highly targeted state; that he gained vote share in every single state relative to his last election; that his party now holds four additional Senate seats; or that he managed all of that while becoming only the second president in U.S. history to return to the White House after an electoral defeat. His victory was solid by today's standards, and was historically significant, though the exact nature of its significance will be determined over the next four years and beyond. However, statistically it was not above the middle tier of recent presidential wins.

Who?

The presidency is determined through electoral votes given by states. However, at bottom, voters determine who wins states. So, whose votes did Donald Trump win in order to collect 312 electoral votes?

The single best predictor of the vote is party affiliation, and the same was true in 2024. Harris won 95 percent of self-identified Democrat, while Trump won 94 percent of Republicans despite Harris's efforts to lure disaffected Republicans. In 2016, Trump won self-described independents by a few points, a result that was reversed in 2020. It was widely expected in 2024 that to win the election one would again need to win the independents. Trump lost independents again but won the election anyway because Republicans in the electorate outnumbered Democrats by 35 to 31 percent. Outside of party, exit polls revealed the demographic distribution of the vote along multiple dimensions, most of which show the collapse of the Obama coalition.[66] (See table 5.4.)

Table 5.4. Trump Vote among Groups, 2016–2024 (in percentages)

	2016	*2020*	*2024*
Republicans	88	94	94
Democrats	8	5	4
Independents	46	41	46
Female	41	42	45
Male	52	53	55
18–29	36	36	43
30–44	41	46	48
45–64	52	50	54
65+	52	52	49
First-time voters	38	32	56
White	57	58	57
Black	8	12	13
Latino	28	32	46
Asian	27	34	39
Protestant (total)	56	60	63
Evangelical	80	76	82
Catholic	50	47	58
Jewish	23	*	22
Other	29	29	34
None	25	31	26
College graduate	42	43	42
No college degree	54	50	56
Less than $100,000	45	43	50
More than $100,000	47	54	46
Union household	42	40	45
Urban	34	38	38
Suburban	49	48	51
Rural	61	57	64
Military veteran	60	54	65

* No Jewish results reported in 2020.
Source: CNN Exit Polls 2016, 2020; NBC Exit Polls 2024.

Gender: Though she did not emphasize her potential to be the first woman president, Kamala Harris had hoped to overwhelm Trump with women's votes. In fact, Trump held down his losses among women and fought back by building a big advantage among men; 2024 was his best election in both groups. Nationally, Harris won by 8 percentage points among women while Trump won by 12 among men, building a lead among male voters of every age-group. As usual, what looked like a gender gap actually concealed a marriage gap. Trump lost the women's vote overall because he lost single women by more (38 to 61 percent) than he won married women (52 to 47 percent). He also won married men by 60–38 percent, while breaking even with unmarried men (49–49 percent).

Race: Trump continued making inroads among non-white voters, as he had done since 2016. He beat Harris 57 to 42 percent among whites, but also picked up one-third of the non-white vote. This included 13 percent of the black vote, 39 percent of the Asian vote, and a whopping 46 percent of the Hispanic vote. Though the exit polls may have been skewed by a small sample size, they also recorded that Trump won over two-thirds of the traditionally Democratic Native American vote. Among groups Harris was targeting, Trump won white women and Latino men, and pulled in one in five black men, even after Barack Obama lectured them for being misogynistic if they voted for him and Harris promised "forgivable loans" to start cannabis dispensaries.[67] He even won several Puerto Rican enclaves, such as Florida's Osceola County.[68] Complaints about the comedian in the Garden clearly did not sway the intended audience. The most significant of these shifts was probably Trump's gain among Hispanics, which threatens to upend the partisan balance for years if it is sustained.[69] Overall, the 2024 vote was less racially polarized than any election in recent memory.

Age: Harris won the youngest voters, though not overwhelmingly. She led 18–29-year-olds by 54–43 percent, in contrast to Obama's 60–37 lead in 2012 and Biden's 60–36 lead in 2020.[70] Trump pulled in 47 percent of the 30–44 year olds, 54 percent of the 45–64 year-olds, and broke even with the over-65 set. Consequently, as with race, 2024 saw less polarized results on the basis of age than any recent election.

First-time voters: The improved showing by Trump among the young contributed to the result, unthinkable against Obama or Biden, that the Republican candidate built an 11-point advantage over the Democrat among first-time voters. (In 2020, Biden won first-time voters by a 2–1 margin.[71]) Trump and Harris split non-first-time voters 49–49. Given his loss among 18–29-year-olds, Trump's lead among the first-timers, though it may have been made possible by holding close among the young, ultimately had to come from older first-time voters—individuals who had been disconnected from politics for years, perhaps decades.

Socioeconomic status: The 2024 election continued the trend of socioeconomic sorting of the parties. There were two elements to this trend: education and income.

Voters with no college at all gave Trump their biggest majority, 62 to 36 percent. He also won, by smaller margins, voters with some college but no degree and voters with an associate's degree. Harris won voters with a bachelor's degree, and won by a 21 point margin those with an advanced degree such as a PhD or law degree. Education and race trumped gender; white women with no college degree voted nearly 2–1 for Trump.

Trump built a coalition of the middle, winning voters from $30,000 to $100,000 annual income. Harris built a coalition of the top and the bottom, winning those under $30,000 and over $100,000. If categories were collapsed, Trump won the bottom, whether cut off at $50,000 or $100,000. Again, though, the differences were muted in comparison to differences in income-level voting 20 or 30 years ago. Dividing voters more finely into five income groups, neither candidate received more than 52 percent in any group. Trump's 2024 showing was the first time in his three elections that he won voters making under $100,000.

If Trump did well in the "working-class" vote, defined as non–college graduates making under $100,000, he did not fare quite as well among union households, representing nearly one-fifth of voters, where Harris won by a 53–45 percent margin. Trump won the non-union households 51–47 percent. His 45 percent among the unionized was nevertheless higher than he received in 2016 (42 percent) or 2020 (40 percent).[72] In any case, given the vast increase in government employee unions representing teachers and other professionals, the correlation between "unionized" and "working class" is much more tenuous than it used to be. Nevertheless, Teamsters and Firefighters unions, stereotypical working-class unions, declined to endorse Harris.

Religion: Protestants supported Trump by nearly a 2–1 margin, while the subset of Protestants who self-identified as "white born-again or evangelical Christian" gave Trump 82 percent of their votes. Harris won 78 percent of Jewish voters (despite concerns about antisemitism visibly subsisting in some reaches of the Democratic Party), 71 percent of voters identifying as "nones," and 64 percent of voters who said they were "something else" (such as believers in other religions including Buddhism, Hinduism, and Islam). In between, as usual for the last 50 years, were Catholic voters, who were once a reliable part of the Democratic coalition but are now the single most crucial swing group on the religious front. In 2016, Catholics narrowly preferred Trump; in 2020, their coreligionist Biden. In 2024, Catholics swung back hard to Trump, giving him the lead over Harris by 20 percentage points. White Catholics picked Trump by a 28-point margin. Helped by a federal raid on an Amish dairy farm in January 2024, Trump apparently succeeded in mobilizing the Amish vote in Pennsylvania, contributing to his victory there.[73] (The last time the Amish turned out in large numbers was for George W. Bush in 2004.)

Other swings back to Trump: In 2016, Trump won the suburbs narrowly and won groups such as rural voters and military voters overwhelmingly. He lost in 2020 partly because he lost the suburbs and won core groups like veterans and rural voters much more narrowly than before (veterans by 10, rural voters by 15). In 2024, the outcomes of 2016 returned with a vengeance. Trump won the suburban vote by 4 points, the rural vote by 30 points, and veterans by 31, surpassing his 2016 numbers. In this way and others, in 2020, it had seemed like 2016 might have been an aberration. Now it looks more as if 2020 was the aberration. Moreover, in 2024 Trump surpassed both his 2016 and 2020 showings among both men and women; the young and the middle-aged; blacks, Latinos, and Asians; Catholics, Protestants, and members of "other" religions; suburbanites and rural voters; veterans and union households; and voters with no college degree and with incomes under $100,000.

Why?

What accounts for Trump's win? Exit polls help illuminate how issues played with the voters, and they make it clear that the issues Trump highlighted worked to his advantage more fully than Harris's issues worked for her.

Trump's issues were the economy, immigration, and, to a lesser extent, disorder in the world that he laid at Joe Biden's feet. About one-third of voters listed economy as the primary issue driving their vote, and they split about 4–1 for Trump.[74] More than two-thirds of voters said the economy was "not so good" or "poor," and 70 percent of them voted for Trump. Nearly half described their family's financial state as worse than four years before, and 82 percent voted for Trump. Slightly more than half said their condition was the same (29 percent) or better (24 percent) than in 2020, and Harris won them, but by a smaller margin. Only a quarter said inflation had caused them no hardship in the last year, and Harris won 77 percent of them. On the other hand, another quarter said inflation had caused them severe hardship, and half said moderate hardship. Trump won those voters convincingly. Economists were divided over whose economic plans would be most damaging in the future—big tariffs or big regulation and price controls—but Americans rendered a much clearer verdict on the past four years.

Another 12 percent said immigration was their number one issue, and Trump won them by a 9–1 margin. Voters did indicate a preference for a policy of building a pathway to citizenship for illegal immigrants in the country, as opposed to deportation of all illegals, but the desire to deport migrant criminals and the imperative of preventing additional future illegal migration was at the top of voters' minds.

Foreign policy was mentioned as the number one issue by only 4 percent of voters, a number in line with previous elections when the United States was not at war. Trump led in that group by a 56–39 percent margin.

Overall, most voters said they trusted Trump more than Harris on the economy (53–46 percent), immigration (53–44 percent), crime and safety (52–47 percent), and to lead in crisis (51 to 47 percent).

Harris only led Trump in voter trust on abortion, and there only by 49–46 percent. She had expected the abortion issue to work to her favor—and it did, but only a little. Harris won three-fourths of voters who said it was the issue most driving their vote, but those voters were only 14 percent of the electorate. And, as we have seen, Harris did not do nearly as well with women voters as she needed to. What happened? Trump's states rights position, aside from being constitutionally plausible, deflected the issue to lower levels. In some ways, Harris was arguably the more extreme candidate on abortion. While two-thirds of voters said that abortion should be always legal or mostly legal, only one-third held Harris's position of nearly unlimited legality, and it was the only group Harris won. It turned out that even women are divided and ambivalent on the issue, and relatively few give it high priority.

Aside from abortion, Harris's other major campaign theme was democracy. According to exit polls, 34 percent of voters identified the state of democracy as their number one issue, slightly more than said the same about the economy. Harris won 80 percent of those voters. Other questions, however, raised the possibility that the issue was more complicated. When asked whether democracy was secure or threatened, many more than 34 percent—73 percent—said it was threatened. Of those, Trump voters outnumbered Harris voters 50 percent to 48 percent. Both sides cited things to fear. Harris voters could point to Trump's attempt to overturn his 2020 election defeat, as well as his threats to jail his opponents and his generally demagogic approach. Trump voters could point to Democratic attempts to keep Trump off the ballot and burden him with prosecutions, not to mention their century-long project of shifting power to unelected bureaucracies. Trump himself said that Democratic rhetoric was a threat to democracy: "Remember the words they use: 'They are a threat to democracy.' They've been saying that about me for seven years. I think I got shot because of that, okay? People said 'he's a threat to democracy.'"[75] Democracy was also an issue that could cut more than one way.

Specific issues were subsumed in broader aggregated evaluations. Only 40 percent of voters said they approved of the job Joe Biden was doing as president, while 59 percent said they did not approve. The approvers voted for Harris 96 percent to 3 percent. The much larger group of disapprovers voted for Trump 82 percent to 16 percent. This evaluation was clearly tied to feelings of satisfaction or dissatisfaction about the country. Only a quarter were satisfied or enthused about the state of the country, and Harris garnered 85 percent of their votes. Three-quarters described themselves as dissatisfied or angry. They gave 62 percent of their votes to Trump, including 73 percent of the angry.

How did the candidates themselves appear to the voters? Of course, each candidate had a coterie of enthusiastic advocates. Trump, however, seemed to have an edge in terms of enthusiasm. Of the three-quarters of voters who said they were primarily voting *for* their candidate, Trump led, 55–44 percent. Among the quarter who said they were voting *against* the opponent, Harris led 60–36 percent. At the other end of the spectrum, Trump won the "double-haters," the 8 percent who said they had an unfavorable view of both candidates, by a 52–32 percent margin.

On the whole, though, neither candidate broke out, which accounts for the close final result in the popular vote. Voters were evenly divided, 49–49 percent, about whether they would be excited or optimistic if Trump won versus concerned or scared. In Harris's case, 48 percent were excited or optimistic, 50 percent concerned or scared. Trump was seen favorably by 46 percent and unfavorably by 53 percent; Harris received favorable marks from 46 percent and unfavorable evaluations from 52 percent.

After the election, Trump claimed that the failed assassination attempt in Butler, Pennsylvania had caused Americans to look at him more favorably, an argument buttressed by a piece in the *Washington Examiner* on the "humanization of Trump."[76] Trump's exit poll assessment was several steps up from 2016, when 60 percent saw him unfavorably and only 38 percent favorably.[77] Nevertheless, it was basically unchanged from 2020, when he was seen favorably by 46 percent and unfavorably by 52 percent.[78] Compared with Harris's 46.7 percent, Trump's RealClearPolitics average favorability sat at 44.9 percent on November 4, modestly but not massively higher than the 42.5 percent recorded on July 13, the day of the assassination attempt.[79]

Voters thought Trump had the edge on ability to lead and ability to bring needed change, where he had an advantage over Harris of 50 percentage points. They said Harris was more likely to care about people like them and to exercise better judgment (by a margin of 68 percentage points). Good judgment is always useful, it seems, but ability to bring change is especially useful when an overwhelming majority are dissatisfied or angry with the state of the country. Each of the major contenders was half a candidate, locked in a battle of nearly equal unpopularity.

Both also seemed to be victims of foreign interference, though there was no reason to believe it had much effect on voters. There was evidence that covert Russian accounts on X, Telegram, and YouTube had posted AI-doctored videos attacking Harris and Walz, while Chinese hackers invaded the phones of Trump, Vance, and Harris. Iran conducted cyber reconnaissance on swing-state election websites. Most dramatically, Iran also authorized its agents to assassinate Trump himself, leading to indictments from the U.S. Department of Justice.[80] The latter revelation, which would have occasioned a bipartisan uproar among Americans in an earlier election, was shrugged off, if it was noticed at all. In 2024, Americans were polarized, jaded, and suffering from political sensory overload.

* * *

Political scientists assume that presidential election outcomes are baked into the "fundamentals." In this view—and we share it—the objective situation of the country, and the state of public sentiment surrounding it, meant that any Democratic candidate, whether Biden, Harris, or a new candidate, would have faced an uphill climb. Inflation, Biden's low approval rating, and general public dissatisfaction would have guaranteed that. Consequently, any Republican candidate, whether Trump, Haley, or DeSantis, would have been more or less well-positioned to win under the circumstances.

As we noted early in this book, a number of highly unusual features of the contest left open until the end whether the old rules were still operational. Biden's age and incapacity, and then Trump's age; Harris's unconventional and arguably undemocratic means of ascent to her party's nomination; Trump's indictments and convictions; the heavy baggage carried by Trump from his previous term in the White House; the oddity of a losing president seeking and winning renomination; all threatened to upend the dominance of the fundamentals. In the end, most of it was noise. Gravity reasserted itself, the referendum took place, and the incumbent party lost when the president's approval rating was 40 percent and two-thirds of the country thought things were on the wrong track.

Yet this account is too simple and discounts too much the importance of human agency. For one thing, candidates and campaigns can matter, at least on the margins. Both candidates had serious deficiencies. It would be difficult to deny, for example, that Harris's structural predicament of being the vice president to an unpopular president was exacerbated by her widely-broadcast declaration on *The View* that she could not think of anything the Biden administration did that she would do differently. Indeed, following the 2000 election, which George W. Bush won despite the unanimous prediction of political science models, some election modelers grudgingly admitted that candidates and campaigns can be important on the margins, and hence decisive in a close race. And 2024 was, after all, a closely decided election. Not as close as 2020, when 43,000 votes in Wisconsin, Arizona, and Georgia would have altered the outcome, but close enough that the contingencies cannot be declared inconsequential. A switch of less than half a percent in Wisconsin and less than 1 percent in Michigan and Pennsylvania from Trump to Harris would have given Harris 270 electoral votes and the win.

Could a different Democratic candidate less tainted with the Biden administration, perhaps Josh Shapiro or Mark Kelly, have made up that little extra ground needed for victory, or at least pulled a few more Democratic House candidates over the line, depriving Republicans of unified control of government at the outset of the second Trump presidency? It would be difficult to dismiss that possibility.

On the other side, though a Republican candidate may have been likely to win, did it make any difference which Republican candidate? Might Nikki Haley or Ron DeSantis have won by more, perhaps carrying into office a larger Republican House contingent and a few more Senate seats? It is not inconceivable. In fact, it may be probable. In the spring of 2024, Haley was polling much better against Biden than Trump was. Given the constellation of factors working against the Democrats, it was surprising that the race was as close as it was. Donald Trump may have been the only available Republican who could have found himself ahead of Joe Biden by only 3 percentage points after the June 27 debate.

And, of course, the most momentous contingency of all, largely lost in the postelection analysis: What if the Butler assassin had succeeded in killing Donald Trump two days before the opening of the Republican convention? Aside from chaos and bitterness, what would have resulted? It is impossible to know, just as it is impossible to know what would have resulted—maybe less Republican voter enthusiasm?—had the assassination attempt not been made at all.

It is also worth observing that the boundary between fundamentals and contingencies is often less solid than we imagine. Political actors can make decisions upstream that have an important impact on the fundamentals later. The state of the economy and the president's approval rating do not spring full-blown from the earth, untouched by human hands. In 2024, the fact that one of the candidates was a sitting vice president and the other former president Trump was also a product of discretionary political decisions. The decisions that had hardened into fundamentals by November 2024 were many.

TRUMP'S SECOND IMPEACHMENT

On January 13, 2021, the House of Representatives impeached President Trump for inciting the January 6 attack on the Capitol. No Democrats voted against the resolution and 10 Republicans voted for it, more party defections than in any previous presidential impeachment. Conviction in a Senate trial would have transformed the 2024 race by barring Trump from holding federal office again. The GOP would have had to run somebody else.

But on the day of the House vote, Senate Republican Leader Mitch McConnell announced that he would not support a move by Democratic Leader Charles Schumer to call an emergency Senate session for the purposes of an impeachment trial. McConnell's consent was necessary, so the Senate could not try Trump before he left office on January 20. Senators did not vote to start the proceeding until February 9.

The delay had consequences. In the immediate wake of January 6, many Republicans criticized Trump's actions before and during the attack. Senator Lindsay Graham (R-SC) famously proclaimed: "All I can say is count me out. Enough is enough."[81] Surveys in early February showed that most Americans supported the impeachment move.[82] But as the days ticked by, grassroots Republicans rallied behind the 45th president and GOP lawmakers soberly appraised the risk of angering their base. Despite an 1876 precedent, questions about the constitutionality of impeaching a former official provided a handy rationale for opposing a trial. By the time the verdict came up for a roll call on February 13, the chances for conviction had vanished. Only seven Republican senators joined all 50 Democrats in voting "guilty." The total was short of the necessary two-thirds, so Trump could run again.

After voting "not guilty," McConnell said that Trump was morally responsible for the attack. He added: "We have a criminal justice system in this country. We have civil litigation. And former Presidents are not immune from being held accountable by either one."[83] In 2024, however, Trump's election effectively ended federal criminal proceedings against him.

THE 2021–2022 SPENDING BINGE

Although the Biden and Harris campaigns would blame corporations and a number of impersonal forces for the upsurge of inflation in 2021 and 2022, government spending was also an obvious culprit. Early on, Bill Clinton's Secretary of the Treasury Larry Summers publicly warned policymakers that spending plans on the drawing board would be inflationary.

Despite these red flags, Biden, Nancy Pelosi, and Chuck Schumer pushed through Congress almost $4.3 trillion, not counting substantial spending increases in already-existing programs. As a result, the federal deficits were larger as a proportion of GDP than during the Great Depression. This spending binge was accompanied by a regulatory binge in which the Biden administration issued rules costing the economy $1.7 trillion, more than three times the cost of new Obama regulations at that point in his presidency.[84] And to make matters worse for Harris, as vice president she cast the tiebreaking votes in the Senate for the American Rescue Plan and the Inflation Reduction Act. On the other hand, American grocery shoppers and a host of Democrats who narrowly won their Senate races should send thank-you notes to Joe Manchin and Kyrsten Sinema for cutting Build Back Better by 75 percent.

AFGHANISTAN

If the American Rescue Plan was the Biden administration's first important domestic policy decision, the withdrawal from Afghanistan was the first important foreign policy decision. Donald Trump had bequeathed to Biden a rickety withdrawal agreement with the Taliban. Biden, like Trump, was anxious to end the "forever war" against the group that had provided the refuge from which al Qaeda launched the 9-11 attacks.

Biden surveyed the scene and ordered the withdrawal completed. It is now clear that his military advisors had advised him against it. The withdrawal led to chaos in Afghanistan and a quick takeover by the Taliban

The immediate political impact in the United States was profound. According to the RealClearPolitics poll aggregator, Joe Biden's job approval rating was about 52 percent, with 42 percent disapproving, at the beginning of July 2021. On August 23, Biden went underwater, with more Americans disapproving than approving. By October 15, his numbers were a mirror image of early July: 44 percent approve, 52 percent disapprove.[85] Biden's approval rating never recovered, and was undoubtedly limited by further disorder in the world that was arguably invited by the debacle in Afghanistan.

PROSECUTIONS

Prior to 2023, no former president had faced state or federal prosecution. This was at least in part because they were generally a law-abiding lot. There was also an underlying concern: prosecuting a former president could open the door to partisan recriminations and a never-ending cycle of payback.

Between March and August 2023, that concern was set aside in four different cases, two federal and two state, in which charges were brought against Donald Trump. A charge of mishandling classified documents was preceded by a dramatic FBI raid on Trump's Mar-a-Lago estate in August 2022.

The relative legal merits and demerits of the cases have been widely discussed and debated, though it does seem probable that some of the charges were on stronger legal ground than others. (Only one went to trial and resulted in a conviction before Election Day, and it is being appealed as of this writing.) The political effect of the blizzard of prosecution is clearer: Donald Trump gained support in his primary election fight during a crucial period in 2023 when Florida governor Ron DeSantis was challenging. More generally, the prosecutions strengthened the determination of Republican voters to see Trump reelected. Most Republicans did not distinguish among the cases and saw them as part of a coordinated attempt by Democrats to abuse the justice system against Biden's political opponent. No Mar-a-Lago raid and prosecutions? Less likelihood that Trump is renominated by Republicans and, if renominated, less intensity by Republican voters in the general election. That doesn't mean that Trump was not hurt at all among independents by the prosecutions, but it seems likely the net effect worked in his favor.

THE BORDER AND BIDEN'S ASYLUM ORDER

During the first three and a half years of the Biden-Harris administration, U.S. Customs and Border Protection (CBP) logged nearly eight million encounters with migrants illegally crossing the border with Mexico. Migrants faced squalid conditions, and border communities strained to deal with the influx. The issue threatened to be a major liability for the Democrats, as polls showed that a great majority of Americans thought that the federal government was doing a poor job. Accordingly, Biden proposed a bill he called "the toughest set of border security reforms we've ever seen."[86] Trump came out against the bill, and Senate Republicans backed away from it.

In June, Biden issued an executive order temporarily suspending the entry of migrants who crossed the southern border illegally. Illegal border crossings declined substantially, but politically, it was too little, too late. The immigration issue still worked for Trump in the November election. It did not help Harris that Biden in 2021 had said she would "lead our diplomatic effort and work with those nations to . . . enhance migration enforcement at their borders," allowing Republicans to tag her as the "failed border czar."

Perhaps Biden hesitated to act on asylum because he feared a backlash from his own party. The fear was unjustified: once he made the decision, Democrats were more likely to support than oppose it. If Biden had issued the order sooner, he could have taken some of the sting out of the border crisis, which in turn could have helped Harris carry Arizona, Nevada, and perhaps other states as well.

RFK JR.

By August, Robert F. Kennedy Jr.'s money was running low and it began to appear that remaining in the race would hurt Trump more than Harris. He ended his third-party campaign and endorsed Trump. But suppose that Democratic super PAC donors had decided to prop him up and help him stay in the race. (It would have been a deeply cynical move, but faulting outside spending groups for cynicism is like handing out speeding tickets at the Indy 500. Democratic super PACs had helped beatable MAGA candidates in Republican primaries in 2022.) There is no way that Kennedy could have won the popular vote, especially after revelations that he had once dumped a dead bear in Central Park and that he had gotten a brain worm from eating roadkill. But there might have been enough anti-vaccine zealots to earn him 3–5 percent of the vote in key states. And that showing could have helped tip those states to Harris.

THE BIGGEST DECISION OF ALL: BIDEN'S DECISION TO RUN AGAIN

Joe Biden, the oldest president in American history to date, was older when he took office than Ronald Reagan was when he left it. In 2024, he was 81. Long before his disastrous debate with Trump, it was painfully evident that he had lost a step or two. Or three.

If Biden had been able to swallow his pride and pull out by mid-2023, there would have been a competitive race for the Democratic nomination. The nominee might have been a senator or governor without close connections to Biden, which would have made it much harder for Trump to tie that candidate to the Biden record. Even if it had ended up being Kamala Harris, she at least would have had more time to figure an answer to the question of how her presidency would be different from the incumbent's. George H. W. Bush threaded that needle in 1988, thanks in part to starting his unofficial campaign years before. (Bush had the added advantage, though, of serving as vice president with a president who was riding high in the polls in 1988.)

Of course, we cannot be certain how this or any of our other scenarios would have worked out in the real world. We could only test these ideas by rerunning the election in alternate universes, and we are not living in a Marvel movie. Still, it seems reasonable to suggest that a number of individual decisions shaped the fundamentals of the campaign. Different decisions earlier would have meant different fundamentals and possibly a different outcome or even different contestants.

Chapter 6

Congressional and State Elections

In 2024, Republicans clung to a hairsbreadth margin in the House while wresting control of the Senate from the Democrats. That outcome was typical of the closely contested politics of the early 21st century—and quite different from the pattern of the late 20th century.

Democrats held the majority in the House between 1954 and 1994, the longest stretch of one-party dominance in U.S. history. After the LBJ landslide of 1964, they held more than two-thirds of all the seats in both chambers. Republicans did control the Senate from 1980 to 1986, but at the time, it appeared that their majority stemmed mainly from a streak of good luck in small states.[1] The 1986 midterm strengthened Democrats in the House, restored their majority in the Senate, and set congressional politics back to normality. Or so it seemed.

Starting in 1994, however, things were different. In that year, Republicans swept the House and Senate. And at least for the next 30 years, control of the House and Senate would be in play. That shift in the political plates changed life on Capitol Hill. As Frances E. Lee put it: "A secure majority party behaves differently from a party that fears losing power. A minority party optimistic about winning a majority behaves differently from a hopeless minority. Members of insecure minorities worry more about partisan advantage and work harder to win it."[2] Congressional parties put much more emphasis on campaign organization and fundraising through their traditional campaign committees and outside spending groups. "Messaging" bills proliferated, and members extended partisan warfare into cyberspace.

On the floor of each chamber, lawmakers faced intense pressure to vote with their team. At the start of Biden's term in 2021, Democrats held a narrow House majority and controlled the 50–50 Senate only because of Harris's tiebreaking vote. By historical standards, it was an inauspicious beginning

101

for a president with significant legislative ambitions. And yet Senate Majority Leader Charles Schumer and House Speaker Nancy Pelosi were highly skillful in holding in holding their troops together and avoiding roll calls they knew they would lose. Despite nearly unanimous Republican opposition, Biden won most of the floor votes on which he took a position in 2021 and 2022.[3]

Democrats had little choice but to accomplish as much as possible in their early days. Historical patterns suggested that they could lose both houses in the 2022 midterm. But they also had reasons for hope.

THE 2022 MIDTERM

Midterm elections typically allow the out-party to check the incumbent administration, especially when the president's party has majorities in both the House and Senate. The midterms of 1994, 2006, 2010, and 2018 all began with unified party control of the federal government, and all ended with the out-party winning control of one or both chambers.

On rare occasions (1998 and 2002), the in-party has picked up House seats in midterms, but there were extremely unusual circumstances those years—a backlash against Republicans for Bill Clinton's prospective impeachment in 1998, a post-9/11 national security swell for them in 2002. The overall pattern has consisted of losses. In the past, the extent of these losses usually depended on the state of the economy and public approval of the president's job performance. When both went south, the in-party took a bigger hit. Accordingly, many predicted a "Red Wave" that would carry the GOP into decisive control of Congress.

Instead, Republicans gained only a perilously thin majority in the House and suffered a net loss of one seat in the Senate. Out of thousands of state legislative elections, they won only a few dozen seats and lost control of four chambers. To top it off, the ranks of GOP governors fell by two. What happened to the Red Wave?

For the first time in modern midterm history, the party with unified control of the federal government could campaign with a "check and balance" narrative of its own. Scholars refer to Congress and the presidency as the "political branches" as opposed to the nonpartisan, unelected judiciary. But the public no longer saw the Court as apolitical. In a Quinnipiac University survey before the *Dobbs* decision, 63 percent of voters agreed that "the Supreme Court is mainly motivated by politics."[4] A Yahoo News/YouGov poll found that 74 percent of adults said the Court has become "too politicized."[5]

If people regard the Court as a political branch, they may view elections as a way to check it—a point Lincoln made in his 1858 debates with Stephen

Douglas. After *Dobbs*, an NPR/PBS NewsHour/Marist poll found that most Americans disagreed with the decision (56–40 percent) and thought it was politically motivated (57–36 percent). By a 51–36 percent margin, the survey's voters said they would be more likely to support a congressional candidate who would back legislation to restore *Roe*.[6] In an Associated Press VoteCast survey around election time, 38 percent of voters said *Dobbs* had a major impact on their decision about whether to vote, and 47 percent said that the decision had a major impact on their candidate choice.[7] Republican governors who had signed stricter abortion limits, such as Ron DeSantis of Florida and Mike DeWine of Ohio, cruised to reelection, so the impact was not a simple one, but overall the issue served as something of a drag on Republican efforts.

Another way for Democrats to seize the "check and balance" mantle was to keep running against Donald Trump. In previous times, the in-party would not see any need to fight the loser of the last presidential election. During the 1994 midterm, it would have been laughable for Democrats to warn about George H. W. Bush. But this time, millions of Republicans believed Trump's claim that he had won the 2020 election, and they were ready to support him again in 2024. Republican elected officials continued to speak of him as the leader of their party, which delighted Democratic opposition researchers. The network exit poll confirmed his impact. As usual for a midterm, many voters (32 percent) saw their House vote as a way to oppose the incumbent president. But almost as many (28 percent) saw it as a way to oppose Trump.[8] (In the 2018 midterm, when Trump was the incumbent, 38 percent said the same of him.[9])

The outcome of the midterm heartened Democrats and disappointed Republicans. Yet the data showed more support for the GOP than the post-election reactions suggested. In the aggregated national vote for the House, Republicans led the Democrats by more than three million ballots. Their percentage was the same as in the 2014 midterm, yet they won 25 fewer seats see table 6.1). "Wasted" votes were one reason for the reduced seat yield. For control of the House, winning more seats by small margins is better than fewer seats by large margins. In 2014, the Democratic vote was more geographically concentrated than the GOP vote, so the average Democratic margin of victory was larger (36.9 percent to 35 percent). In 2022, it was the Republicans—particularly in the rural South—who tended to win by bigger margins (30.2 percent to 27.7 percent).[10] Democrats also benefited from ger-rymanders in Illinois and other states.

On the Senate side, Republicans would have gained control if they had run better candidates in key states. The most glaring example was Georgia, where the GOP contender was former football star Herschel Walker. Because his grasp of policy was shaky at best, Senate Republicans often had to chaperone

Table 6.1. Vote and Seat Shares in House Elections

	GOP Vote Percentage	*GOP Seat Percentage*
2010	51.4	55.6
2012	46.9	53.8
2014	50.6	56.8
2016	48.2	55.4
2018	44.5	45.9
2020	47.0	49.0
2022	50.6	51.0
2024	50.6	50.6

Sources: Molly E. Reynolds, *Vital Statistics on Congress*, https://www.brookings.edu/wp-content/uploads/2024/11/2-2-Full.pdf; Cook Political Report, 2022 National House Vote Tracker, https://www.cookpolitical.com/charts/house-charts/national-house-vote-tracker/2022; 2022 National House Vote Tracker, https://www.cookpolitical.com/vote-tracker/2024/house.

him during media interviews. Revelations about his personal life were so egregious that his son denounced him in viral videos. He ended up with 48.6 percent in a runoff against incumbent Democrat Raphael Warnock. In Arizona, Republican Blake Masters made damaging gaffes, such as blaming gun violence on "Black people, frankly."[11] His staunch antiabortion stand appeared to be another liability: about a third of voters picked abortion as their top issue, and 91 percent of them backed incumbent Democrat Mark Kelly.[12] Although polls had suggested a squeaker, Kelly won by a 4.9 percent margin. In the race to succeed retiring senator Pat Toomey (R-Pennsylvania), celebrity doctor Mehmet Oz suffered from accusations of carpetbagging (he lived in a New Jersey mansion) and flip-flopping (he had recently been pro-choice). Democrat John Fetterman prevailed even though a recent stroke had temporarily impaired his ability to speak and caused him to struggle through his sole debate with Oz. One thread linking the three Republican losers is that they had won their party's nomination because of Trump's support. As Andrew Prokop observed at Vox, all three underperformed Trump's 2020 vote share in their states: "Their poor performances contrast with the more 'ordinary' GOP nominees—former Nevada attorney general Adam Laxalt, two-term incumbent Sen. Ron Johnson (WI), and Rep. Ted Budd (NC), who each outperformed Trump—though in Laxalt's case, not by enough to win."[13]

On the House side, Republicans learned their majority status was a bouquet with thorns. At the start of the congressional session, it took 15 ballots for them to elect party leader Kevin McCarthy (R-CA) as the new speaker. Infighting continued throughout the year, sometimes pitting hard-line conservatives against more pragmatic colleagues and sometimes pitting the conservatives against one another. In the fall, right-wing firebrand Matt Gaetz (R-FL) moved to oust McCarthy from the speakership. Eight Republicans joined all Democrats to pass the motion, making McCarthy the first House speaker to suffer this fate. It took three weeks and several false starts for

Republicans to secure the election of a new speaker, Mike Johnson (R-LA). The hard-liners applauded the selection, but it was unclear whether Johnson would be as successful at fundraising and electoral politics as McCarthy.

Republicans were hoping that control of the House would enable them to dig up damaging information about the president and other administration officials. The new majority found no silver bullets. GOP-led committees investigated the shady business dealings of President Biden's son Hunter. After hyping expectations about what they would find, the Republicans turned up suspicious circumstances but no definitive evidence linking the president to his son's misdeeds.[14] In any case, their internal discord distracted them from the fight against the Democratic administration. Meanwhile, they had a high-profile scandal of their own. In a bizarre case, freshman representative George Santos (R-NY) turned out to have made up large parts of his life story, and the House expelled him for financial misconduct. In a special election early in 2024, former representative Tom Suozzi regained the seat for the Democrats.

Overall, Democrats had reason to feel good about their showing in 2022. They had gained a seat in the Senate and limited their losses in the House. But as investment disclosures remind us, past performance is no guarantee of future results. In 2024, that phrase would apply particularly well to Senate elections.

SENATE ELECTIONS

Class I Flips

The Senate has a unique electoral rhythm. It consists of three "classes" that come before the voters on six-year cycles. If a party has an exceptionally successful showing at the start of a cycle, it will have a challenge at the end. Six years later, it must defend its winnings under very different circumstances: seats it won during a presidential election year will come up again during a midterm, sometimes under a new president. Over those six years, the issues that favored the party might turn against it, and the makeup of state electorates might shift under its feet.

The Class I seats, which were at stake in 2024, have had a distinctive history. In 2006, the Bush administration was unpopular because of the Iraq War and Hurricane Katrina. Voter discontent drove six Republican incumbents out of office. It gave Democrats a narrow majority, thanks to additional votes from Joe Lieberman (CT) and Bernie Sanders (VT), who ran as independents but caucused with Senate Democrats. In 2012, Democrats had 23 seats up for election (including those of Lieberman and Sanders), while the Republicans had only 10. At the start of the campaign, many pundits assumed that these lopsided numbers guaranteed GOP gains. But because of some historically bad GOP candidates, a slight tailwind from President Obama's modest reelection margin, and the wily leadership of Senate Majority Leader Harry Reid, Democrats defied the odds and scored a net gain of two seats. (Connecticut Democrat Chris Murphy replaced the retiring Independent Joe Lieberman, and Maine Independent Angus King succeeded the retiring Republican Olympia Snowe. King would caucus with Democrats.)

In 2018, Class I Democrats faced a daunting challenge. Republicans had gained a majority in the 2014 midterm and maintained control in 2016 despite losing some ground. Democrats only had to flip two seats to get a majority in the chamber. Still, this year, they had to defend 26 seats (including the Alabama seat that Doug Jones had won in a special election and the Minnesota seat of appointed senator Tina Smith). Republicans only had to defend nine. Republicans ended up with a net gain of two, and thus kept control of the chamber. Downplaying the loss of the GOP majority in the House that year, Trump declared the result "a very-close-to-complete victory."[15]

Nevertheless, Democrats still held on to most Class I seats. In the short term, that outcome was good news for the Democrats. It also meant that they would have a big exposure problem six years later, when they would have to defend 23 of 34 seats up for election in 2024. (Republicans were defending 10 Class I seats plus that of appointed senator Deb Fischer of Nebraska, who was running in a special election for the last two years of Senator Ben Sasse's term.) Democrats had a 51–49 margin in the chamber, so losing one seat would mean losing control of the chamber if the election produced a Republican vice president. Losing two or more would mean minority status, whatever happened in the presidential race. In the end, they would lose four. In three of these cases, the smell of defeat was evident throughout the campaign.

West Virginia. On November 9, 2023, West Virginia's Joe Manchin announced that he would not seek reelection, which meant that a Republican would likely pick up his seat. When Manchin began his political career as a state legislator in the 1980s, West Virginia was solidly Democratic. Since the New Deal, it had voted Republican for president only in GOP landslide years (1956, 1972, and 1984). Michael Dukakis carried the state in 1988, as did Bill Clinton in the next two elections. In 2000, however, George W. Bush's campaign strategist Karl Rove reckoned that the coal-mining, Bible-believing state would spurn Al Gore's environmental policies and the Democratic Party's cultural liberalism. Rove ran an extensive grassroots operation, which flipped the state to Bush and gave him the five electoral votes he needed to eke out a national victory. Like much of rural America, West Virginia shifted strongly toward the Republican Party during the early years of the new century.

As governor and then as senator, Manchin managed to buck the GOP tide with his good-old-boy persona and his moderate-to-conservative issue positions. (In one respect, Manchin was a demographic outlier in a WASP state: he was an Italian American Catholic whose original family name was Mancini.) But in April 2023, the state's popular governor, Democrat-turned-Republican Jim Justice, announced that he would run for Manchin's seat. With polls giving Justice a double-digit lead, the 76-year-old Manchin's retirement announcement was no surprise. In November 2024, Justice crushed his Democratic opponent by a 40-point margin.

Montana. Like West Virginia, Montana gained the status of a scarlet-red state only in the recent past. During the latter half of the 20th century, it had elected prominent Democratic senators such as Mike Mansfield (who succeeded LBJ as majority leader) and Max Baucus. In 2000, Republican Conrad Burns won the state's Class I seat. Six years later, his opponent was Jon Tester, a third-generation farmer serving as president of the State Senate. With his beefy frame, flat-top buzz cut, and his two-finger left hand (the result of a childhood meat-grinding accident that cost him three fingers), Tester defied stereotypes about Democratic politicians. His timing was good. Not only was 2006 a favorable year to run as a Democrat, but Burns was an unusually weak incumbent. In one of the first-ever viral YouTube political videos, a Democratic operative caught him falling asleep during a hearing.[16] Tester narrowly won, thanks in part to a Libertarian candidate who drew votes from Burns. The state then started moving to the right, but luck was with Tester. In 2012, a Libertarian candidate again won enough votes to tip the election to Tester. Dark money groups, reportedly with Democratic connections, aided the Libertarian effort by attacking the GOP candidate as weak on big government.[17] Six years later, Tester won a majority of the vote by casting himself as a fighter for Montana, unbeholden to either party. And because it was a midterm, there was no surge of Republican votes as there would be with Trump on the ballot.

Tester's luck ran out in 2024. Trump was sure to win the state in a landslide. The Republican candidate was Tim Sheehy, a young Annapolis graduate and former Navy SEAL. Most important, the state had changed. Decades of steady population growth had brought an influx of Republican-leaning voters who had no memory of Tester's long service to the state.[18] Sheehy won with 52.6 percent.

Ohio. Like Tester, Sherrod Brown of Ohio was a member of the class of 2006. In that year, he challenged incumbent Republican senator Mike DeWine. George W. Bush's unpopularity burdened DeWine, as did a sprawling scandal involving other Ohio Republicans. On *Meet the Press*, Tim Russert asked DeWine: "Are you caught up in a perception of a culture of corruption regarding the Republican Party, particularly in Ohio?" The senator candidly responded: "Tim, the climate, as they say, in politics is not good."[19] Brown romped by a margin of 13 points, though DeWine would later make a comeback as the state's governor.

Ohio had long enjoyed a reputation as a "bellwether" in presidential politics, and it had voted for the winner in every presidential election since 1964. The 2012 campaign was no exception, and Obama carried it for the second time. A slight coattail effect may have helped Brown. Obama won more raw votes, though a smaller percentage of the total vote. Brown easily defeated Republican Josh Mandel. In the 2018 midterm, he won by an even wider margin over Representative Jim Renacci.

Unfortunately for Brown, Ohio was shifting from a purple bellwether to a red base state. It was older, whiter, and less educated than the nation—exactly the demographic profile that characterized Trump country. In 2016, Trump carried the state by a wide margin despite losing the aggregated national popular vote. Four years later, he enjoyed a similar margin in Ohio, even as Biden was winning nationwide. By 2024, Biden was unpopular in the state. Though Brown outperformed Harris both in raw votes and percentages, he could not overcome the drag from the top of the ticket. He lost to Republican Bernie Moreno by 3.6 percent. After the election, he pointed to the Democratic Party's failure to appeal to working-class voters: "I think that we don't appear to be fighting for them. Workers have drifted away from the Democratic Party."[20]

Pennsylvania. Bob Casey was yet another member of the class of 2006, and his electoral career resembled Sherrod Brown's. He first entered the Senate by defeating an unpopular incumbent. In his case, it was Rick Santorum, who had become a target of popular culture for his controversial statements against same-sex marriage. Like Ohio, Pennsylvania voted for Obama in 2012, and Casey got a modest boost from the president. In the 2018 midterm, Casey dispatched an underfunded Republican opponent.

Despite demographic similarities to neighboring Ohio, Pennsylvania followed a different political trajectory Whereas Ohio had shifted strongly to the GOP during the Trump years, Pennsylvania remained a swing state. Biden carried it in 2020, and the 2022 midterm not only brought John Fetterman to the Senate but also elevated Democrat Josh Shapiro to the governorship. So unlike Sherrod Brown, Casey did not appear to be a likely loser throughout the 2024 campaign. Most polls showed him slightly ahead.

Candidate quality was one reason the campaign took an unexpected turn. Republican David McCormick was a West Point graduate who received the Bronze Star for combat service in Iraq during the first Gulf War. He earned a PhD in international relations from Princeton and served in several high positions during the George W. Bush administration, including Under Secretary of the Treasury. He then made a fortune as a hedge fund executive. He sought the GOP Senate nomination in 2022, losing the primary to Trump-endorsed Mehmet Oz. Two years later, he managed the unusual feat of gaining Trump's support while maintaining his image as a mainstream business Republican. With his own deep pockets and corporate connections, he enjoyed ample funding. He linked Casey to the Biden-Harris administration and benefited from Trump's victory in the state. In the end, he barely edged out Casey by two-tenths of one percent.

The Holds

Despite losing four Senate seats, Democrats could take consolation in retaining four seats in states that Trump carried. During the late 20th century, such outcomes were common: in 1988, 17 senators won election in a state that went for the other party's presidential nominee (two Dukakis states elected Republican senators while 15 Bush states elected Democrats.)[21] In the new century, "mismatches" were rarer. In 2020, the only example was Susan Collins (R-ME).

Among the four states, the GOP's best opportunity for a pickup should have been Arizona. Incumbent Kyrsten Sinema had alienated Democratic voters by breaking with her party on issues such as the Senate filibuster. With polls showing that she would lose a Democratic primary, she declared herself an independent and eventually decided to retire. Former two-term governor Doug Ducey could have been a strong GOP candidate, but as in 2022, he opted not to run. Instead, the Republican nominee was Kari Lake, a former local television anchor. During her 2022 gubernatorial race, she embraced the idea that the Democrats had stolen the 2020 election from Trump. Her advocacy was so zealous that even Trump reportedly made fun of her.[22] After narrowly losing her race, she responded with more claims of election fraud that damaged her credibility and generated costly litigation but did not change the result.

The Democratic candidate was Ruben Gallego, a Marine Corps veteran of the Iraq War who had served in the House since 2015. He outraised Lake by a wide margin and focused on bread-and-butter economic issues and border security. His message resonated with fellow Hispanics. "We took a very strong and direct approach at border security because we knew that the Latino community was actually also worried about border security," he told NBC News.[23] His strong performance among Hispanics helped him outperform Harris and defeat Lake 50.1 to 47.7 percent.

Wisconsin Democratic senator Tammy Baldwin first won her seat in 2012, when Obama was carrying the state by seven points. She easily won reelection in the 2018 midterm, and had built a reputation as a hardworking legislator, but faced a serious challenge in 2024. Polls showed that Trump could win the state, as he had in 2016. Her opponent was banker Eric Hovde, who was wealthy enough to lend millions to his campaign.

Hovde proved to be a flawed candidate. At one campaign stop, he flubbed the Pledge of Allegiance.[24] On a conservative podcast, he seemed to raise questions about the competence of senior citizens: "Well, if you're in a nursing home, you only have a five, six-month life expectancy. Almost nobody in a nursing home is in a point to vote."[25] He later explained that he was talking about election integrity, but as the old political saying goes: if you're explaining, you're losing. His most serious gaffe came in his one debate with Baldwin. In response to a question about the farm bill, he whiffed: "I'm not an expert on the farm bill because I'm not in the U.S. Senate."[26] In Wisconsin—America's Dairyland—this blunder gave ammunition to Baldwin. It also reminded voters that, although he grew up in the state, he actually lived and worked in Orange County, California.[27] As Trump was carrying the state, Baldwin squeaked through by less than a percentage point.

In Michigan, the retirement of four-term Democratic incumbent Debbie Stabenow gave Republicans a good opportunity for a pickup. They had a high-quality candidate in Mike Rogers, a former congressman and chair of the House Intelligence Committee. A onetime FBI agent, he had maintained a public profile as a television commentator on national security issues. Though he was a mainstream Republican who had criticized Trump in the past, he won the former president's endorsement.

Democrats had a high-quality candidate of their own in three-term representative Elissa Slotkin. Before serving in the House, she had extensive experience in the CIA, the Defense Department, and the National Security Council. During her time in Congress, she reached beyond the Democratic base in a Republican-leaning district. The Lugar Center found her to be the most bipartisan House member from the state.[28]

Rogers won among voters who thought the economy or immigration was the most critical issue. Slotkin won among those who put a priority on abortion or the state of democracy.[29] She won by about three-tenths of one percent of the vote.

In Nevada, incumbent Democrat Jacky Rosen seemed to have a significant edge throughout most of the campaign. The Republican candidate was Sam Brown, a veteran of Afghanistan who had suffered severe injuries and scarring from a roadside bomb. He had only lived in the state for a few years, and had never won an election. Rosen had the advantage of incumbency, a large war chest, and the support of the Culinary Workers Union, legendary for its effective ground game in the state.[30] She also made effective use of the abortion issue against Brown, who had taken a hard-line antiabortion stance until recently. Nevertheless, Harris's defeat in the state proved to be a burden for Rosen, who won by less than two points.

One Democratic retention in a Harris state is worth a mention. Maryland had supported the Democratic presidential candidate in every election since 1992. It had not elected a Republican senator since 1980. Republicans nevertheless hoped that popular two-term governor Larry Hogan could break their losing streak. Hogan downplayed partisanship and tried to put distance between himself and national Republicans. In speeches and ads, Democratic candidate Angela Alsobrooks countered by framing the election as a choice between parties. "A vote for Larry Hogan is a vote to make Lindsey Graham and Ted Cruz the Chairs of Committees," she said in a social media post. "This is what's on the line this year. The Senate majority will control the agenda, and with your help, I'll be the 51st vote."[31] She prevailed by a double-digit margin. Hogan thus joined the ranks of candidates who had won gubernatorial elections in states favoring the opposite party, only to learn that partisanship usually matters more in Senate races. In recent years, other examples have included Linda Lingle (R-HI), Bill Weld (R-MA), Evan Bayh (D-IN), Steve Bullock (D-MT), and Phil Bredesen (D-TN).[32]

On the other side of the aisle, the story of "holds" was simple: Republicans did not lose any Senate seats. Because of the Class I map, Democrats knew that substantial gains were unlikely. For a while, they thought they might bring down Ted Cruz of Texas, a longtime target of liberal loathing. Their candidate was Representative Colin Allred, a charismatic former NFL player who built a national fundraising base. They had also hoped that the state's changing demographics would turn it from red to purple, but they had failed to anticipate Republican inroads among Hispanic voters. In 2024, Texas stayed red, and Cruz won by eight points.

With adoptive Floridian Donald Trump as the presidential nominee, the state's Democrats understood that the Senate race would be tough. Nevertheless, some thought Representative Debbie Mucarsel-Powell might score an upset by rallying Hispanic support. She did not. As in the past, Florida Hispanics voted Republican, and Rick Scott returned to the Senate.

Overall, the 2024 Senate elections continued a trend that had been underway for decades.

In the late 1970s and early 1980s, about half of the states had split Senate delegations, with one Republican and one Democrat. (New York, for instance, elected the odd couple of erudite Democrat Daniel Patrick Moynihan and earthy Republican Alfonse D'Amato.) As elections polarized, split delegations became less common, and in 2024, they nearly disappeared. While McCormick's victory in Pennsylvania created a split delegation, the Republican pickups in West Virginia, Montana, and Ohio ended them. Besides Pennsylvania, the only split delegations left were Maine and Wisconsin. These three represented the lowest number since the start of direct election of senators.[33]

HOUSE ELECTIONS

At the start of the election cycle, Democrats aspired to retake control of the lower chamber. They fell short. As in the 2022 midterm, Republicans won the aggregated popular vote for the House. Compared with the 2020 election, they made notable gains among Hispanic voters, going from 36 to 45 percent, and they increased their share among residents of small towns and rural areas, from 58 to 65 percent.[34] As for seats, they ended up with a 220–215 majority. That tiny margin was a near-run thing: a switch of 7,309 votes in three districts would have given control to the Democrats, 218–217.[35] Redistricting contributed both to the Democrats' early hope and later disappointment.

After the 2020 census, Democratic supermajorities in the New York Legislature drafted a congressional gerrymander so extreme that the state's highest court threw it out and had a special master draw new lines. Under this map, Republicans gained three seats, including one that had belonged to the chair of the Democratic Congressional Campaign Committee. This outcome was a major reason Democrats lost their narrow majority in the House. After the midterm, they went to court and got a chance to draw the lines again. This time, they drafted a plan that advantaged their candidates, but not so much as to invite another judicial intervention.[36] In 2024, they also ran better campaigns. Hakeem Jeffries of Brooklyn, who became House Democratic Leader after the 2022 midterm, made it a personal mission to improve party organization and fundraising in the state.[37] Following the lead of Tom Suozzi, who earlier won the special election to succeed the disgraced George Santos, they put more emphasis on fighting crime and bolstering border security.[38] In November, Democrats flipped three GOP seats.

As a result of voting rights litigation, Alabama and Louisiana had new district maps, and Black Democrats picked up one seat in each. But redistricting cut both ways. In 2022, the North Carolina Supreme Court ruled that a congressional district map by the state's GOP legislature violated the state constitution. Special masters drew a new map, which resulted in the election of seven Democrats and seven Republicans. Then a partisan judicial election came into play. Republicans defeated two incumbent members of the state's Supreme Court, flipping it from a 4–3 Democratic majority to a 5–2 Republican majority. The court's new majority granted a GOP request to rehear the redistricting case. It reversed the earlier decision. The legislature drew a map that gave Republicans a gain of three House seats—canceling out Democratic gains in New York.

In addition to the North Carolina pickups, Republican challengers defeated Democratic incumbents Susan Wild and Matt Cartwright in Pennsylvania, Yadira Caraveo in Colorado, and Mary Peltola in Alaska. A Republican also flipped the House seat that Elissa Slotkin had vacated for her successful Senate race in Michigan.

As Republican gains piled up, Democrats worried that they would suffer a net loss of a seat or two instead of the takeover that they had imagined just weeks earlier. But California, with its notoriously slow vote count, eventually came through for them. Democrats failed to pick off Republican incumbents David Valadao and Ken Calvert. Still, they successfully defended incumbent Mike Levin and held onto the seat that Katie Porter had vacated for her losing race for the Democratic Senate nomination. Three more Democratic victories in California resulted in a net gain of one seat nationwide (two if one counts the Suozzi pickup in a special election).

In 2020, Republican Mike Garcia flipped a Democratic seat north of Los Angeles. As a Hispanic military veteran, he was a good fit for a district with a significant Hispanic population and many defense-related jobs. He retained the seat in 2022 even though redistricting had made his constituency more Democratic: in 2020, Biden won it with 55 percent.[39] His opponent in 2024 was George Whitesides, a former NASA official and CEO of Virgin Galactic. His background enabled him to campaign as a job creator, and his business connections helped attract millions in direct contributions and outside spending. While stressing his strong stand in favor of abortion rights, he cast himself as a bipartisan problem solver. The appeal worked, and he edged out Garcia by about 8,000 votes.

Like Garcia, Republican Michelle Steel represented a Biden district. This one was in suburban Orange County, a former GOP stronghold that had become more competitive over the previous decade. Steel was an immigrant from Korea, and the district had the highest percentage of Asian Americans of any in Southern California.[40] "Asian American," however, is a broad category that encompasses many disparate groups. In 2022, her opponent was a Taiwanese American whom she attacked as "China's Choice"—a bid for the large bloc of Vietnamese American voters who were anti-China.[41] She won with 52 percent. In 2024, her opponent was not vulnerable to this kind of attack: Derek Tran, a consumer lawyer and Army veteran, was the son of Vietnamese refugees. Criticizing Steel's inconsistent positions on abortion and rallying voters in the Little Saigon area, Tran won a narrow victory, becoming the first Vietnamese American to represent the district.

And one month after Election Day, Democrat Adam Gray won the very last House race to reach a conclusion. By just 187 votes, he defeated Republican incumbent John Duarte, who in turn had narrowly bested Gray two years earlier. In this Central Valley district, the Democratic Party had a strong edge in voter registration, but many of its nominal members were rural conservatives who often voted Republican. Gray had served in the State Assembly, where he built a "radical centrist" record that appealed to these voters.[42] Same-day registration may have put him just over the top. In the precinct containing the University of California at Merced, same-day registrants broke 267–47 in his favor.[43]

In addition to the party flips, four incumbents lost primaries:

- Bob Good (R-VA), chair of the House Freedom Caucus, picked the wrong enemies. He endorsed Ron DeSantis for president, so Trump endorsed his primary opponent John McGuire. He joined the effort to oust Speaker Kevin McCarthy, who returned the favor by steering outside spending against him.[44]
- Jerry Carl (R-AL) lost to Barry Moore (R-AL) in an incumbent-vs.-incumbent primary stemming from the Alabama redistricting. Trump did not endorse either candidate, but Moore put more emphasis on his support for Trump.[45]
- Cori Bush (D-MO) vociferously attacked Israel's actions in the Gaza War, so the pro-Israel United Democracy Project poured in millions to defeat her. The outside spending amplified her weaknesses, including ethics problems, enabling local prosecutor Wesley Bell to come out ahead.[46]
- Jamal Bowman (D-NY) lost to Westchester County Executive George Latimer. Like Bush, Bowman was an opponent of Israel, and pro-Israel groups spent heavily to oust him. In 2023, Bowman achieved national notoriety when a security camera caught him pulling a fire alarm in a futile attempt to delay a House floor vote. He pleaded guilty to a misdemeanor and paid a fine. In December 2024, he reflected: "I wish I didn't pull that damn fire alarm, you know what I'm saying?"[47] The defeats of Bowman and Bush called into question the future of the "Squad," the young radical progressives led by Ayanna Pressley, Rashida Tlaib, Ilhan Omar, and Alexandria Ocasio-Cortez, who until recently had seemed to be on the upswing in the Democratic House contingent.

The incumbent defeats are noteworthy because they were so rare. About 96 percent of House members who sought another term in 2024 were successful, a rate consistent with long-standing patterns in congressional elections. But while the reelection rate has remained steady, the reasons behind it have changed. Through the 1980s, incumbents built their support base by bringing federal dollars to their districts, providing services to individuals, and casting key roll call votes in line with constituent opinion. (Rural Democrats, for instance, often broke with their party on issues such as gun control and environmental regulation.) Many held on even where voters tended to support the opposite party in races for higher office.[48] Incumbents still cater to district interests, but partisanship has increasingly dominated House elections.[49] By and large, Republican candidates win Republican districts, and

Democrats win Democratic districts, with relatively few seats seriously in play.

At the same time, it would be an exaggeration to say that individual members' Washington activity was irrelevant to their reelection chances. In some key swing districts, moderates on both sides outperformed their parties' presidential candidates. Rural Democrats Marie Gluesenkamp Perez (WA) and Jared Golden (ME), co-chairs of the centrist Blue Dog Coalition, opposed student loan forgiveness and favored tougher measures on border security. Trump carried both districts, but Gluesenkamp Perez won by 4 percent and Golden won by 1 percent.[50] Pennsylvania Republican Fitzpatrick, co-chair of the moderate Problem Solvers Caucus, won a Harris district by 12.8 percent. In Nebraska's famously Democratic-leaning "Blue Dot" district, which gave Harris one electoral vote, Republican Don Bacon survived a tough challenge by 1.9 percent.[51] They are all exceptions, of course, but in a chamber where three seats can make the difference between majority and minority status, exceptions are consequential.

STATE AND LOCAL ELECTIONS

Eleven states held gubernatorial elections in 2024, none resulting in a change in party control. In most cases, Republican and Democratic candidates prevailed in states that normally favored their own party. One outlier was Vermont, where Republican governor Phil Scott won a third term in a state that had long been a deep shade of blue. Next door in New Hampshire, former U.S. senator Kelly Ayotte (R) made a comeback. In 2016, she lost her seat to Democrat Maggie Hassan by just 743 votes. This time, with Republican incumbent Chris Sununu declining to seek reelection. Ayotte got 53.6 percent against former Manchester mayor Joyce Craig. Ayotte and Scott, both with reputations as pragmatists, became the only Republicans to win 2024 gubernatorial elections in states that Kamala Harris carried.

The strangest gubernatorial race took place in North Carolina. Democratic attorney general Josh Stein won his party's nomination to succeed the term-limited governor, Roy Cooper (D). The GOP candidate was Mark Robinson, the state's first Black lieutenant governor and first Black major party nominee for governor. In a state that had voted Republican in all but one presidential election since 1976, a good GOP candidate could have defeated Stein.

Instead, Robinson was a terrible candidate. Among his many outlandish statements, he questioned the Holocaust, wished for a return to a time when women could not vote, and threatened to use his AR-15 against the government if it got too big.[52] Despite this baggage, polls showed a competitive race through the middle of 2024. In September, however, the race effectively ended. First, local news outlets reported claims—which he denied—that he had once been a regular at porn shops.[53] Accusations about Robinson's past went national when CNN reported that he had made incendiary comments on a pornography message board years earlier, calling himself a "black NAZI!" and suggesting that he wanted to bring back slavery.[54] Robinson also denied these allegations, but his campaign money soon dried up, and most of his staff melted away.

Earlier in the year, Trump had endorsed Robinson with effusive praise: "This is Martin Luther King on steroids; I told that to Mark. I said: 'I think you're better than Martin Luther King. I think you are Martin Luther King times two.'"[55] After the scandal broke, Trump did not appear with Robinson again, telling reporters: "I'm not familiar with the race. I haven't seen it."[56]

Even as Trump was narrowly carrying North Carolina, Stein won with 54.9 percent of the vote, and his victory helped Democrats sweep all races for statewide office, including a close race for the state's Supreme Court.

In the state legislatures, the 2024 election brought relatively slight change. Voters in 44 states elected 5,808 legislators, or about three-quarters of all seats nationwide.[57] Compared with their numbers just before the election, Republicans scored a net gain of just 70 seats.[58] The GOP picked up the Michigan House and broke Democratic control of the Minnesota House. (The Minnesota outcome embarrassed Governor Tim Walz, who spent the fall of 2024 campaigning for vice president.) Republicans ended the year with control of 58 legislative chambers, up one from just before the election. Democrats had 38, down two. One had no majority. Nebraska's legislature is unicameral and officially nonpartisan.

If the year-to-year shifts seem unremarkable, consider how legislatures have changed over the decades. For many years, Democrats had a substantial lead in legislative chambers, mainly because of the party's dominance in the South. In midcentury, some Southern chambers literally had no Republican members at all. As late as the 2008 election, Democrats won 60 chambers to the GOP's 37. Republicans made huge gains in the 2010 midterm, which became entrenched as a result both of shifting voter behavior and aggressive redistricting.

Another set of results offered clues about voters' issue positions, as 41 states voted on 146 statewide ballot measures.[59] Ten states considered constitutional amendments protecting abortion rights.[60] The measures passed in Arizona, Colorado, Maryland, Missouri, Montana, and New York. (Four states—California, Michigan, Ohio, and Vermont—had already enacted such provisions.) Nevada voters approved an amendment, but under state rules, it will require repassage in 2026 to take effect. In Florida and South Dakota, abortion rights amendments failed to win enough votes. Nebraska voters not only rejected such an amendment, but they also passed one to ban abortion after the first trimester. These results suggest that while voters continued to disapprove of the *Dobbs* decision, this sentiment was far from universal. Democrats hoped the issue might generate enough turnout to move some states out of the Trump column, but his victories in Arizona, Missouri, Montana, and Nevada indicated otherwise.[61] Trump's late-blooming opposition to a national abortion ban probably gave him some insulation on the issue.

Concerns over immigration cropped up in ballot measures to ban noncitizen voting. In 2022, six states passed such measures. In 2024, legislatures in eight states asked voters to approve constitutional amendments to forbid noncitizens from voting in state or local elections. All passed. Opponents said the effect is largely symbolic because federal law already forbids noncitizen voting in federal elections (18 USC 611) or claiming citizenship to vote in any election at any level (18 USC 1015). Supporters said such measures could prevent cities from changing their municipal codes to allow noncitizen participation in local elections.

Our previous book noted that California voters showed a slight conservative streak in 2020 by rejecting ballot measures that would have repealed a 1996 ban on affirmative action and changed Proposition 13, the historic 1978 measure that limited property taxes. That streak reappeared in 2024. Voters turned down propositions to raise the state's minimum wage and end a ban on local rent control. Another outcome shocked advocates of prison reform. The state legislature proposed a constitutional amendment to forbid forced labor in jails and prisons. There was no organized opposition to the measure, and no one submitted an argument against it for publication in the state's ballot pamphlet. Nevertheless, 53 percent voted no. Concern about crime contributed to the outcome, though supporters of the measure speculated that the ballot language—specifically the phrase "involuntary servitude"—might have confused many voters.[62]

There was no confusion about the meaning of another crime-related measure. In 2014, a ballot proposition reduced penalties for drug possession and theft of items worth $950 or less. In 2024, Proposition 36 proposed to change that law by increasing penalties and allowing felony charges in certain circumstances. Supporters of this proposition argued the earlier law had fostered open-air drug use, shoplifting, and smash-and-grab robberies, all of which had proliferated in the previous decade. Opponents said it would have little effect on crime and increase the burden on an already-strained correctional system. With polls showing that Proposition 36 would win easily, Vice President Harris declined to take a public position. It passed by a two-to-one margin.

The crime issue sealed the fate of two prominent district attorneys. In Alameda County (encompassing Oakland and other Bay Area communities), Pamela Price had sought to reduce incarceration rates despite a surge in violent and property crime. In a recall election, 63 percent voted to oust her and have the county board of supervisors pick a replacement. In Los Angeles County, whose population exceeds that of 40 states, incumbent George Gascon faced fierce criticism for pursuing similar policies. In a nominally nonpartisan race, Republican-turned-independent Nathan Hochman defeated him with 60 percent of the vote.

THE TRUMP EFFECT

This chapter would not be complete without a discussion of Trump's down-ballot impact. Unlike Reagan in the early 1980s, Trump could not claim that his coattails pulled congressional Republicans out of the wilderness. Before his election in 2016, Republicans had 247 seats in the House and 54 in the Senate. With his return to power after the 2024 elections, they were down to 220 House seats and 53 Senate seats (see table 6.2). As we have seen, the party's Senate gains in 2024 occurred mostly because several Democratic incumbents could no longer survive long-standing partisan trends in their home states.

Coattails did not give Trump power over congressional Republicans. Primaries did. From 2016 onward, Trump enjoyed near-universal approval from GOP voters. If Trump gave a thumbs-down, Republican incumbents feared these voters could turn against them in the next primary. They had reason to worry. In 2018, after Representative Mark Sanford (R-SC) faulted his policies, Trump tweeted his endorsement of a primary challenger. Even though he waited until voting had begun, the tweet helped end Sanford's long career. During the same year, Senators Bob Corker (R-TN) and Jeff Flake (R-AZ) retired after polls showed that their criticism of Trump was likely to doom their chances of renomination.

In 2021, 10 House Republicans voted for his impeachment. Liz Cheney (R-WY), the most prominent of the 10, was chair of the House Republican

Table 6.2. Party Gains in House and Senate Elections, 2016–2024

	House	*Senate*
2016	6D	2D
2018	40D	1R
2020	12R	3D
2022	9R	1D
2024	2D	4R

Note: The data refers to the difference between the number of seats won by the party gaining seats in that election and the number of seats that party won in the preceding general election.
Source: Molly E. Reynolds, *Vital Statistics on Congress*, https://www.brookings.edu/wp-content/uploads/2024/11/2-2-Full.pdf.

Conference. After she refused to back down from her criticism of Trump, House Republicans ousted her from that post. She then joined Adam Kinzinger (R-IL), who had also voted for impeachment, on the House committee investigating the January 6 attack on the Capitol. Trump and House GOP leader Kevin McCarthy supported Cheney's primary opponent, who won with 66 percent of the vote. Kinzinger decided not to run for reelection, though partly because a Democratic gerrymander had put him in the same district as another Republican incumbent.

Of the other pro-impeachment Republicans, three lost primaries, and three retired in 2022. As of the 2024 election, only two remained: David Valadao (R-CA) and Dan Newhouse (R-WA). Newhouse might have lost a closed Republican primary in 2024. But in Washington State's top-two system, the candidates who get the most primary votes advance to the general election, regardless of party. A moderate Republican group stealthily promoted Newhouse's weakest Republican opponent.[63] The ploy worked, resulting in a Republican-on-Republican general election where Democrats and independents helped Newhouse prevail.

Of the seven senators who voted to convict Trump in the 2021 impeachment trial, only Lisa Murkowski (R-AK) won in 2022. Like Newhouse, she probably would have lost a closed primary, but the state's ranked-choice voting system enabled her to get support from Democrats. Susan Collins (R-ME) and Bill Cassidy (R-LA) did not have to face voters until 2026. Richard Burr (R-NC), Pat Toomey (R-PA), and Ben Sasse (R-NE) declined to seek reelection. After Sasse announced that he would not run again, he resigned from the Senate for what turned out to be a brief stint as president of the University of Florida. Mitt Romney (R-UT), who had also been the only Republican to vote for conviction in Trump's first impeachment, decided to step aside after a single term. Despite his stature as the party's 2012 presidential candidate, polls showed that most Utah Republicans did not want him to run again.[64] In a social media post, Trump reveled in Romney's withdrawal, saying that he "did not serve with distinction."[65]

Sometimes, Trump signaled his attitude through catty nicknames. When he referred to "Liddle Bob Corker" and "Jeff Flake(y)," ambitious Republicans got the hint that those seats would soon be open. At other times, he would make a preemptive threat. Urging the House to censure Adam Schiff (D-CA) for alleged misconduct in investigating him, he said on social media: "Any Republican voting against his CENSURE, or worse, should immediately be primaried. There are plenty of great candidates out there!"[66] Republicans got the message, and none voted against the censure motion.

Trump's sway had limits. After House Republicans ousted Kevin McCarthy as speaker, Trump endorsed Jim Jordan (R-OH) to replace him. Jordan still could not muster enough Republicans to get a majority on the House floor. If Trump could not elevate a leadership candidate, he showed that he could bring one down. When it looked as if the Republicans might get behind Tom Emmer (R-MN), Trump denounced him on social media and in private phone calls. He soon withdrew and Trump reportedly gloated: "He's done. It's over. I killed him."[67]

In December 2024, Trump demanded that a continuing resolution immediately raise the debt limit so that he would not have to deal with it after he became president. Dozens of House Republicans voted no, and eventually, Congress passed the measure without a debt limit provision. Why was this issue different? Trump derived his power from Republican primary voters, and in this case, he wanted something that they strongly opposed. In a 2023 survey for CBS, YouGov found that 69 percent of Republicans were against increasing the debt limit, and 44 percent said they would still oppose it even if it meant the United States would default on its existing debt.[68] On most issues, Trump was going to get his way with congressional Republicans, but he needed the support or acquiescence of the GOP base.

In state politics, as in Congress, most Republican candidates and officeholders accepted Trump as party leader. Even so, it was possible to survive after getting on his bad side. In Georgia, Governor Brian Kemp and Secretary of State Brad Raffensperger drew his wrath by refusing to go along with his scheme to reverse Biden's 2020 victory in the state. In 2022, they defeated Trump-backed primary challengers by keeping their focus on state issues instead of the last presidential election.

Aside from such unusual cases, however, one thing was clear by 2024: the GOP was Trump's party.

Chapter 7

Trump Returns

What Comes Next? Policy, Politics, and Institutions

The election of 2024 capped a year of unexpected twists and turns, probably the strangest campaign since 1968. In some ways, however, the election itself was almost anticlimactic. The only suspense remaining by dawn the next day was whether Donald Trump would hold on to his constitutionally irrelevant lead in the nationally aggregated popular vote and whether Republicans or Democrats would hold a tiny advantage in the House of Representatives. In another sense, the result was dramatic, as Trump became only the second president of the United States to be defeated for reelection and then be returned to the White House. It was, as many noted, one of the greatest political comebacks in American history.

Needless to say, Trump's win in 2024 represented a big change for him since 2020. Less remarked on was that it also represented a stronger showing than in 2016, when he won with very small margins in three "Blue Wall" states and ended with three million fewer votes nationally than Hillary Clinton. In the end, 2024 was not radically different from 2016—Trump only won one state, Nevada, that he had not won eight years before. But it was different enough to mark a solid win. Trump gained vote share in every state, and gained among most key demographic groups.

As for the passions stirred by Trump, for and against, one is hard pressed to find an analogy in presidential history. Certainly not Grover Cleveland, the last two-time nonconsecutive winner. Some possibilities come to mind, but fall short. Arguably, Richard Nixon was never loved by his supporters, nor Ronald Reagan and Franklin Roosevelt hated by their opponents, with as much passion as Trump—nor were Reagan's and Roosevelt's supporters and opponents as closely divided as Trump's. The fiery Andrew Jackson—perhaps not coincidentally, beloved by Trump—may come closer to fitting the bill, a full two centuries ago.

Trump's strongest supporters see him as an indefatigable fighter, fist raised in the air on behalf of political, cultural, and economic groups who feel ignored at best, if not positively attacked, by liberal and corporate elites. They believe that his defeat in 2020 was illegitimate and the January 6, 2021 attack on the Capitol was exaggerated, if not a leftist "false flag" operation.[1] His strongest critics see him as a looming authoritarian, perhaps even a fascist, a man who has already proven his willingness to upend the Constitution in narcissistic pursuit of his own power. In between are the people who have now given him two wins and one loss.

For all the drama, the last three elections have sustained a predictable rhythm in American politics. When Americans believe the country is off track, they throw the bums out. In 2016, Trump was the beneficiary; in 2020, he was the victim. In 2024, Trump and Biden were both unpopular before Biden dropped out, to be replaced by the unpopular Kamala Harris. In the great unpopularity contest of 2024, Trump had one irreducible advantage. Americans were unhappy, for many sound reasons ranging from inflation to uncontrolled immigration to woke madness to world disorder, and he was running against the bums.

Yet this, perhaps, does not give Trump enough credit. Most political figures would have thrown in the towel after 2020. Trump did not. As president trying to govern, he may find again, as he did the first time, that focusing exclusively on his role as pugilist-in-chief is not enough. The bottomless well of self-regard that fueled his comeback may lead to triumph or disaster, for him and his country; it may prove a harbinger of national renewal or of abuse. But without it, no comeback would have been possible.

Moreover, Trump may have been unpopular in 2024, but he was much less unpopular than he had been eight or even four years before. On November 1, 2016, his RealClearPolitics favorability average was −19.7 percentage points. Following a modest improvement during his first term, his post-January 6 favorability (as of January 15, 2021), was back down to −20.4. By July 18, 2024, however, Trump had improved to −12.0. On Election Day 2024, his favorability was −7.0.[2] There was a decisive group of voters that, to put it simply, he grew on over time.

The election of 2024 will have important implications for policy, politics, and American institutions.

POLICY

The Senate filibuster and tight margin in the House will continue to limit controversial legislative action except on a couple of budget-related bills per year that can be passed on "reconciliation" rules that require only a bare majority to pass, even in the Senate. And the more disparate elements that are crammed into a reconciliation bill, the more challenging it will be to hold the narrow GOP House majority together.[3] Like Harris, Trump ran a largely thematic campaign that left questions about exactly how he planned to execute his promises. Even after the flurry of activity after he was sworn in, many questions remained. Some policy predictions seem plausible, however:

Immigration: As expected, Trump concentrated first on plugging the porous border, deporting illegal immigrants with a criminal record, and limiting asylum claims. The Trump administration claimed that this focus bore early fruit, telling Fox News that illegal border crossings declined sharply.[4] What he will do beyond that will depend on politics and logistics.[5] H-1B visa policies will continue to present a sticking point within his coalition. His Day One executive order declaring birthright citizenship ended was stayed by a federal judge within hours and may or (more likely) may not survive judicial scrutiny.

Foreign policy: The United States will demand that allies take up a greater burden. Beyond that, Trump's desire to project a strong America will be in tension with his desire to disengage from security responsibilities. Will he abandon Ukraine? Will he withdraw from NATO? Will he look the other way if China threatens Taiwan? He has intimated as much, and there are certainly those in his entourage who would celebrate. Yet his national security appointees also include more traditional hawks. Despite his "America First" slogan, hearkening back to 1940 isolationism, Trump did not go full isolationist in his first term. Will he in his second? And will the aggressive noises he made during the presidential transition about taking over Greenland, the Panama Canal, and perhaps even Canada mean anything, or were they just noise? (After a strong statement by Secretary of State Marco Rubio, Panama announced it would not renew its contract with a Hong Kong company to manage the canal.)

Trade: In his first term, Trump used tariffs or tariff threats as a tool to get more favorable trade terms for the United States, not to construct a generally protectionist economic policy. In 2024, he seemed to be advocating a more general embrace of tariffs, which he called "the most beautiful word in the dictionary."[6] Was he just laying the groundwork for another round of the art of the deal, or is he really committed to taking the United States back to the high-tariff days of William McKinley (and, it should be remembered, Herbert Hoover)? Voters who pulled the lever for Trump to defeat "Bidenflation" may be unpleasantly surprised to discover that a new round of tariffs has suddenly made everything at Walmart more expensive. Or, perhaps early successes using tariff threats to get concessions from Colombia and Mexico will serve as the pattern.

Wokeness: Trump made it clear that his administration would wage war on the whole complex of federal, state, and local policies that reflect what many critics call "wokeness" (or, for an earlier era, "political correctness"). Among other things, this would include Diversity, Equity, and Inclusion (or DEI) policies in schools or workplaces and policies requiring males who identify as females to be allowed to play girls' sports. Here, one should expect Trump to give no quarter. As chief executive, he will be able to do much within the federal government, and made a big start as soon as he was inaugurated. Outside of it, he will have to rely on strings attached to federal grants or civil rights actions brought by the Justice Department or Department of Education, with a more uncertain outcome. Trump will, it seems, be moving with the tide. DEI is facing a backlash nationwide, and he may get help from some moderate Democrats who see excessive commitment to wokeness as one reason for their party's 2024 losses. In 2020, Black Lives Matter was a force to be reckoned with; in 2024 it was largely defunct and discredited, its coffers drained by its leaders.[7]

Fiscal issues: Trump will certainly fight to extend his 2017 tax cuts, which would otherwise expire in 2025. Even before entering office, he also set in motion an attempt to identify government efficiencies through the new Department of Government Efficiency, or DOGE (though it is not an official cabinet-level department), and his Secretary of Treasury has announced a goal of reducing the deficit to 3 percent of GDP. Though Trump has talked of shaving $2 trillion from federal spending by trimming wasteful discretionary spending, the real engine driving the federal debt crisis is the entitlement programs, especially Social Security, Medicare, and Medicaid. While Medicaid goes to the poor and will be on the chopping block, Medicare and Social Security are middle-class entitlements paying benefits to the elderly. Trump vowed in 2016 not to touch them, and he did so again in 2024, even attacking Nikki Haley for suggesting raising the Social Security retirement age. Only a major economic crisis traceable to the deficit is likely to move him off this position. Like Kamala Harris, he also proposed numerous tax breaks and spending programs that seemed primarily to serve a political purpose (for example, ending taxes on tips, a policy that appealed to the outsized hospitality industry in the swing state of Nevada). Overall, in his first term, Trump showed little interest in addressing the fiscal catastrophe bearing down on the United States. When the shouting dies down, will he actually do better the second time around?

In each of these issues and more, general outlines are visible, but many questions remain. The more that can be done unilaterally without relying on Congress, and the closer the policy hews to Trump's main themes of 2024, the more likely it will happen, and will last for the duration of his presidency. The more Trump and Republicans attempt to convert a narrow win on the basis of inflation and immigration into a "mandate" for a rang departures on unrelated issues, the greater the difficulty will be.

POLITICS

In the wake of the election, it was common for casual analysts to proclaim that 2024 represented a "realignment." In the everyday usage of the term, there was clearly a movement of voters toward the Republicans. Groups including Hispanics (and to a lesser extent other non-white voters), union families, 18–29 year olds, first-time voters, Catholics, and voters with incomes under $100,000 moved substantially in Trump's direction, though in only a few cases (such as Catholics, first-timers, and incomes under $100,000) did Trump go from losing in 2020 to winning in 2024.[8] More often, he continued losing groups he lost before, but by smaller margins, and continued winning groups he had won before, but by bigger margins. His gains were almost across-the-board demographically and geographically.

In the political science usage of the term realignment, though, the jury is out. By realignment, political scientists generally mean a substantial and enduring shift in voter preferences, usually producing a new and reliable majority coalition. By this definition, it is not yet possible to say whether 2024 has inaugurated a realignment. There are two open questions: whether the 2024 shift in voter preferences will prove enduring, and whether it will broaden into a more substantial Republican majority than a plurality of 1.4 percent of the popular vote and a razor-thin edge in the House of Representatives.

The key group is the Hispanic vote, where exit polls say Trump grew from 32 percent support in 2020 to 46 percent in 2024.[9] This gain pushed Trump over the top in Nevada and Arizona and possibly other states as well. Hispanics were 12 percent of the electorate even though they are around 20 percent of the population. As more Hispanics reach voting age and become citizens, their weight in the electorate will grow. Democratic hopes for a "coalition of the ascendant" hinged both on the expansion of the Hispanic electorate and its overwhelming support for the party. But if Republicans can keep matching their 2024 showing, that coalition will turn out to be a mirage. On the other hand, Republican hopes for a permanent, solid majority in the national electorate could prove ephemeral unless they can push their Hispanic vote share above 50 percent. Geographically, 2024 points to the potential for Republicans to become competitive at the presidential level in a number of states that have been out of reach, such as New York, New Jersey, Illinois, Minnesota, and Virginia—though, so far, it is still only a potential.

Whether Republicans succeed in consolidating and broadening their 2024 gains will depend on their own skill, the speed with which Democrats recover, and above all, events. Many might have thought Dwight D. Eisenhower's win in 1952—a much bigger win than Trump's—to mark lasting shift in party strength, but by 1954 Democrats had retaken control of Congress and by 1961 they were back in the White House. One analyst surveyed Lyndon Johnson's 1964 landslide—bigger than Ike's—and declared that Republicans would probably not win another presidential election until 1988.[10] Vietnam, riots, and stagflation then led to five GOP wins in the next six elections, including two 49-state wipeouts. For all of the Republican triumphalism and all the Democratic gloom, the most that can be said after 2024 was that Republicans had edged ahead for the moment in a seesaw political environment in which small shifts can have big consequences.

In the midterm elections of 2026 the Senate map might seem to be tilted nearly as heavily for Democrats as it was tilted against them in 2024, 22 Republican seats up for election to only 13 Democratic seats (if there are no additional special elections).[11] Unfortunately for the Democrats, only one of those 22 GOP seats—that held by Susan Collins of Maine—is in a state that Kamala Harris won. Two Democratic seats, those of Gary Peters of Michigan and Jon Ossoff of Georgia, are in states that Trump won. In the House, by contrast, Democrats will need only to pick up a handful of seats—far fewer than the average midterm gain by the opposition party—to regain their majority. Given the narrow margin after 2024, a few vacancy elections could put Democrats in control of the House even before the midterms. If Republicans are still holding on to their congressional majorities after 2026, one will be on firmer ground seeing their 2024 wins as something other than another bump in the three-decade-long ebb and flow of a 50–50 country.

For now, given the tight margins involved, the biggest realignments may be taking place within the parties rather than between them. On the Republican side, MAGA is ascendant, and the traditional Republicans are on the downswing. Trump is clearly in control of his party now, and J. D. Vance seems positioned to carry that transition into the future beyond 2028. Limited government is no longer the watchword, arguably leaving the country without any major party committed to the principle. The new Republican Party bears an uncanny resemblance to the (very) old Republican Party, at least in terms of trade, immigration, and foreign policy (though fiscal sobriety remains a question mark).[12] MAGA argues that it is time for a readjustment on the world stage that once again gives priority to American interests. Critics answer that American interests will not be well-served by disregarding the expensive lessons that led postwar Republicans to adopt free trade and international security engagement. Time will tell.

Nor is MAGA itself unified. Even before Trump was sworn in for his second term, fissures appeared in the MAGA coalition between immigration hard-liners and "tech bros" such as Musk and Ramaswamy. The latter ignited a firestorm by suggesting that H-1B visas for foreign tech workers be expanded, leading to the former to complain of betrayal. In response, Musk declared that there were "hateful and unrepentant racists" burrowed into the GOP who needed to be rooted out. Trump tried to calm the ruckus by taking Musk's side—the H-1B program was, Trump said, a "great program"—but longtime MAGA guru Steve Bannon told Musk to "sit in the back and study" or "we're going to rip your face off."[13] The underlying conflict is unlikely to go away.

Of course, postelection conflicts among the losers are almost always more serious than among the winners, and there were many reasons to expect conflicts to erupt regularly on the Democratic side. Unsurprisingly, an ideological dispute rose to the fore almost immediately. Did Harris lose because Democrats (including Harris in her 2019 presidential run) had veered too far left, or because Harris had tacked too much to the center during the fall campaign, shedding some of her 2019 stands and campaigning with Liz Cheney?

Within a few days of Election Day, Democratic congressman Seth Moulton of Massachusetts spoke out against males playing girls' sports and denounced what he called a progressive litmus test that has kept Democrats silent about such issues.[14] Days later, Ritchie Torres of New York, the only gay black House member, told the *Washington Post* that "I worry that our party has been hijacked by far-left elites whose sensibilities and priorities are out of touch with those of working-class people on the ground," conceding that issues like transgender surgeries for minors and males playing girls' sports were "complicated" and that critics had a point.[15] Throughout the postelection period, a number of Democrats both publicly and privately pointed the finger at the party's leftward lunge. Alexandria Ocasio-Cortez answered by blaming other factors, including sexism in the electorate and backlash against the pro-Israel advocacy group AIPAC.[16] Bernie Sanders, like Ocasio-Cortez a self-described "democratic socialist," said "It should come as no great surprise that a Democratic Party which has abandoned working class people would find that the working class has abandoned them."[17] Analysts will continue collecting evidence on that score, but critics of the Democrats' leftward move would seem to have the better argument. At least on issues such as affirmative action and immigration, data showed that the positions of Republicans and independents had barely moved since the mid-1990s, while Democrats had veered sharply left of the median voter in the last 15 years.[18]

Less ideologically driven postelection disputes tore at Democrats, as well. Nancy Pelosi blamed Biden for not leaving the race sooner, or perhaps for endorsing Harris rather than letting an open convention play out.[19] Some

Democrats took shots at Pelosi and Obama.[20] Biden himself said he regretted leaving the contest, claiming against all evidence that he would have won.[21]

Speaking of Biden, Democrats will also have to grapple with the odium of having collectively covered up or ignored Joe Biden's incapacity as president for years. In December 2024, the *Wall Street Journal* published an investigative report revealing that Biden was known by his staff and key congressional Democrats to be failing as early as 2021, his first year in office.[22] Not only was no move made to trigger the 25th amendment, but Democrats almost uniformly assailed anyone else who raised the issue of Biden's capacity—except for Congressman Dean Phillips, who ran a quixotic campaign for president on that basis and was himself assailed when he was not ignored. Republicans got a two-for-the-price-of-one bonus here, as large parts of the Democratic-leaning major media were discredited when they had to acknowledge that they had "underreported" Biden's travails. Former MSNBC host Mehdi Hasan, for instance, admitted that "Like many others, I was completely, utterly, totally, embarrassingly wrong, about Biden's lack of mental competence."[23]

If Democrats could agree on anything, it was that they had lost touch with large parts of the American electorate that had once seen themselves as Democrats, including the working class. What route they will take to try to find their way back is unclear, but it will necessarily involve serious contestation.

INSTITUTIONS

Electoral College

The first important institutional effect of the 2024 election is that pressure to alter or abolish the Electoral College will abate, at least for a time. Had Trump won again while trailing in the aggregated popular vote, as in 2016, or had he nearly done so, as in 2020, demands for change would have become louder. Instead, he won a solid victory in the Electoral College propelled by a modest lead in the popular vote, taking the wind out of the sails of the agitation against the Electoral College.

Because actual change in the Electoral College would normally require a constitutional amendment which would have little chance of being ratified by the requisite 38 states, agitation for change would take one of two destructive paths. On one hand, the party that considers itself aggrieved—in recent years, Democrats—would see itself as trapped beyond remedy and would become increasingly bitter and alienated from the Constitution, with unpredictable results. That process may already have begun, but has probably been arrested.

On the other hand, pressure would increase to find a way around the high obstacles of the constitutional amendment process. Since 2006, the proposed workaround has taken the form of the National Popular Vote Interstate

Compact. The Compact would commit states to delivering their electoral votes to the leader of the nationally aggregated popular vote even if another candidate won their state contest. It would take effect as soon as states with 270 electoral votes have signed on. As of December 2024, 17 states and the District of Columbia, with 209 electoral votes, had joined. Critics have pointed out a number of flaws to the compact: there is no official national vote, there could be no mechanism to trigger a national recount if the vote were very close, interstate compacts require approval by a vote of Congress, and the entire mechanism is an attempt to amend the Constitution without amending the Constitution.

If the compact had been operating in 2024, states like California and Colorado would have been forced to cast their electoral votes for Trump even though he lost there by lopsided margins. Mature reflection could lead to a serious rethinking of the strategy. At the least, the ardor for the compact has undoubtedly cooled.

Election Access/Security

Since the election controversies of 2020, state and federal officeholders have been occupied with questions of election access and election integrity. At the federal level, Democrats in 2021 made a priority of legislation that would have required states to open up mail ballot elections, expanded early voting, allowed automatic and same-day voter registration, and made it more difficult for states to remove inactive voters from the rolls. Their HR 1 also imposed new campaign finance restrictions and required states to use independent commissions for congressional redistricting.[24] Seeing the measure as an unprecedented grab for centralized power over election administration, Senate Republicans filibustered the bill. Democrats threatened to abolish the filibuster (for voting rights legislation only, they said), but Senators Joe Manchin (WV) and Kyrsten Sinema (AZ) would not go along, so the effort died.

At the state level, Republicans in several states passed legislation to correct what they saw as loose procedures encouraging fraud. In Georgia, one of the most high-profile instances, the legislature enhanced voter ID requirements for mail ballots, both codified ballot drop boxes and established more stringent security measures for their use, tightened the time frame for requesting an absentee ballot but also expanded opportunities for in-person early voting, and took steps to limit the amount of time Election Day voters wait in line.[25] Joe Biden attacked the measure as "Jim Crow 2.0," but its resemblance to literacy tests, poll taxes, the all-white primary, and KKK intimidation at the polls was unclear at best.

When Senate Democrats were unable to defeat the filibuster and Republicans ran out of state governments that would entertain new voting integrity measures, an uneasy truce set in. For a time in the fall of 2024, things began to sound like a replay of 2020. In Pennsylvania, controversy erupted over whether (despite state law) mail ballots would be counted if the envelopes were not correctly dated; in mid-September, the Pennsylvania Supreme Court ruled they would be invalid.[26] When several irregularities became apparent in Pennsylvania in late October, Trump seized on them as evidence of wide-scale fraud, and it seemed clear he was preparing the battleground in the event the reported results again turned against him.[27] In Virginia, a purge of inactive voters was momentarily stopped by a lawsuit from the U.S. Justice Department, though the Supreme Court ultimately allowed it to go forward.[28] Exit polls showed that only a third of voters were very confident the election was being conducted fairly and accurately; Kamala Harris won those voters overwhelmingly. Another one-third reported being only somewhat confident, and the remaining one-third said they were either "not very" or "not at all" confident. Those voters were much more likely to be supporters of Donald Trump.[29]

The actual result went Trump's way and was decisive enough that fraud simply disappeared as a theme. It will probably remain largely submerged until there is another very close election. Voter turnout also did not suffer some drastic decline. In Georgia, for example, turnout in 2024 was 5,270,912. Four years earlier it was 5,025,683.[30] The involuntary truce that fell into place in 2022 seems destined to hold awhile longer. Republicans did not make significant state gains in 2024, and Democrats have no base in Congress from which to launch a new effort in their direction. A Republican push in Congress for national legislation requiring voter ID and prohibitions on non-citizen voting in local elections will have to overcome the filibuster and federalism, as the Constitution assigns most election administration to the states. And, with the possible exception of noncitizen voting, the fire has seemingly gone out of the issue. Trump's victory put a damper on it in two ways. Since he won, no one can claim that fraud in the election of 2024 robbed him of the presidency. More subtly, his 2024 victory might introduce some doubts about 2020 in the minds of introspective Trump supporters. If it was so easy for Democrats to cheat their way into the White House in 2020, why didn't they just do it again four years later?

Campaign Finance

The 2024 election broke all records for spending on a presidential race. On the Democratic side, after the votes were counted, it became clear that Harris had spent around $1.5 billion in 15 weeks, leading outraged Democrats to wonder how anyone could spend that much money in three months and still lose. There were two answers. First, as Hillary Clinton also showed in

2016 when she outspent Donald Trump, money is not e\
other things must be married to financial resources, such a
biography, an effective organization, and a compelling messa
To be compelling, the message must comport with voters' own
and perceptions. As long as one's opponent has sufficient (not   ..y
superior) resources and a compelling message, money itself is nev\ . enough.
Second, the Harris campaign wasted an enormous amount of money on
consultants, campaign luxuries, and fees for celebrities who interviewed or
endorsed the vice president. As Shane Goldmacher reported in the *New York
Times*, "Her cash-rich campaign spared no expense as it hunted for voters—
paying for an avalanche of advertising, social-media influencers, a for-hire
door-knocking operation, thousands of staff, pricey rallies, a splashy Oprah
town hall, celebrity concerts and even drone shows."[31] Just as the election
result takes the air out of the rage against fraud or the Electoral College, it
may also undermines the impetus for campaign finance reform. If Kamala
Harris can spend $1.5 billion and lose, is controlling campaign money really
that important?

Yet there is one feature of the 2024 election finance picture that may lead
to greater scrutiny, though probably not in the short term: the role of hyper-
billionaires in the election. This, of course, is not really new. Since the 2010
rise of "super PACs" with the right to raise and spend unlimited contributions
on independent expenditures, the rich and very rich have established Super
PACs to support their favorite candidates. Then in 2020, Facebook's Mark
Zuckerberg contributed an estimated $400 million in grants to local campaign
offices ostensibly to help them navigate the difficulties of administering
elections during a pandemic. Critics, however, argued that his contributions
favored Democratic-leaning jurisdictions and noted that they often came
with strings attached, including a requirement that the recipient partner with
a (generally left-wing) advocacy group.[32]

In 2024, it was Elon Musk who jumped into the ring, contributing $250
million in independent expenditures to help elect Trump. Some $40 million
of that took the form of $1 million "lottery" payments to swing-state vot-
ers who signed a petition supporting the Constitution. Philadelphia District
Attorney Larry Krasner sued in October to stop the payouts, but was unsuccessful, largely because Musk's lawyers argued it was not really a lottery at
all, as winners were not chosen randomly as the program had promised.[33]
Zuckerberg's 2020 intervention rendered the outrage hollow. Unlike Zuckerberg after 2020, Musk immediately took a very public role as an informal
adviser to Trump. Eight days after the election, Trump announced that he
would co-chair DOGE with Vivek Ramaswamy (Ramaswamy stepped away
from the role after a couple of months). The question was naturally raised:
Did he buy his way into government?

In the wake of 2020, a few states passed laws to prohibit state or local election administration offices from accepting private donations, but only Republicans were concerned. Now, both sides have their tech billionaires, and Democrats are concerned about Musk. One can anticipate some state laws being passed to limit the kind of programs Musk funded in 2024. Federal action is off the table for now and the Supreme Court is committed for the foreseeable future to the not-implausible proposition that spending your own money is a form of protected political speech.

The Presidency and the Administrative State

More than a century ago, the Progressive Movement advanced two principles regarding the institutions of the executive branch. Both have taken root and changed the federal government substantially, though they are not fully compatible. One was that the presidency as an institution should be given greater power and made more central to American government and life. No longer would the institution of Article II play second fiddle to Congress. Theodore Roosevelt and Woodrow Wilson launched this project and Franklin Roosevelt built on it. The other Progressive principle was that bureaucratic experts should be given significantly more power and independence, hence the raft of independent regulatory commissions and agencies that now issue thousands of detailed regulations with the force of law on the basis of vague guidance from Congress. Although the president can appoint the top few layers of administrators, he cannot even fire all of them (the independent regulatory commissions have fixed terms), and he can neither hire nor fire the 97 percent working under civil service protections. Consequently, while there is a certain coherence to these principles—executive powers should be enhanced and Congress diminished—there is also a tension between the president and the bureaucracy.

The second Trump administration is committed to a wholesale revamping of this picture. To be sure, Donald Trump embraces the cross-partisan progressive vision of the presidency and began pushing in that direction as soon as he was inaugurated. Trump initiated several dozen unilateral executive actions in his first two weeks, including important and durable decrees such as ending Lyndon Johnson's order establishing "affirmative action" for federal contractors, pardons of every January 6 rioter, symbolic measures such as claiming to change the name of the Gulf of Mexico to the Gulf of America, and measures like the birthright citizenship order and freezing of federal grants that would be highly significant in the uncertain event they are upheld. In this, he is standing on ground cleared by Wilson and the two Roosevelts, and takes inspiration as well from George W. Bush's executive, Barack Obama's "pen and phone," and Joe Biden's aggressive (though often futile) attempts to leverage executive power. It is not clear that, in principle, Trump has any use for an independent Congress at all. As discussed in chapter 6, he will insist on personal loyalty from Republicans in Congress and will threaten to "primary" deviants. This will not always work—and may become much less useful after the 2026 midterm elections—but when it comes up short, Trump will not hesitate to fall back on the varying forms of unilateral executive action dramatized by Bush, Obama, and Biden.

More generally, Trump will continue on the path of 20th- and 21st-century presidents who have emphasized their role as party leader and rhetorical figure at the expense of their bedrock unifying role as head of state.[34] In particular, many critics are concerned that Trump's rhetorical style, which at its best uses demotic language to appeal to otherwise disengaged citizens, also veers frequently into demagoguery—an unfortunate, even dangerous, but predictable effluence of Woodrow Wilson's deliberate elevation of presidential rhetoric. Trump may seek to push the boundaries out farther, but in these ways he will be acting along lines already established. Perhaps the modern presidency has already gone too far, in which case Americans will need to give serious thought to how to rein it in.

It is the second area—the vast extent and power of the administrative state—that Trump will seek to disrupt rather than merely accelerate. Already, near the end of his first term, he issued an executive order that sought to strip civil service protections from around 50,000 mid-level policymaking bureaucrats (so-called "Schedule F"). Before it could be implemented, Joe Biden took office and revoked it, but a second Trump term will see it return, along with a whole range of other efforts to bring the administrative state under political control.[35] This, indeed, was a central goal of Project 2025 dismissed by Trump on the campaign trail but apparently back in vogue in time for the inauguration.[36]

On one hand, the administrative state poses a real challenge for democratic self-governance. Consent of the governed, a core principle of American government, is arguably incompatible with lodging tremendous power in the hands of officials who are unelected and cannot be fired. Moreover, doing so has actually encouraged the elected officials in Congress to delegate increasing responsibility to the unelected—i.e. become increasingly irresponsible themselves. Scholars such as Philip Hamburger question whether the administrative state is constitutionally acceptable in its current form.[37]

On the other hand, unwinding the administrative state is itself a task fraught with difficulties and dangers. As political scientist Herbert Kaufman wrote decades ago, "Every restraint or requirement originates in somebody's demand for it."[38] And once a piece of red tape is in place, individuals and groups come to rely on it. Tens of thousands of rules, even if of dubious democratic legitimacy, have served as the basis for decades' worth of business decisions and case law. For another, there are roughly three million civilian employees of the federal government, most of whom are currently under civil service protection. It is one thing to remove a small but politically important sliver of that number and make them political hires, but another thing altogether to attempt a wholesale elimination of civil service protections. Is the Office of Personnel Management prepared to process hundreds of thousands of Schedule G appointments? And are Republicans prepared for the angry pushback from the government employee unions, now among the wealthiest and most powerful unions in the country?

Not least, attempting to simply undo the quasi-independence of the federal bureaucracy as if there has not been a massive growth in its power and size since the late 1800s would, unlike an increase in the use of executive orders, actually result in a fundamental transformation of presidential power, especially in the absence of an assertive Congress. Although one possible consequence would be that voters would focus more attention on the administrative competence of presidential contenders, it is at least as likely that the partisan, demagogic presidency that has evolved would remain intact, simply with much greater power at its disposal. Does Donald Trump want to take apart the administrative state because he has read Philip Hamburger and has deep concern for the principle of consent of the governed or because he is nonplussed that the bureaucracy is not loyal to him personally? Even if one is inclined to trust Trump with the full power of the bureaucracy, can all future presidents be so trusted?

Of course, the presidency does not exist in a vacuum. The system can tolerate a strong presidency—indeed it arguably requires one—but must be matched with a strong Congress and a strong Supreme Court, each with its own will. Yet Congress continues to devolve its responsibilities to the executive branch and to become less jealous of its own prerogatives. Its own dysfunction, born of extremely narrow margins and deep partisanship, even invites presidential supervision. For its part, the Court is facing a dual challenge. Its legitimacy has been under fire for several years from Democrats who did not appreciate its originalist rulings. In Trump, it is now confronted with a president who admires Andrew Jackson's willingness to simply ignore judicial decisions he disliked and who in the past has expressed disappointment that his first-term appointees to the Supreme Court were insufficiently loyal to him. At the end of 2024, Chief Justice John Roberts issued a report warning about the potential decay of judicial independence.[39] How far will Trump push to assert himself over the coordinate branches and the bureaucracy? And how successful will he be? These momentous institutional questions could come to dominate the next four years.

* * *

One final potential institutional effect of the election of 2024 s raised, and it is an effect that may serve to limit both Trump's push anu the reactions of his partisan rivals. The election produced several important reversals: Trump restored to the White House, this time with a popular vote plurality; Republicans back in the majority in the Senate; a Republican trifecta for the first time since 2016, if only by the barest of margins in the House. We can hope that these reversals may occasion greater institutional caution by political forces that are suddenly aware that the proverbial shoe really can wind up on the other foot. We have alluded to the possibility that ardor will cool for the National Popular Vote Interstate Compact. Within days of the election, it was already evident that Democrats had a newfound appreciation for the Senate filibuster. On the Republican side, allegations of fraud are suddenly unfashionable, and one can assume that Republicans are relieved that the principles of the Eastman memos of December 2020—holding that the vice president possesses essentially unlimited discretion to count or not count states' electoral votes—were not operational when Kamala Harris was the vice president tasked with counting Donald Trump's electoral votes.[40] An important ballast in our constitutional republic, though one too often taken for granted, is the leavening impact of knowing that the wheel always turns. That valuable lesson has been reinforced.

CIVIC HEALTH

At the intersection of policy, politics, and institutions sits what one might call "civic health." The election of 2024 took place after a decade or more of growing concern about political polarization and extreme rhetoric, including talk of civil war or national divorce and an assassination attempt against Supreme Court Justice Brett Kavanaugh. The 2024 campaign itself produced more extreme rhetoric, whether Trump's fulminations against "the enemy within" or Harris's association of Trump with Hitler, and two more assassination attempts, this time on Trump himself. By Election Day, 70 percent of voters said they feared postelection violence.[41]

In the midst of this bleak picture, there were two signs of hope. First, though rhetoric remained polarized, actual voting behavior became less so. As we noted in chapter 5, voting patterns by racial groups, age-groups, and income groups were less differentiated than at any time in recent memory; the gaps in candidate preference between whites and non-whites, between young and old, and between classes all declined. When voters were divided into five distinct income groups, neither major candidate received more than 52 percent of the vote in any group. In that sense, Americans were drawing closer to each other, not being split farther apart.

Second, numerous signs pointed to a certain degree of exhaustion that, at least for a time, might drain American politics of some its venom. Unlike 2016, there were no riots protesting Trump's election. A few Democrats made noises about applying the "insurrection clause" of the 14th Amendment to try to deny Trump a victory in Congress.[42] Nevertheless, the post-election maneuvering seemed perfunctory in comparison with 2016, when a serious campaign was launched to convince Republican electors to abandon Trump, or 2020, when Trump engaged in a variety of schemes to forestall defeat and his supporters stormed the Capitol. Instead, in the wake of the election, a parade of previously hostile business and media figures including Jeff Bezos, Mark Zuckerberg, Google CEO Sundai Pichai, and MSNBC hosts Joe Scarborough and Mika Brzezinski arrived at Mar-a-Lago to meet with the president-elect and offer him congratulations.[43] (Beyond a desire for political peace, one motive may have been Trump's overt threat to use antitrust enforcement and FCC licensing power against corporations he dislikes.[44]) Viewership of MSNBC and CNN fell dramatically, as many liberals apparently showed their exhaustion with politics by tuning out.[45] It seemed possible that a boil had been lanced. For the first time in years, it appeared that the conditions might be right for America to depolarize, at least to a degree.

Yet a number of contrary indicators call into question this hopeful interpretation. One is that it will depend on the right kind of political leadership. Donald Trump, whose favorability ratings rose to match his unfavorability in the wake of the election for the first time since he entered politics, might be able to build on this moment, if can control his worst impulses to a degree heretofore unseen. If not, he could easily provoke his opponents into new paroxysm of hostility, and the postelection moment will evaporate. Trump's Christmas 2024 message, in which he wished "Merry Christmas to the Radical Left Lunatics, who are constantly trying to obstruct our Court System and our Elections, and are always going after the Great Citizens and Patriots of the United States but, in particular, their Political Opponent, ME" was not a good start.[46] To see Trump as a potentially depolarizing figure represents, like all second marriages, the triumph of hope over experience.

Another is the bracing possibility that democratic political exhaustion on the left may lead not to quietude but an upsurge in political violence. The assassination of United Health CEO Brian Thompson shortly after the election, and the outpouring of support for his accused murderer, are an indication of where things could be headed.[47] Clearly, Trump and the far left feed off each other. Moreover, the New Year's Day terror attack in New Orleans by a homegrown jihadist and kamikaze demonstration in Las Vegas by a disillusioned patriot showed that the motivation and propensity for political violence is quite broad and hardly limited to trust-fund Bolsheviks.

In the long run, to restore civic health will require a number of developments that are not wholly or even primarily political. Among other things, a deeper rot will have to be addressed in American politics—the death of truth. Democratic politics has always involved some choices about what to emphasize and what to de-emphasize, what to avoid talking about and what to shade in a certain way. We now seem to have entered a political world in which campaigns run on the basis of obvious falsehoods, essentially demanding that voters deny clear realities as a price of loyalty to their partisan tribe. In 2024, voters were told that the economic harm they had suffered from inflation was not real, that the evident decline in Joe Biden's mental and physical capacities was not real, that Donald Trump's defeat in 2020 was not real, and that the January 6 Capitol riot was not real. Who are you going to believe, the campaigns seemed to be asking, us or your lying eyes? Though postmodern relativism had its birth on the left, it is now firmly ensconced on the right, as well. This tendency cannot be considered anything but troubling, regardless of whatever short-term hopes may be raised by the paucity of postelection riots. The sacrifice of truth to political narrative is a hallmark of societies that slip into a totalitarian stupor. It is difficult to imagine a full recovery of civic health until that tendency is reversed and political leaders and their followers are willing to police their own tribe in accordance with the truth.

Moreover, as Alexis de Tocqueville argued nearly two centuries ago, American civic health is also dependent on a number of ostensibly nonpolitical social institutions that nevertheless establish the foundation for political society. Among the most important of these building blocks of civil society are religion, family, and private associations. Each of these have suffered blows, as family breakdown has proceeded apace, a smaller percentage of Americans participate in organized religious life, and whole swaths of associational life (such as bowling leagues and the Elks Club) have shriveled, especially among working-class Americans.[48] To this challenge neither candidate offered much of a solution, except for the rhetorical and symbolic support Trump offered religion. At the same time, there are signs that traditional Christianity is making something of a comeback among both intellectuals and the broader public.[49] Here, though the two may be intertwined, culture will drive politics more than the other way around.

Not least, over the past several decades, Americans have grossly neglected the task of ensuring that future generations understand how American government works and what principles undergird it. Civics surveys of high school students and adults show that a shocking number of Americans, young and old, do not know that the federal government has three branches or what they are called, understand the powers and limits of the presidency, understand their basic constitutional rights, or understand the federal system of national, state, and local governments.[50] According to surveys, younger

Americans are also less committed to freedom of speech and less convinced of the benefits of a free exchange of ideas than their elders.[51] A belated recognition of this threat has led a number of states to launch institutes or schools of civics at state universities and colleges, and there is a growing movement to require and improve the teaching of civics in grade school.[52] When Benjamin Franklin left the constitutional convention upon adjournment, he was reportedly asked by a Philadelphian, "What have you given us?" "A republic," was said to be Franklin's answer, "if you can keep it." In the long run, our capacity to keep it will be powerfully influenced by whether the country does a better job of forming citizens. This is an educational task, and hence at least partly a political one, but it should not be a partisan one.

A FINAL WORD

Though November's election result was perhaps predictable, the political world in 2024 was deeply unsettled from beginning to end. It will remain so for some as time, as Republicans and Democrats sort out what they stand for and as political outsiderism continues to have an appeal across the spectrum. Underlying the political jumble is a moment of deeper uncertainty in society, as the ground seems to be shifting in many ways. Americans now doubt the efficacy of both our governmental and social institutions, have lost confidence in the mainstream media, and increasingly see higher education as a dubious investment. On right and left, norms of political behavior have eroded and made way for a normalization of a rougher style of politics that may or may not be capable of holding the country together. The nation's place in the world is in flux and may be challenged more forcefully by its authoritarian enemies at any moment.

Into this maelstrom steps Donald Trump for a second try. Early indications are that his second administration will be more focused and more consistent than before—but also less internally constrained, with fewer independent voices reining in potential excess. At once it promises greater achievement and greater disaster. Americans must be prepared for either—or, perhaps, generous helpings of both.

This time, Trump brings to the White House two advantages and two disadvantages that he did not have in 2017. On one hand, he now has a better sense of how Washington operates; he is an outsider with a term in the White House under his belt. He also enjoys a modicum of popular legitimacy owing to his narrow plurality in the aggregated popular vote. On the other hand, he cannot run for reelection and entered office as a lame duck from day one. Moreover, time marches on, and he also began his second term at 78 years of age, the same age Joe Biden was when he took office (and about the same age Ronald Reagan was when he left office after two terms).

Trump's unflinching determination—his instinct to rise from the floor, thrust his fist in the air, and fight, no matter the circumstance—will be an asset, until it isn't. Determination produced his historic comeback. It can also turn to stubbornness, and stubbornness to futility or abuse. There is perhaps no president in recent history whose primary qualities of personality are capable of producing such radically opposite results. For better and worse, in 2024 Trump tapped into Americans' frustrations and rode the failures of the Biden administration back to power. He will face the daunting task of governing in a way that validates his supporters' confidence without confirming his critics' worst fears.

Notes

CHAPTER 1

1. Michael Cavna, "How 'Doonesbury' predicted Donald Trump's Presidential Run 29 Years Ago," *Washington Post*, June 23, 2016, https://www.washingtonpost.com/news/comic-riffs/wp/2016/06/23/how-doonesbury-predicted-donald-trumps-presidential-run-29-years-ago.

2. We are indebted to Professor Jacob Smith for this insight.

3. Bruce Mehlman, "The Morning After," Age of Disruption Blog, November 6, 2024, https://brucemehlman.substack.com/p/the-morning-after.

4. Gallup, "Satisfaction With the United States," https://news.gallup.com/poll/1669/general-mood-country.aspx.

5. "Public Trust in Government: 1958–2024," Pew Research Center, June 24, 2024, https://www.pewresearch.org/politics/2024/06/24/public-trust-in-government-1958-2024.

6. Megan Brenan, "Americans' Trust in Media Remains at Trend Low," Gallup, October 14, 2024, https://news.gallup.com/poll/651977/americans-trust-media-remains-trend-low.aspx.

7. Tom Nichols, *The Death of Expertise*, 2d ed. (New York: Oxford University Press, 2024), 247.

8. Cary Funk et al., "Americans Reflect on Nation's COVID-19 Response," Pew Research Center, July 7, 2022, https://www.pewresearch.org/science/2022/07/07/americans-reflect-on-nations-covid-19-response.

9. "As Partisan Hostility Grows, Signs of Frustration With the Two-Party System," Pew Research Center, August 9, 2022, https://www.pewresearch.org/politics/2022/08/09/as-partisan-hostility-grows-signs-of-frustration-with-the-two-party-system.

10. Exit poll data at "How Groups Voted," Roper Center for Public Opinion Research, https://ropercenter.cornell.edu/how-groups-voted-1988 and https://ropercenter.cornell.edu/how-groups-voted-2008.

11. Oscar Holland, "Republicans are red and Democrats blue. But it wasn't always that way," CNN, September 20, 2024, https://www.cnn.com/style/why-republicans-red-democrats-blue/index.html.

12. Brian Arbour, "'All Politics Is Local'? Not Anymore." *Washington Post*, December 9, 2014, https://www.washingtonpost.com/news/monkey-cage/wp/2014/12/09/all-politics-is-local-not-anymore.

13. *Vital Statistics on Congress*, Brookings, 2022, https://www.brookings.edu/wp-content/uploads/2017/01/vitalstats_ch2_tbl16.pdf.

14. Kitty Kelley, "Death and the All-American Boy," *Washingtonian*, June 1, 1974, https://www.washingtonian.com/1974/06/01/joe-biden-kitty-kelley-1974-profile-death-and-the-all-american-boy.

15. Alan I. Abramowitz,. "The Polarized American Electorate: The Rise of Partisan-Ideological Consistency and Its Consequences," *Political Science Quarterly* 137 (2022): 645–74, https://doi.org/10.1002/polq.13388.

16. Mark Jurkowitz et al., "U.S. Media Polarization and the 2020 Election: A Nation Divided," Pew Research Center, January 24, 2020, https://www.pewresearch.org/journalism/2020/01/24/u-s-media-polarization-and-the-2020-election-a-nation-divided.

17. Carroll Doherty et al., "Partisan Antipathy: More Intense, More Personal," Pew Research Center, October 10, 2019, https://www.pewresearch.org/politics/2019/10/10/partisan-antipathy-more-intense-more-personal.

18. Zach Goldberg, "The Rise of College-Educated Democrats," *City Journal*, February 2, 2023, https://manhattan.institute/article/the-rise-of-college-educated-democrats.

19. Carroll Doherty et al., "Changing Partisan Coalitions in a Politically Divided Nation," Pew Research Center, April 9, 2024, https://www.pewresearch.org/politics/2024/04/09/changing-partisan-coalitions-in-a-politically-divided-nation.

20. Carroll Doherty et al., "As Partisan Hostility Grows, Signs of Frustration With the Two-Party System," Pew Research Center, August 9, 2022, https://www.pewresearch.org/politics/2022/08/09/as-partisan-hostility-grows-signs-of-frustration-with-the-two-party-system.

21. "Fractured Nation: Widening Partisan Polarization and Key Issues in 2020 Presidential Elections," Public Religion Research Institute, October 20, 2019, https://www.prri.org/research/fractured-nation-widening-partisan-polarization-and-key-issues-in-2020-presidential-elections.

22. Daniel A. Cox, "Democrats and Republicans Believe Their Opponents' Policies Threaten the National Interest," Survey Center on American Life, September 30, 2020, https://www.americansurveycenter.org/democrats-and-republicans-believe-their-opponents-policies-threaten-the-national-interest.

23. Daniel A. Cox, "After the Ballots are Counted: Conspiracies, Political Violence, and American Exceptionalism," Survey Center on American Life, February 11, 2021, https://www.americansurveycenter.org/research/after-the-ballots-are-counted-conspiracies-political-violence-and-american-exceptionalism.

24. Hannah Fingerhut, "AP-NORC Poll: Most Republicans Doubt Biden's Legitimacy," Associated Press, February 5, 2021, https://apnews.com/article/joe-biden

-donald-trump-capitol-siege-coronavirus-pandemic-elections-79599e3eef68732134c
94375a26897f7.

25. James Ceaser and Andrew Busch, *Upside Down and Inside Out: The 1992
Elections and American Politics* (Lanham, MD: Rowman & Littlefield, 1993), 2–3.

26. For the most detailed account of how government enriched Fred Trump, see
Russ Buettner and Susanne Craig, *Lucky Loser* (New York: Penguin Press, 2024),
part I.

27. Jon Shields and Stephanie Muravchik, *Trump's Democrats* (Washington, DC:
Brookings Institution Press, 2020).

28. Donald J. Trump (1st Term), The President's News Conference, August 19,
2020. Online by Gerhard Peters and John T. Woolley, The American Presidency
Project https://www.presidency.ucsb.edu/node/343453.

29. For example, Governor Andrew Cuomo of New York insisted that nursing
homes admit COVID-19-positive patients. In the realm of social health, California's
state government, overseen by Governor Gavin Newsom, declared that churches must
close but liquor stores could remain open as "essential" businesses.

30. John Whitesides, "Trump's Handling of Coronavirus Pandemic Hits Record
Low Approval: Reuters/Ipsos Poll," Reuters, October 8, 2020, https://www.reuters
.com/article/world/us-politics/trumps-handling-of-coronavirus-pandemic-hits-record
-low-approval-reutersipsos-idUSKBN26T3OE.

31. Presidential Approval Ratings—Joe Biden, Gallup, https://news.gallup.com/
poll/329384/presidential-approval-ratings-joe-biden.aspx.

32. Joseph R. Biden, Remarks and a Question-and-Answer Session at a CNN
Presidential Town Hall in Cincinnati, Ohio, July 21, 2021. Online by Gerhard Peters
and John T. Woolley, The American Presidency Project https://www.presidency.ucsb
.edu/node/336967.

33. Jill Barshay, "Proof Points: Three Views of Pandemic Learning Loss and
Recovery," *The Hechinger Report*, August 28, 2023, https://hechingerreport.org/
proof-points-three-views-of-pandemic-learning-loss-and-recovery.

34. Federal Reserve Bank of St. Louis, "Real Disposable Personal Income: Per
Capita (A229RX0)," June 20, 2023, https://fred.stlouisfed.org/series/A229RX0.

35. Virginia de Rugy, "The Not-So-Stimulative $1.9 trillion Package," *National
Review*, March 19, 2021, https://www.nationalreview.com/corner/the-not-so
-stimulative-1-9-trillion-package.

36. Oliver Knox, "Why 'Bidenomics' Falls Flat," *Washington Post*, November 7,
2023, https://www.washingtonpost.com/politics/2023/11/07/why-bidenomics-falls
-flat.

37. The Conference Board, "US Consumer Confidence Increased Again in
December," December 20, 2023, https://www.conference-board.org/topics/consumer
-confidence/press/CCI-Dec-2023.

38. Carroll Doherty et al., "Americans More Upbeat on the Economy; Biden's
Job Rating Remains Very Low," Pew Research Center, January 28, 2024, https://
www.pewresearch.org/wp-content/uploads/sites/20/2024/01/PP_2024.1.25_biden
-economy_REPORT.pdf.

39. Jim Geraghty, "The Eye-Opening Numbers on Biden's Economic Record," *National Review*, January 7, 2025, https://www.nationalreview.com/corner/the-eye -opening-numbers-on-bidens-economic-record.

40. John Burn Murdoch, X post, November 7, 2024, https://x.com/jburnmurdoch/ status/1854559598574784631.

41. Presidential Debate at Belmont University in Nashville, Tennessee, October 22, 2020, https://debates.org/voter-education/debate-transcripts/october-22-2020 -debate-transcript.

42. U.S. Customs and Border Protection, "Southwest Land Border Encounters," https://www.cbp.gov/newsroom/stats/southwest-land-border-encounters.

43. Carroll Doherty et al., "Most Americans Are Critical of Government's Handling of Situation at U.S.-Mexico Border," Pew Research Center, May 3, 2021, https://www.pewresearch.org/politics/2021/05/03/most-americans-are-critical-of -governments-handling-of-situation-at-u-s-mexico-border.

44. Eugene Daniels, "Biden makes Harris the point person on immigration issues amid border surge," *Politico*, March 24, 2021, https://www.politico.com/news/2021 /03/24/kamala-harris-immigration-border-surge-477810.

45. Joseph R. Biden, Remarks with Vice President Harris in a Meeting on Immigration, March 24, 2021. Online by Gerhard Peters and John T. Woolley, The American Presidency Project, https://www.presidency.ucsb.edu/node/348935.

46. Rob Garver, "Huge Number of Migrants Highlights Border Crisis," Voice of America, January 3, 2024, https://www.voanews.com/a/huge-number-of-migrants -highlights-border-crisis/7424665.html; U.S. Customs and Border Protection, "Southwest Land Border Encounters."

47. Holly Otterbein, "Fetterman Defends 'Reasonable' Border Talks as Fellow Dems Fume," *Politico*, December 7, 2023, https://www.politico.com/live-updates /2023/12/07/congress/fetterman-on-border-00130639.

48. Joseph R. Biden, Statement on Bipartisan Senate Negotiations Regarding Border Security Legislation, January 26, 2024. Online by Gerhard Peters and John T. Woolley, The American Presidency Project, https://www.presidency.ucsb.edu/node /369434.

49. Donald J. Trump, Truth Social post, February 5, 2024, https://truthsocial.com/ @realDonaldTrump/posts/111879340091575646.

50. "Undocumented Immigrant Offending Rate Lower than U.S.-Born Citizen Rate, National Institute of Justice, September 12, 2024, https://nij.ojp.gov/topics /articles/undocumented-immigrant-offending-rate-lower-us-born-citizen-rate; Sean Kennedy, Jason Richwine, and Steven A. Camarota, *Misuse of Texas Data Understates Illegal Immigrant Criminality*, Center for Immigration Studies, October 11, 2022, https://cis.org/Report/Misuse-Texas-Data-Understates-Illegal-Immigrant -Criminality.

51. "6 in 10 See Illegal Immigration as Very Serious Problem," Monmouth University Polling Institute, February 26, 2024, https://www.monmouth.edu/polling -institute/reports/monmouthpoll_us_022624.

52. Federal Bureau of Investigation, "FBI Releases 2023 Crime in the Nation Statistics," September 23, 2024, https://www.fbi.gov/news/press-releases/fbi-releases

-2023-crime-in-the-nation-statistics Lori Robertson, "Crime Stats Still Show a Decline Since 2020," FactCheck.org, October 23, 2024, https://www.factcheck.org /2024/10/crime-stats-still-show-a-decline-since-2020.

53. Bureau of Justice Statistics, "Criminal Victimization, 2022," September 14, 2023, https://bjs.ojp.gov/library/publications/criminal-victimization-2022; Bureau of Justice Statistics, Criminal Victimization, 2023," September 12, 2024, https://bjs.ojp .gov/document/cv23_sum.pdf.

54. Joseph R. Biden, Remarks on the Situation in Afghanistan Online by Gerhard Peters and John T. Woolley, The American Presidency Project https://www.presi-dency.ucsb.edu/node/352279.

55. United States Senate Committee on Foreign Relations, Minority, "Left Behind: A Brief Assessment of the Biden Administration's Strategic Failures during the Afghanistan Evacuation," February 2022, https://www.foreign.senate.gov/imo/media /doc/Risch%20Afghanistan%20Report%202022.pdf; Ellie Kaufman, "First on CNN: US left behind $7 billion of military equipment in Afghanistan after 2021 withdrawal, Pentagon report says," CNN, April 28, 2022, https://www.cnn.com/2022/04/27/poli-tics/afghan-weapons-left-behind/index.html.

56. Shannon K. Crawford, "2 years on, Afghanistan withdrawal continues to cast pall on Biden administration: ANALYSIS," ABC News, August 31, 2023, https:// abcnews.go.com/Politics/2-years-withdrawal-afghanistan-continues-cast-pall-biden/ story?id=102837216.

57. Kathy Frankovic, "Americans Who Think the Withdrawal from Afghanistan Went Poorly Blame Biden," YouGov, August 26, 2021, https://today.yougov.com/ topics/international/articles-reports/2021/08/26/americans-blame-biden-withdrawal -afghanistan.

58. Michael Kranish and Dan Lamothe, Harris was 'last person in the room' on Afghan exit, but her influence is unclear," *Washington Post*, August 7, 2024, https://www.washingtonpost.com/politics/2024/08/07/kamala-harris-biden-afghani-stan-withdrawal.

59. "Presidential Approval Ratings—Joe Biden," Gallup, https://news.gallup.com /poll/329384/presidential-approval-ratings-joe-biden.aspx.

60. "After Kabul: Veterans, America, and the End of the War in Afghanistan," More in Common, November 2021, https://www.moreincommon.com/media/vvjp-do2k/after-kabul-more-in-common.pdf.

61. William A Galston, "Anger, Betrayal, and Humiliation: How Veterans Feel About the Withdrawal from Afghanistan," Brookings, November 12, 2021, https:// www.brookings.edu/articles/anger-betrayal-and-humiliation-how-veterans-feel -about-the-withdrawal-from-afghanistan.

62. Richard Wike et al., "Growing Partisan Divisions Over NATO and Ukraine," Pew Research Center, May 8, 2024, https://www.pewresearch.org/wp-.content/ uploads/sites/20/2024/05/pg_2024.05.08_russia-nato_report.pdf.

63. Carroll Doherty et al., "Americans' Views of the Israel-Hamas War," Pew Research Center, December 8, 2023, https://www.pewresearch.org/politics/2023/12 /08/americans-views-of-the-israel-hamas-war.

64. Calvin Woodward and Emily Swanson, "Biden is widely seen as too old for office, an AP-NORC poll finds. Trump has problems of his own," Associated Press, August 28, 2023, https://apnews.com/article/biden-age-poll-trump-2024-620e0a5cfa0039a6448f607c17c7f23e.

65. Eli Stokols et al., "'We've All Enabled The Situation': Dems Turn On Biden's Inner Sanctum Post Debate," *Politico*, July 2, 2024, https://www.politico.com/news/2024/07/02/biden-campaign-debate-inner-circle-00166160; Peter Baker, David E. Sanger, Zolan Kanno-Youngs and Katie Rogers, "Biden's Lapses Are Said to Be Increasingly Common and Worrisome," *New York Times*, July 2, 2024, https://www.nytimes.com/2024/07/02/us/politics/biden-lapses.html.

66. Ian Ward, " Conservatives See a Conspiracy Around Joe Biden's Stumbles," *Politico*, July 11, 2024, https://www.politico.com/news/magazine/2024/07/11/biden-age-conservatives-conspiracy-00167438.

67. Harry Enten, "Why it will be tough for Biden to Defeat Trump," CNN, March 9, 2024, https://www.cnn.com/2024/03/09/politics/election-president-trump-biden/index.html.

68. Caitlin McCabe, "Bettors See Higher Chance of Trump Election Victory After Assassination Attempt," *Wall Street Journal*, July 15, 2024, https://www.wsj.com/livecoverage/stock-market-today-bank-earnings-07-15-2024/card/bettors-see-higher-chance-of-trump-election-victory-after-assassination-attempt-bCoaMgTJqJzEfOzKkwlc.

69. Jonathan V. Last, "The Christian-Nationalist Rot Runs Deep. Also: Kamala Harris Skips the Start-Up Phase," The Bulwark, July 23, 2023, https://www.thebulwark.com/p/the-christian-nationalist-rot-runs.

70. Speech: Donald Trump Holds a Political Rally in Bozeman, Montana—August 9, 2024, https://rollcall.com/factbase/trump/transcript/donald-trump-speech-political-rally-bozeman-montana-august-9-2024.

71. Jeffrey M. Jones, "2024 Election Environment Favorable to GOP," Gallup, September 25, 2024, https://news.gallup.com/poll/651092/2024-election-environment-favorable-gop.aspx.

72. Scott Keeter, "Public Opinion Polling Basics," Pew Research Center, https://www.pewresearch.org/course/public-opinion-polling-basics.

73. Harry Enten, X post, October 4, 2024, https://x.com/ForecasterEnten/status/1842374580519817349.

74. Theodore Roosevelt, Calvin Coolidge, Harry Truman, and Lyndon Johnson all chose not to run for a second consecutive term, but each had served part of his predecessor's term after the latter's death.

75. "Harris and Walz's Exclusive Joint Interview with CNN," August 30, 2024, https://www.cnn.com/2024/08/29/politics/harris-walz-interview-read-transcript/index.html.

76. Donald J. Trump, Truth Social post, August 23, 2024, https://truthsocial.com/@realDonaldTrump/posts/113015293839304595.

77. Daniel Marans, "The TV Moment That Might Have Been Kamala Harris' Biggest Mistake," Huffpost, November 11, 2024, https://www.huffpost.com/entry/kamala-harris-the-view-mistake_n_6730f276e4b0231a203ab696.

78. Lydia Saad, "Socialism and Atheism Still U.S. Political Liabilities," Gallup, February 11, 2020, https://news.gallup.com/poll/285563/socialism-atheism-political -liabilities.aspx.

79. Jamie Ballard and David Montgomery, "What Americans Believe About the Attempted Assassination on Donald Trump," YouGov, July 24, 2024, https:// today.yougov.com/politics/articles/50154-what-americans-believe-about-attempted -assassination-donald-trump-poll.

80. C-SPAN and Pierrepont Consulting, "Supreme Court Survey Agenda of Key Findings," March 2022, https://static.c-spanvideo.org/assets/documents/scotusSurvey /fullSurvey.2022.b.pdf.

81. Karlyn Bowman and Samantha Goldstein, "Attitudes About Abortion: A Comprehensive Review of Polls from the 1970s to Today," American Enterprise Institute, November 2, 2021, https://www.aei.org/research-products/report/attitudes -about-abortion-a-comprehensive-review-of-polls-from-the-1970s-to-today.

82. Craig Palosky, "New KFF Survey Finds Abortion Remains Key Issue for Voters with Democrats Holding a Sizeable Edge over Republicans; A Third of Women Say They'll Only Vote for Someone Who Shares Their Views," Kaiser Family Foundation, May 26, 2023, https://www.kff.org/womens-health-policy/press-release/new -kff-survey-finds-abortion-remains-key-issue-for-voters-with-democrats-holding-a -sizeable-edge-over-republicans-a-third-of-women-say-theyll-only-vote-for-someone -who-shares-their-views.

83. Julie Carr Smyth, "Ohio Voters Enshrine Abortion Access in Constitution in Latest Statewide Win For Reproductive Rights," Associated Press, November 7, 2023, https://apnews.com/article/ohio-abortion-amendment-election-202f-fe3e067 47b616507d8ca21ea26485270.

CHAPTER 2

1. "Democrats Are Supportive of Harris, but Many Adults Think Trump Has the Electoral Advantage," AP-NORC survey, July 31, 2024, https://apnorc.org/projects /democrats-are-supportive-of-harris-but-many-adults-think-trump-has-the-electoral -advantage.

2. Veera Korhonen, "Educational Attainment in the U.S. 1960–2022," Statista, July 5, 2024, https://www.statista.com/statistics/184260/educational-attainment-in-the-us.

3. Joseph R. Biden, Remarks at a Campaign Reception in Weston, Massachusetts, December 5, 2023. Online by Gerhard Peters and John T. Woolley, The American Presidency Project https://www.presidency.ucsb.edu/node/368341.

4. Harry Enten, "RFK Jr. Has a Big Primary Problem: Democrats Like Joe Biden," CNN, June 18, 2023, https://www.cnn.com/2023/06/18/politics/robert -kennedy-democratic-primary-joe-biden/index.html.

5. Jon Levine, "RFK Jr. Says COVID May Have Been 'Ethnically Targeted' to Spare Jews," *New York Post*, July 15, 2023, https://nypost.com/2023/07/15/rfk-jr -says-covid-was-ethnically-targeted-to-spare-jews.

6. Anthony Salvanto, Kabir Khanna, Fred Backus, Jennifer De Pinto, "CBS News Poll Analysis: Some Democrats Don't Want Biden to Run Again. Why Not?" CBS News, December 13, 2023, https://www.cbsnews.com/news/democrats-dont -want-biden-to-run-again-poll-analysis.

7. Bloomberg did win the Democratic caucus in American Samoa.

8. Steve Peoples, "Bernie Sanders Endorses Biden, Rules Out 2024 Bid of His Own," Associated Press, April 25, 2023, https://apnews.com/article/bernie-sanders -biden-endorsement-2024-d8f0772b117e2bf83e1062708ea651c0.

9. Niels Lesniewski and Ryan Kelly, "Biden's support from Democrats Held Steady in Senate, Fell in GOP-led House," *Roll Call*, February 15, 2024, https:// rollcall.com/2024/02/15/bidens-support-from-democrats-held-steady-in-senate-fell -in-gop-led-house.

10. "The Most Popular Democrats (Q3 2024)," YouGov, https://today.yougov .com/ratings/politics/popularity/Democrats/all.

11. David Smith, "'There's a Very Real Danger Here': AOC On 2024, The Climate Crisis And 'Selling Out," *The Guardian*, September 3, 2023, https:// www.theguardian.com/us-news/2023/sep/03/aoc-interview-2024-election-climate -democrat.

12. Alex Thompson, "Dean Phillips' Lonely Campaign Cuts Deeper at Biden's Age," Axios, January 20, 2024, https://www.axios.com/2024/01/20/dean-phillips -new-hampshire-biden-age.

13. Chris Wallace. Interview with Senator Joe Biden. Fox News Network. August 27, 2006 Sunday. https://advance-lexis-com.ccl.idm.oclc.org/api/document?collection =news&id=urn:contentItem:4KRS-4S60-TWD3-12B4-00000-00&context=1516831.

14. Asma Khalid, "Biden Campaigns in South Carolina," National Public Radio, August 30, 2019, https://www.npr.org/2019/08/30/755752326/biden-campaigns-in -south-carolina.

15. Steve Kornacki, "Journey to Power: The History of Black Voters, 1976 to 2020," NBC News, July 19, 2019, https://www.nbcnews.com/politics/2020-election/ journey-power-history-black-voters-1976-2020-n1029581.

16. Joe Biden, X post, May 29, 2024, https://x.com/JoeBiden/ status/1795941949221798200.

17. "National Exit Polls: How Different Groups Voted," *New York Times*, November 3, 2020, https://www.nytimes.com/interactive/2020/11/03/us/elections/exit-polls -president.html.

18. Roper Center for Public Opinion Research, "How Groups Voted," https:// ropercenter.cornell.edu/how_groups_voted.

19. William Frey, "Census Shows Pervasive Decline in 2016 Minority Voter Turnout," Brookings, May 18, 2017, https://www.brookings.edu/articles/census -shows-pervasive-decline-in-2016-minority-voter-turnout.

20. "Read the Full Transcript of the South Carolina Democratic Debate," CBS News, February 25, 2020, https://www.cbsnews.com/news/south-carolina-democratic -debate-full-transcript-text.

21. Joseph R. Biden, Fact Sheet: The Biden-Harris Administration Advances Equity and Opportunity for Black Americans and Communities Across the Country,

February 6, 2024. Online by Gerhard Peters and John T. Woolley, The American Presidency Project https://www.presidency.ucsb.edu/node/369574.

22. Cleve R. Wootson Jr., Emily Guskin and Scott Clement, "Fewer Black Americans plan to vote in 2024, Post-Ipsos poll finds," *Washington Post*, May 6, 2024, https://www.washingtonpost.com/politics/2024/05/06/poll-biden-black-voters.

23. Kiana Cox, "An Early Look at Black Voters' Views on Biden, Trump and Election 2024," Pew Research Center," May 20, 2024, https://www.pewresearch.org /race-and-ethnicity/2024/05/20/an-early-look-at-black-voters-views-on-biden-trump -and-election-2024.

24. Ubi Sommer and Idan Franco, "Trump's African Americans? Racial resentment and Black Support for Trump in the 2020 Elections, *Politics, Groups, and Identities*, 12(#4, 2023): 921–947. https://doi.org/10.1080/21565503.2023.2265899.

25. Joseph R. Biden, Remarks on the United States Supreme Court Decision on Affirmative Action in College Admissions and an Exchange with Reporters, June 29, 2023. Online by Gerhard Peters and John T. Woolley, The American Presidency Project https://www.presidency.ucsb.edu/node/363474/

26. Kamala Harris, Statement by the Vice President on the Supreme Court's ruling in Students for Fair Admissions v. Harvard and Students for Fair Admissions v. University of North Carolina, June 29, 2023. Online by Gerhard Peters and John T. Woolley, The American Presidency Project https://www.presidency.ucsb.edu/node /363655.

27. Justin McCarthy, "Post-Affirmative Action, Views on Admissions Differ by Race," Gallup, January 16, 2024, https://news.gallup.com/poll/548528/post-affirmative-action-views-admissions-differ-race.aspx.

28. Eli Yokley, "What Voters Think of the Affirmative Action Ruling," Morning Consult, July 11, 2023, https://pro.morningconsult.com/analysis/affirmative-action -ruling-polling.

29. "National Exit Polls."

30. Luis Noe-Bustamante, "Latinos' Views on the Migrant Situation at the U.S.-Mexico Border," Pew Research Center, March 4, 2024, https://www.pewresearch .org/race-and-ethnicity/2024/03/04/latinos-views-on-the-migrant-situation-at-the-us -mexico-border.

31. UnidosUS, National Survey of Latino Voters, November 2023, https://unidosus .org/wp-content/uploads/2023/11/unidosus_national_surveyoflatinovoters.pdf.

32. Russell Contreras, "Democrats' Big Vulnerability: Why They're Losing Black, Hispanic Voters," Axios, March 13, 2024, https://www.axios.com/2024/03/13 /why-democrats-black-hispanic-vote-republican.

33. Cary Funk and Mark Hugo Lopez, "A Brief Statistical Portrait of U.S. Hispanics," Pew Research Center, June 14, 2022, https://www.pewresearch.org/science /2022/06/14/a-brief-statistical-portrait-of-u-s-hispanics.

34. Jens Manuel Krogstad et al., "Key Facts About Hispanic Eligible Voters in 2024," Pew Research Center, January 10, 2024, https://www.pewresearch.org/short -reads/2024/01/10/key-facts-about-hispanic-eligible-voters-in-2024.

35. Diana Orcés, "Exploring the Diverse Religious and Political Affiliations of Hispanic Americans," Public Religion Research Institute, October 13, 2023, https://

www.prri.org/spotlight/exploring-the-diverse-religious-and-political-affiliations-of -hispanic-americans.

36. Noe-Bustamante, "Latinos' Views on the Migrant Situation."

37. Abby Budiman Jeffrey S. Passel, and Carolyne Im, "Key Facts about Asian American Eligible Voters in 2024," Pew Research Center, January 10, 2023, https:// www.pewresearch.org/short-reads/2024/01/10/key-facts-about-asian-american -eligible-voters-in-2024.

38. Mychael Schnell, "Warnock campaign releases ads in Vietnamese, Mandarin, Korean to mobilize AAPI voters," *The Hill*, November 30, 2022, https://thehill .com/homenews/campaign/3755689-warnock-campaign-releases-ads-in-vietnamese -mandarin-korean-to-mobilize-aapi-voters.

39. Kimmy Yam, "Asian Americans Heavily Favored Warnock in Georgia Run-off, Exit Poll Shows," NBC News, December 8, 2022, https://www.nbcnews.com /news/asian-america/asian-americans-heavily-favored-warnock-georgia-runoff-exit -poll-shows-rcna60639.

40. Joshua Grossman, et al., "The Disparate Impacts of College Admissions Policies On Asian American Applicants," National Bureau of Economic Research, Working Paper 31527, August 2023, https://www.nber.org/system/files/working_papers/ w31527/w31527.pdf.

41. Luis Ferré-Sadurní and Ellen Yan, "Crime Concerns Drove Asian Americans Away From New York Democrats," *New York Times,* January 10, 2023, https:// www.nytimes.com/2023/01/10/nyregion/asian-voters-republican-crime-nyc.html; Seth Moskowitz, "Will Asian Americans Retreat from Democrats?" The Liberal Patriot, July 9, 2023, https://www.liberalpatriot.com/p/will-asian-americans-retreat -from.

42. "Vice President Kamala Harris Leads New Campaign Effort to Reach Out to Asian American Voters," Associated Press, July 9, 2024, https://apnews.com/article /kamala-harris-biden-asian-americans-nevada-pennsylvania-2024-ab6de235e8d1921 6aa0f65559e6515da.

43. Audrey Kearney et al., "KFF Survey of Women Voters: Key Takeaways," KFF, June 20, 2024, https://www.kff.org/womens-health-policy/poll-finding/kff -survey-of-women-voters-key-takeaways.

44. Theodore H. White, *The Making of the President, 1968* (New York: Pocket Books, 1970), 497.

45. Ruy Teixera, "Brahmin Left vs. Populist Right," American Enterprise Institute, August 10, 2023, https://www.aei.org/op-eds/brahmin-left-vs-populist-right.

46. National Exit Polls: How Different Groups Voted."

47. CNN, "Exit Polls," https://www.cnn.com/election/2020/exit-polls/president/ national-results.

48. Stef W. Kight, "Dramatic Realignment Swings Working-Class Districts Toward GOP," Axios, April 16, 2023, https://www.axios.com/2023/04/12/house -democrats-winning-wealthier-districts-middle-class-gop.

49. Nicholas Short, "The Politics of the American Knowledge Economy," *Studies in American Political Development* 36 no. 1 (2022): 41–60. https://doi.org/10.1017/ S0898588X21000134.

50. "Union Members—2023," Bureau of Labor Statistics, January 23, 2024, https://www.bls.gov/news.release/pdf/union2.pdf.

51. Economic Policy Institute, "Who Are Today's Union Workers?" April 21, 2021, https://www.epi.org/publication/who-are-todays-union-workers.

52. Matt Grossmann and David A. Hopkins, *Polarized By Degrees* (New York: Cambridge University Press, 2024), 121–124.

53. "The Biden-Harris Record," https://www.whitehouse.gov/therecord.

54. Nicole Narea, "Biden Is Betting in Impossible Promises to Progressives," Vox, July 18, 2024, https://www.vox.com/politics/361389/biden-progressives-supreme -court-rent-cap-assault-weapons.

55. Collin Binkley and Linley Sanders, "Biden's Student Loan Work Gets Tepid Reviews—Even Among Those With Debt, an AP-NORC Poll Finds," Associated Press, June 11, 2024, https://apnews.com/article/student-loan-cancellation -forgiveness-college-debt-e5ad2748058cfd037e0323321f532836.

56. Grossmann and Hopkins, *Polarized by Degrees*, 159–161.

57. Nicholas F. Jacobs and Daniel M. Shea, *The Rural Voter: The Politics of Place and the Disuniting of America* (New York: Columbia University Press, 2024), 122.

58. Mayhill Fowler, "Obama Exclusive (Audio): On V.P And Foreign Policy, Courting the Working Class, and Hard-Pressed Pennsylvanians," *Huffington Post*, April 19, 2008, https://www.huffpost.com/entry/obama-exclusive-audio-on_b _96333.

59. Carl Hulse, "Tester's Fight for Political Survival Is Democrats' Last Stand on the Great Plains," *New York Times*, October 12, 2024, https://www.nytimes.com /2024/10/12/us/politics/jon-tester-democrats-great-plains.html.

60. This claim emerged on the internet in mid-2024 and was rated "True" by the fact-checking site Snopes. Anna Rescouet-Paz, "Kamala Harris' Father Is a 'Marxist Economist'?", Snopes, August 4, 2024, https://www.snopes.com/fact-check/harris -father-marxist-economist/.. Others disagree with this assessment. See Robert Draper, "Kamala Harris and the Influence of an Estranged Father Just Two Miles Away," *New York Times*, October 4, 2024, https://www.nytimes.com/2024/10/04/us/politics /kamala-harris-father.html. In any case, he was largely absent from her life after he divorced her mother.

61. Dan Morain, *Kamala's Way: An American Life* (New York: Simon & Schuster Paperbacks, 2022), 54.

62. Kamala Harris, *The Truths We Hold: An American Journey* (New York: Penguin Books, 2019), 37.

63. Harris, for Law and Order. *The San Francisco Chronicle*, December 7, 2003: D4. NewsBank: America's News—Historical and Current. https://infoweb -newsbank-com.ccl.idm.oclc.org/apps/news/document-view?p=AMNEWS&docref =news/0FF4C213363173C0.

64. David Siders, "'Ruthless': How Kamala Harris Won Her First Race," *Politico*, January 24, 2019, https://www.politico.com/magazine/story/2019/01/24/kamala -harris-2020-history-224126.

65. Phillip Matier, "Brains, Brio, Beauty—and Wounded Feelings." *The San Francisco Chronicle*, November 10, 2003: A13. NewsBank: America's News—Historical

and Current. https://infoweb-newsbank-com.ccl.idm.oclc.org/apps/news/document -view?p=AMNEWS&docref=news/0FEBDE3E1C581966.

66. Dan Morain, "High Stakes, National Spotlight in Campaign For Attorney General," *Sacramento Bee*, October 23, 2010: A13. NewsBank: America's News— Historical and Current. https://infoweb-newsbank-com.ccl.idm.oclc.org/apps/news/ document-view?p=AMNEWS&docref=news/1330E62D0CD0DA70.

67. Morain, Kamala's Way, 85.

68. State of California Department of Justice, "Attorney General Kamala D. Harris Issues Statement on Prop. 8 Arguments," March 26, 2013, https://oag.ca.gov/news/ press-releases/attorney-general-kamala-d-harris-issues-statement-prop-8-arguments.

69. State of California Department of Justice, "Attorney General Kamala D. Harris Issues Statement on Appeal of Court Ruling on California's Death Penalty," August 21, 2014, https://oag.ca.gov/news/press-releases/attorney-general-kamala-d-harris -issues-statement-appeal-court-ruling-california.

70. Lara Bazelon, "Kamala Harris Was Not a 'Progressive Prosecutor.'" *New York Times*, January 17, 2019, https://www.nytimes.com/2019/01/17/opinion/kamala -harris-criminal-justice.html.

71. State of California Department of Justice," California and the Fight Against Transnational Organized Crime." March 2014, https://oag.ca.gov/sites/all/files/agweb /pdfs/toc/report_2014.pdf.

72. Seema Mehta, "Exclusive: Kamala Harris Makes 'No Apologies' For Aggressive Senate Campaign," *Los Angeles Times*, February 18, 2015, https://www.latimes .com/local/political/la-me-pc-harris-speaks-out-on-senate-run-20150218-story.html.

73. Roy Behr, quoted in Michael Finnegan, "Rep. Loretta Sanchez enters race for Barbara Boxer's Senate seat*,"* *Los Angeles Times*, May 14, 2015, https://www .latimes.com/local/political/la-me-pc-loretta-sanchez-senate-campaign-20150414 -story.html.

74. Jeffrey B. Lewis, Keith Poole, Howard Rosenthal, Adam Boche, Aaron Rudkin, and Luke Sonnet (2024). *Voteview: Congressional Roll-Call Votes Database*. https://voteview.com/person/41701/kamala-devi-harris.

75. Monica Hesse, "Kamala Harris Said 19 Words in 2018 That Taught Us All We Need to Know," *Washington Post*, July 22, 2024, https://www.washingtonpost.com/ style/power/2024/07/22/kamala-harris-brett-kavanaugh.

76. Of course, critics saw Harris's question as inane. Though Kavanaugh struggled, some would say it is not hard to think of laws that tell males what they can or cannot do with their bodies, such as mandatory seat belt laws, antidrug laws, and prohibitions on rape and (in some states) suicide. As of 2024, all males had to register for Selective Service, potentially putting their bodies at risk of injury or death.

77. Andrew Stanton, "Four Issues Kamala Harris Has Changed Her Position On," *Newsweek*, September 9, 2024, https://www.newsweek.com/kamala-harris-changed -stances-issues-future-policies-1950985.

78. Dan Diamond, "What Kamala Harris Learned from Embracing, Abandoning Medicare-for-all," *Washington Post*, September 10, 2024, https://www.washingtonpost .com/health/2024/09/10/kamala-harris-medicare-for-all.

79. Morain, *Kamala's Way*, 211–212.

80. Li Zhou, "Kamala Harris Drops Out of The 2020 Presidential Race" Vox, December 3, 2019, https://www.vox.com/2019/12/3/20993805/kamala-harris-drops -out-of-the-2020-presidential-race.

81. Kate Sullivan, "More Than 200 Black Women Urge Biden To Pick Black Woman As Running Mate," CNN, April 24, 2020, https://www.cnn.com/2020/04/24 /politics/black-women-letter-joe-biden-running-mate/index.html.

82. Caroline Kelly, "Rep. Jim Clyburn Says He Urged Biden to Choose A Black Woman As His Running Mate," CNN, November 7, 2020, https://www.cnn.com /2020/11/07/politics/clyburn-biden-black-woman-running-mate-cnntv/index.html.

83. Rober Caro, *The Years of Lyndon Johnson: The Passage of Power* (New York: Knopf Doubleday, 2012), 198.

84. Edward-Isaac Dovere," The Inside Story of the Biden-Harris Debate Blowup," *Politico*, May 19, 2021, https://www.politico.com/news/magazine/2021 /05/19/edward-isaac-dovere-2020-campaign-book-excerpt-joe-biden-kamala-harris -489347.

85. United States Senate, Votes to Break Ties in the Senate, "https://www.senate .gov/legislative/TieVotes.htm.

86. Haley Strack, "Harris's Personnel Problem: Over 90 Percent of VP's Staff Left in Last Three Years," *National Review*, July 22, 2024, https://www.nationalreview .com/news/harriss-personnel-problem-over-90-percent-of-vps-staff-left-in-last-three -years/; John L. Dorman, "Ex-Harris Staffer Says She gives 'Soul-destroying Criti- cism," *Business Insider*, December 5, 2021, https://www.businessinsider.com/kamala -harris-former-staffer-soul-destroying-criticism-aides-report-2021-12; Christopher Cadelago, Daniel Lippman, and Eugene Daniels, "'Not a healthy environment': Kamala Harris's office rife with dissent," *Politico*, June 30, 2021, https://www .politico.com/news/2021/06/30/kamala-harris-office-dissent-497290.

87. The latter statement was made at a 2023 White House ceremony immediately after Harris noted that "My mother used to—she would give us a hard time some- times, and she would say to us, 'I don't know what's wrong with you young people. You think you just fell out of a coconut tree?'" The coconut tree reference became a staple of both pro- and anti-Harris memes.

88. Thomas Lifson, "Report: White House directs all agencies to refer to 'Biden-Harris administration,'" The American Thinker, March 23, 2021, https:// www.americanthinker.com/blog/2021/03/report_white_house_directs_all_agencies _to_refer_to_bidenharris_administration.html#ixzz8pjVsCPme; Noah Bierman and Matt Stiles, "For Kamala Harris, a shifting role: Fewer public events with Biden," *Los Angeles Times*, October 25, 2021, https://www.latimes.com/politics/story/2021-10-25 /for-kamala-harris-a-shifting-role-fewer-events-with-biden.

89. "Biden and Harris Earn Similar Job Ratings," Monmouth University Poll, March 21, 2023, https://www.monmouth.edu/polling-institute/reports/monmouthpoll _us_032123.

90. Christopher Cadelago, "New Poll Goes Deep on Kamala Harris' Liabilities and Strengths As A Potential President," *Politico*, June 12, 2024, https://www .politico.com/news/2024/06/12/kamala-harris-favorability-poll-00162093.

CHAPTER 3

1. RealClearPolitics, President Trump Job Approval, https://www.realclearpolling.com/polls/approval/donald-trump/approval-rating; Trump Favorable/Unfavorable, https://www.realclearpolling.com/polls/favorability/donald-trump.

2. The American Presidency Project. "Seats in Congress Gained/Lost by the President's Party in Mid-Term Elections." Santa Barbara: University of California. Available from the World Wide Web: https://www.presidency.ucsb.edu/node/332343.

3. Emma Hurt, "'A Hostage Situation Every Day': Strategists Blame Trump For Georgia Senate Losses," NPR, January 29, 2021, https://www.npr.org/2021/01/29/961837774/a-hostage-situation-every-day-strategists-blame-trump-for-georgia-senate-losses.

4. See John Ganz, *When the Clock Broke: Con Men, Conspiracists, and How America Cracked Up in the 1970s* (New York: Farrar, Straus and Giroux, 2024).

5. "Over four decades, Trump's one solid stance: A hard line on trade," *Washington Post*, March 7, 2018, https://www.washingtonpost.com/business/over-four-decades-trumps-one-solid-stance-a-hard-line-on-trade/2018/03/07/4b1ed250-2172-11e8-badd-7c9f29a55815_story.html.

6. See Bojan Pancevski, "Inside the Strange New World of Tucker Carlson," *Wall Street Journal*, July 20–21, 2024, pp. C1–3.

7. Steven E. Schier. "Challenging the World: Trump Foreign Policy" in Steven E. Schier and Todd E. Eberly, *The Trump Effect: Disruption and Its Consequences in U.S. Politics and Government* (Lanham, MD: Rowman & Littlefield, 2022).

8. Andrew E. Busch, "Domestic Policy Legacies of the Trump Presidency," in Steven E. Schier and Todd E. Eberly, *The Trump Effect: Disruption and Its Consequences in U.S. Politics and Government* (Lanham, MD: Rowman & Littlefield, 2022).

9. "The Art of Triangulation in Politics: Examining Trump's Evolution," The Politics Watcher, August 23, 2024, The Art of Triangulation in Politics: Examining Trump's Evolution (thepoliticswatcher.com); Julia Manchester, "Trump's shifting abortion stance raises questions for evangelical support," The Hill, October 8, 2024, https://thehill.com/homenews/campaign/4921783-trump-abortion-stance-evangelicals.

10. Charles R. Kesler, "Trump, the Republican Party, and American Conservatism: Retrospect and Prospect," in Andrew E. Busch and William G. Mayer, *The Elephant in the Room: Donald Trump and the Future of the Republican Party* (Lanham, MD: Rowman & Littlefield, 2022), 126–129.

11. National Conservatism: A Statement of Principles, https://nationalconservatism.org/national-conservatism-a-statement-of-principles.

12. Emily Ekins, "The Five Types of Trump Voters," Democracy Fund, June 2017, https://www.voterstudygroup.org/publications/2016-elections/the-five-types-trump-voters.

13. Verlan Lewis and Hyrum Lewis, *The Myth of Left and Right: How the Political Spectrum Misleads and Harms America* (New York: Oxford University Press, 2022).

14. Pew Research Center, Beyond Red vs. Blue: The Political Typology, Pew Research Center, November 9, 2021, https://www.pewresearch.org/politics/2021/11 /09/beyond-red-vs-blue-the-political-typology-2.

15. For a view of this phenomenon in the 19th century, see James Bryce, *The American Commonwealth* Vol I (Chicago: Charles H. Sergel & Co., 1890), chapter 8 ("Why Great Men Are Not Chosen Presidents"). For more recent analysis in the era of presidential primaries, see Alan I. Abramowitz, "Viability, Electability, and Candidate Choice in a Presidential Primary Election: A Test of Competing Models," *The Journal of Politics* 51(4): 977–992 (1989); Jill Rickershauser and John H. Aldrich, "'It's the electability, stupid' or maybe not? Electability, substance, and strategic voting in presidential primaries," *Electoral Studies* 26(2), 371–380 (2007); and Elizabeth N. Simas, "The effects of electability on US primary voters," *Journal of Elections, Public Opinion and Parties* 27(3), 274–290 (2017).

16. Dan McLaughlin, "How Trump Cost Republicans the Senate," *National Review*, December 19, 2022, https://www.nationalreview.com/2022/12/how-trump -cost-republicans-the-senate.

17. James Politi, "Joe Biden attacks 'extremist' Republicans as a 'threat to America,'" *Financial Times*, September 1, 2022, https://www.ft.com/content/3b484025 -eb31-4dc9-bdbd-850b23a6e0cb.

18. ABC News, National Exit Poll: House, https://abcnews.go.com/Elections/ exit-polls-2022-us-house-election-results-analysis#:~:text=View%20latest%202022 %20election%20exit%20polls%20results,%20including%20by%20demographic.

19. Andrew E. Busch, *Outsiders and Openness in the Presidential Nominating System* (Pittsburgh: University of Pittsburgh Press, 1997).

20. Donald J. Trump, Twitter post, June 22, 2020, https://twitter.com/ realDonaldTrump/status/1275024974579982336.

21. Jonathan Swan and Zachary Basu, "Episode 1: A Premeditated Lie Lit the Fire," Axios, January 16, 2021, https://www.axios.com/trump-election-premeditated -lie-ebaf4a1f-46bf-ba0d-3ed5536ef537.html.; "Donald Trump 2020 Election Night Speech Transcript," Rev, https://rev.com/transcripts/donald-trump-2020-election -night-speech-transcript.

22. Reuters, "Trump cancels news conference to release report on 2020 election," August 17, 2023, https://www.reuters.com/legal/trump-cancels-news-conference -release-report-2020-election-2023-08-18.

23. Dinesh D'Souza, *2,000 Mules: They Thought We'd Never Find Out. They Were Wrong.* (Salem Press, 2022).

24. Rasmussen Reports, "One-in-Five Mail-In Voters Admit They Cheated in 2020 Election," December 12, 2023, https://www.rasmussenreports.com/public_content/ politics/partner_surveys/one_in_five_mail_in_voters_admit_they_cheated_in_2020_ election#:~:text=More%20than%2020%%20of%20voters%20who%20used%20mail -in%20ballots%20in.

25. Zachary Leeman, "Ben Shapiro Dismisses Dinesh D'Souza's Stolen Election Opus 2000 Mules: 'Conclusions of the Film' Not 'Justified' by Its Premises," Mediaite, May 17, 2022, https://www.mediaite.com/politics/ben-shapiro-dismisses-dinesh

-dsouzas-stolen-election-opus-2000-mules-conclusions-of-the-film-not-justified-by
-its-premises/.

26. Kate Brumback, "Georgia man falsely accused of ballot fraud in the film," AP,
May 31, 2024, https://apnews.com/article/2000-mules-film-apology-f1c2de96f17
e72241761b4e6deaee5cb.

27. Kate Brumback, "Creator of '2000 Mules' apologizes to Georgia man falsely
accused of ballot fraud in the film," AP, December 2, 2024, https://apnews.com/arti-
cle/2000-mules-film-dinesh-dsouza-apology-91d6c3c80e6c56e89684a12111f92319.

28. Rasmussen Reports, "One-in-Five Mail-In Voters Admit They Cheated in
2020 Election."

29. Mollie Hemingway, *Rigged: How the Media, Big Tech, and the Democrats
Seized Our Elections* (Washington, DC: Regnery, 2022).

30. RealClearPolitics, 2020 General Election: Trump vs Biden, https://www
.realclearpolling.com/polls/president/general/2020/trump-vs-biden; 2020 Electoral
College Map, https://www.realclearpolitics.com/epolls/2020/president/2020_
elections_electoral_college_map.html.

31. ABC News: National Exit Polls: House, https://abcnews.go.com/Elections/
exit-polls-2022-us-house-election-results-analysis#:~:text=View%20latest%202022
%20election%20exit%20polls%20results,%20including%20by%20demographic.

32. Jennifer Agriesta and Ariel Edwards-Levy, "CNN Poll: Percentage of Republicans who think Biden's 2020 win was illegitimate ticks back up near 70%," CNN,
August 3, 2023, https://www.cnn.com/2023/08/03/politics/cnn-poll-republicans-think
-2020-election-illegitimate/index.html.

33. David A, Graham, "Has Anyone Noticed That Trump Is Really Old?," *The
Atlantic*, November 20, 2023, https://www.theatlantic.com/ideas/archive/2023/11/
donald-trump-old-age-biden/676052.

34. Calvin Woodward and Emily Swanson, "Biden is widely seen as too old for
office, an AP-NORC poll finds. Trump has problems of his own," AP, August 28,
2023, https://apnews.com/article/biden-age-poll-trump-2024-620e0a5cfa0039a6448
f607c17c7f23e.

35. "Trump challenges Biden to drug test before debate," BBC, August 26, 2020,
https://www.bbc.com/news/election-us-2020-53927766.

36. CNN, Exit Polls, https://www.cnn.com/election/2020/exit-polls/president/
national-results.

37. Jonathan D. Karl, "Inside William Barr's Breakup With Trump," *The Atlantic*,
June 27, 2021, https://www.theatlantic.com/politics/archive/2021/06/william-barrs
-trump-administration-attorney-general/619298.

38. Veronica Stracqualursi, "Pence announces 2024 White House run, arguing
Trump 'should never' be president again," June 7, 2023, https://edition.cnn.com/2023
/06/07/politics/pence-2024-presidential-campaign/index.html.

39. United States Attorney's Office, District of Columbia, "40 Months Since the
Jan. 6 Attack on the Capitol," May 6, 2024, https://www.justice.gov/usao-dc/39
-months-since-the-jan-6-attack-on-the-capitol.

40. Mike Gooding, "Jan. 6 Capitol riot: Law enforcement didn't share critical
information, report says," WVEC, July 25, 2023, https://www.13newsnow.com

/article/news/crime/cost-of-capitol-riot-january-6/291-6fb5117e-dea1-4631-a76a
-76e87b268bfd.

41. *Congressional Record* (daily), February 13, 2021, S730, https://www
.govinfo.gov/content/pkg/CREC-2021-02-13/html/CREC-2021-02-13-pt1-PgS717
-2.htm.

42. Noah Manskar, "Riots following George Floyd's death may cost insurance
companies up to $2B," *New York Post*, September 16, 2020, https://nypost.com/2020
/09/16/riots-following-george-floyds-death-could-cost-up-to-2b/; Tom Kerscher,
"Fact-checking claim about deaths, damage from Black Lives Matter protests," *Austin American-Statesman*, August 10, 2020, https://www.statesman.com/story/news/
politics/elections/2020/08/10/fact-checking-claim-about-deaths-damage-from-black
-lives-matter-protests/113878088.

43. Daniel Dale and Marshall Cohen, "Fact check: Five enduring lies about the
Capitol insurrection," CNN, January 5, 2022, https://www.cnn.com/2022/01/04/
politics/fact-check-capitol-insurrection-january-6-lies/index.html.

44. United States Attorney for the District of Columbia, "Member of Oath Keepers
Indicted for Conspiracy and Other Offenses Related to U.S. Capitol Breach". June 24,
2022. https://www.justice.gov/usao-dc/pr/member-oath-keepers-indicted-conspiracy
-and-other-offenses-related-us-capitol-breach.

45. Dale and Cohen, "Fact Check."

46. For an extended presentation of this argument, see Julie Kelly, *January 6: How
Democrats Used the Capitol Protest to Launch a War on Terror Against the Political
Right* (Bombardier Books, 2021).

47. Madison Czopek, "The FBI didn't orchestrate Jan. 6, but a poll shows the
false belief has staying power," Poynter, January 8, 2024, https://www.poynter.org/
fact-checking/2024/fbi-organize-encourage-january-6-capitol-attack-insurrection/#:~
:text=%E2%80%9CIf%20you%20are%20asking%20whether%20the%20violence
%20at%20the%20Capitol.

48. Saranac Hale Spencer, Robert Farley and D'Angelo Gore, "Explaining the
Missing Context of Tucker Carlson's Jan. 6 Presentation," FactCheck.org, March 10,
2023, https://www.factcheck.org/2023/03/explaining-the-missing-context-of-tucker
-carlsons-jan-6-presentation/#:~:text=On%20the%20evening%20of%20Jan.%206,
%202021%20%E2%80%94%20after%20a.

49. Aaron Blake, "Key findings from the Jan. 6 committee's final report,"
Washington Post, December 23, 2022, https://www.washingtonpost.com/politics/
interactive/2022/jan-6-final-report-findings.

50. Dan Barry and Alan Feuer, "How Trump Flipped Script and Made Jan. 6 an
Asset," *New York Times*, January 6, 2024, p. 1.

51. At the end of Trump's first term, one estimate held that Trump had uttered
30,573 misleading or untrue claims. Even correcting for possible bias—the estimate
was compiled by the liberal Washington Post—the number is astounding. Glenn
Kessler, Salvador Rizzo, and Meg Kelly, "Trump's false or misleading claims
total 30,573 over 4 years," *Washington Post*, January 24, 2021, https://www
.washingtonpost.com/politics/2021/01/24/trumps-false-or-misleading-claims-total
-30573-over-four-years.

52. David A. Graham, "The Cases Against Trump: A Guide," *The Atlantic*, September 13, 2024, https://www.theatlantic.com/ideas/archive/2024/09/donald-trump-legal-cases-charges/675531.

53. See "The Trump Indictment Is Damning," *National Review*, June 10, 2023, https://www.nationalreview.com/2023/06/the-trump-indictment-is-damning.

54. https://www.businessinsider.com/donald-trump-mar-a-lago-raid-boost-ron-desantis-poll-2022-8.

55. Robert K. Hur, "Report on the Investigation Into Unauthorized Removal, Retention, and Disclosure of Classified Documents Discovered at Locations Including the Penn Eiden Center and the Delaware Private Residence of President Joseph R. Eiden, Jr.," US Department of Justice, February 2024, https://www.justice.gov/storage/report-from-special-counsel-robert-k-hur-february-2024.pdf.

56. Michael W. McConnell, "Why Republicans Don't Abandon 'Felon' Trump," *Wall Street Journal*, June 20, 2024, p. A15.

57. Jonathan Turley, "Buzz Kill: The Trump Conviction Presents a Target-Rich Environment for Appeal," June 3, 2024, https://jonathanturley.org/2024/06/03/buzz-kill-the-trump-conviction-presents-a-target-rich-environment-for-appeal/comment-page-1/#:~:text=Below%20is%20my%20column%20in%20the%20Hill%20on%20the%20most.

58. J. T. Young, "In Prosecuting Trump, Democrats Have Exonerated Him," *The American Spectator*, March 12, 2024, https://spectator.org/in-prosecuting-trump-democrats-have-exonerated-him/#:~:text=In%20Prosecuting%20Trump,%20Democrats%20Have%20Exonerated%20Him%20Their%20actions%20now.

59. Cumulative Confirmed Covid-19 Deaths, https://ourworldindata.org/covid-deaths.

60. RealClearPolitics, Direction of Country, https://www.realclearpolling.com/polls/state-of-the-union/direction-of-country.

61. RealClearPolitics, President Biden Job Approval, https://www.realclearpolling.com/polls/approval/joe-biden/approval-rating.

62. Cumulative Confirmed Covid-19 Deaths, https://ourworldindata.org/covid-deaths.

63. "Ramaswamy labels Trump 'best president' of 21st Century,'" *Politico*, August 24, 2023, https://www.politico.com/video/2023/08/24/vivek-ramaswamy-praises-trump-best-president-of-the-21st-century-1037286#:~:text=Politicians%20react%20to%20Jack%20Smith's%20Trump%20election%20case%20filing.%20 10/03/24.

64. See "Who's ahead in the national Republican primary polls?," FiveThirtyEight, https://projects.fivethirtyeight.com/polls/president-primary-r/2024/national/#:~:text=Who%E2%80%99s%20ahead%20in%20the%20national%20Republican%20primary%20polls?%20Updating%20average.

65. Curt Anderson and Alex Castellanos, "The DeSantis Team Ran the Worst Campaign in History," *Politico*, January 19, 2024, https://www.politico.com/news/magazine/2024/01/19/the-desantis-team-ran-the-worst-campaign-in-history-00136527#:~:text=The%20mantle%20of%20Worst%20Republican%20Presidential%20Campaign%20Ever%20has%20been.

66. Who's ahead in the national Republican primary polls?, FiveThirtyEight.

67. According to the FiveThirtyEight average, she led the Florida governor 11.9 percent to 11.6 percent Who's ahead in the national Republican primary polls?, FiveThirtyEight.

68. F. Amanda Tugade, "Birdcages and 'new blood': Tensions between Nikki Haley, Donald Trump boil over after Republican debate," *USA Today*, October 21, 2023, https://www.usatoday.com/story/news/politics/elections/2023/10/01/donald -trump-nikki-haley-second-republican-debate/71025264007.

69. Diana Glebova, Samuel Chamberlain, Steven Nelson and Josh Christenson, "Trump easily wins Iowa caucus in historic landslide, urges unity to 'straighten out death and destruction,'" *New York Post*, January 15, 2024, https://nypost.com/2024 /01/15/news/trump-wins-iowa-caucuses-in-landslide-first-election-of-2024.

70. Ben Kamisar, "Nikki Haley: 'Diminished,' 'unhinged' Trump has changed since she backed him," NBC News, February 14, 2024, https://www.nbcnews.com /politics/2024-election/nikki-haley-diminished-unhinged-trump-changed-backed -rcna138667.

71. Natalie Allison, "RNC installs new leadership as Trump tightens hold on GOP," *Politico*, March 8, 2024, https://www.politico.com/news/2024/03/08/rnc -new-leadership-donald-trump-00146032#:~:text=While%20assembled%20for%20a %20hastily%20called%20meeting%20in%20Houston,%20the.

72. Busch, *Outsiders and Openness in the Presidential Nominating System*.

CHAPTER 4

1. Marty Cohen, David Karol, Hans Noel, and John Zaller, *The Party Decides: Presidential Nominations Before and After Reform* (Chicago: University of Chicago Press, 2008).

2. Trevor Hunnicutt and James Oliphant, "US presidential debate: takeaways as Trump and Biden took the stage," Reuters, June 28, 2024, https://www.reuters.com/ world/us/takeaways-biden-trump-presidential-debate-2024-06-28.

3. Annie Linskey and Siobhan Hughes, "Behind Closed Doors, Biden Shows Signs of Slipping," *Wall Street Journal*, June 4, 2024, https://www.wsj.com/politics/ policy/joe-biden-age-election-2024-8ee15246.

4. "For presidents, it's not age but judgment that matters," *Washington Post*, June 9, 2024, https://www.washingtonpost.com/opinions/2024/06/09/wall-street-journal -biden-slipping-article/; Oliver Darcy, "The Wall Street Journal's story about Biden's mental acuity suffers from glaring problems," CNN, June 6, 2024, https://www.cnn .com/2024/06/06/media/wall-street-journal-biden-mental-acuity/index.html.

5. Danielle Wallace, "Harris claims Biden fit to continue in office, despite more than 80 documented encounters in past year," Fox News, July 29, 2024. https://www .foxnews.com/politics/harris-claimed-biden-completely-fit-continue-office-despite -many-documented-encounters-past-year.

6. Jake Sherman, X post, June 28, 2024, https://x.com/JakeSherman/ status/1806698131578388485.

7. Andrew Solender, "These Congressional Democrats Are Demanding Biden Withdraw," Axios, July 19, 2024, https://www.axios.com/2024/07/06/list-house -democrats-biden-withdraw-2024-campaign.

8. Lauren Sforza and Mychael Schnell, "Pelosi Says It's Up To Biden 'To Decide If He's Going To Run,'" *The Hill*, July 10, 2024, https://thehill.com/homenews/ campaign/4763484-nancy-pelosi-joe-biden-reelection-campaign-post-debate/mlite.

9. "Most Say Biden Should Withdraw from the Presidential Race," AP-NORC, July 17, 2024, https://apnorc.org/projects/most-say-biden-should-withdraw-from-the -presidential-race.

10. Jonathan Alter, "How Nancy Pelosi Ripped Off the Band-Aid for Democrats to Force Joe Biden Out," *Vanity Fair*, October 14, 2024, https://www.vanityfair.com /news/story/nancy-pelosi-democrats-force-joe-biden-out.

11. Carl Hulse, "How Biden's Senate Allies Helped Push Him From the Race," *New York Times*, August 29, 2024, https://www.nytimes.com/2024/08/29/us/politics/ senate-democrats-biden-drop-out.html

12. Bob Woodward, *War* (New York: Simon & Schuster, 2024), 338–339.

13. Monica Alba, "'A commander in chief moment': Inside Biden's response to the Trump rally shooting," NBC News, July 14, 2024, https://www.nbcnews .com/politics/white-house/-commander-chief-moment-bidens-response-trump-rally -shooting-rcna161809.

14. Margaret Hartmann, "J.D. Vance Wins Trump Veepstakes. Here's Everyone He Beat Out." *New York Intelligencer*, July 15, 2024, https://nymag.com/intelligencer /article/trump-vp-pick-2024-candidates-odds.html.

15. Kelsey Vlamis, "GOP Senate candidate JD Vance said he doesn't 'really care what happens to Ukraine'," *Business Insider*, February 20, 2022, https://www .businessinsider.com/gop-candidate-jd-vance-i-dont-care-what-happens-ukraine -2022-2.

16. Amy Sherman, "Fact-checking Kamala Harris' claim that JD Vance said he would have overturned the 2020 election," Politifact, July 18, 2024, https://www .politifact.com/factchecks/2024/jul/18/kamala-harris/fact-checking-kamala-harris -claim-that-jd-vance-sa.

17. J. D. Vance, Address Accepting the Vice Presidential Nomination at the Republican National Convention in Milwaukee, Wisconsin Online by Gerhard Peters and John T. Woolley, The American Presidency Project https://www.presidency.ucsb .edu/node/373579.

18. Donald J. Trump (1st Term), Address Accepting the Presidential Nomination at the Republican National Convention in Milwaukee, Wisconsin Online by Gerhard Peters and John T. Woolley, The American Presidency Project https://www .presidency.ucsb.edu/node/373582.

19. Keith Naughton, "Trump's acceptance speech should have been a home run. It wasn't," The Hill, July 19, 2024, https://thehill.com/opinion/campaign/4781405 -trump-speech-rnc-lost-opportunity.

20. Eli Stokols et al., "Why Biden Finally Quit," *Politico*, July 21, 2024, https:// www.politico.com/news/2024/07/21/why-biden-dropped-out-00170106.

21. Sarah Ferris and Christopher Cadelago, "Pelosi Voiced Support for an Open Nomination Process If Biden Drops Out," *Politico*, July 19, 2024, https://www

.politico.com/news/2024/07/19/pelosi-support-open-nomination-biden-drop-out -00169893.

22. Rick Hasen, "Biden-Harris Campaign Funds Is Unlikely to Get Anywhere at the FEC or In Court, and If It Does It Will Likely Take Years," Election Law Blog, July 23, 2024, https://electionlawblog.org/?p=144771.

23. Jasmine Wright, "Black Women Leaders See Decades of Struggle Vindicated in Kamala Harris' Ascension," NOTUS, August 23, 2024, https://www.notus.org/ harris-2024/kamala-harris-black-women-democrats.

24. Dave Lawler, "Hindsight 2024: Pelosi questions Biden's handling of Harris endorsement," Axios, November 8, 2024, https://www.axios.com/2024/11/08/pelosi -biden-endorsement-harris.

25. Zachary Leeman, "Kamala Harris Campaign Surrogate Tells Fox Biden's Endorsement Was a 'Big F You' to Democrats: 'This Is a $1 Billion Disaster,'" Mediaite, November 9, 2024, https://www.mediaite.com/tv/kamala-harris-campaign -surrogate-tells-fox-bidens-endorsement-was-a-big-f-you-to-democrats-this-is-a-1 -billion-disaster.

26. Lazaro Gamio et al., "Many Elected Democrats Quickly Endorsed Kamala Harris. See Who Did," *New York Times*, July 24, 2024, https://www.nytimes.com/ interactive/2024/07/22/us/politics/kamala-harris-democrats-endorsement-list.html.

27. Shane Goldmacher and Reid J. Epstein, "Harris Clinches Majority of Delegates as She Closes In on Nomination," *New York Times*, July 22, 2024, https://www .nytimes.com/2024/07/22/us/politics/kamala-harris-trump-2024-election.html.

28. Anna Massoglia and Jimmy Cloutier, "Kamala Harris Drives Record Fundraising After Biden Exit," Open Secrets, July 25, 2024, https://www.opensecrets.org /news/2024/07/kamala-harris-drives-record-fundraising-after-biden-exit.

29. Nick Evans, "Better Safe Than Sorry: Democrats Prepare for Virtual Roll Call Despite Ohio Deadline Changes," *Ohio Capital Journal*, July 30, 2024, https://ohio-capitaljournal.com/2024/07/30/better-safe-than-sorry-democrats-prepare-for-virtual -roll-call-despite-ohio-deadline-changes.

30. Shane Goldmacher, "How Kamala Harris Took Command of the Democratic Party in 48 Hours," *New York Times*, July 24, 2024, https://www.nytimes.com/2024 /07/24/us/politics/kamala-harris-democrats-nomination.html.

31. Seung Min Kim And Linley Sanders," About 8 In 10 Democrats Are Satisfied With Harris In Stark Shift After Biden Drops Out: AP-NORC Poll," Associated Press, July 31, 3024, https://Apnews.Com/Article/Poll-Joe-Biden-Kamala-Harris-Donald-Trump-1feb5ed3c2e29623ce3cec3565b487cd.

32. Irie Sentner and Liz Crampton, "Often Split Over Israel, Dems Rally Around Walz As GOP Slams Shapiro Snub As Antisemitic," *Politico*, August 7, 2024, https:// www.politico.com/news/2024/08/07/jewish-leaders-walz-shapiro-00172960.

33. Ron Kampeas, "Did Harris opt against Josh Shapiro because he is Jewish? Campaign calls accusation 'ridiculous,'" *The Jerusalem Post*, August 7, 2024, https:// www.jpost.com/american-politics/article-813639.

34. Meredith Lee Hill, "With Tim Walz, Dems See a Path to Winning Back Rural Districts," *Politico*, August 12, 2024, https://www.politico.com/news/2024/08/11/tim -walz-democrats-rural-districts-00173450.

35. Some commentators asserted that the law required tampon dispensers to be placed in boys' restrooms, leading Walz to acquire the derisive nickname "Tampon Tim." Snopes judged the claim "mostly false," but its explanation left it somewhat unclear whether the claim was mostly false or mostly true: "The language of the statute was gender neutral and therefore compelled schools to make menstrual products available to transmasculine (trans boys and male-presenting) students, although that would not necessarily entail stocking them in boys' bathrooms." Anna Rascouet-Paz, "Tim Walz Signed Bill Requiring Tampons in Boys' Bathrooms?," Snopes, August 12, 2024, https://www.snopes.com/fact-check/tim-walz-tampons.

36. Kamala Harris, Address Accepting the Democratic Presidential Nomination in Chicago, Illinois, August 22, 2024. Online by Gerhard Peters and John T. Woolley, The American Presidency Project https://www.presidency.ucsb.edu/node/373892.

37. Reagan used the phrase in dozens of speeches. One example is his 1985 inaugural address: "Let us resolve that we, the people, will build an American opportunity society in which all of us—white and black, rich and poor, young and old—will go forward together, arm in arm." Ronald Reagan, Inaugural Address, January 21, 1985. Online by Gerhard Peters and John T. Woolley, The American Presidency Project https://www.presidency.ucsb.edu/node/259910.

CHAPTER 5

1. 2024 National: Trump vs. Harris, RealClearPolitics, https://www.realclearpolling.com/polls/president/general/2024/trump-vs-harris.Throughout this chapter, we are largely relying on RCP, which, among poll aggregators, was closest to the actual result at the end of the race. Mark Mellmon, "Were the Polls Right? It's Complicated," *The Hill*, November 20, 2024, https://thehill.com/opinion/campaign/4999776-polls-accuracy-2024-election/; Andy Puzder, "How the RCP Averages Got It Right—and NYT Got It Wrong," *New York Post*, November 26, 2024, https://www.realclearpolitics.com/2024/11/26/how_the_rcp_averages_got_it_right—and_nyt_got_it_wrong_636386.html.

2. 2024 RCP Electoral College Map, RealClearPolitics, https://www.realclearpolling.com/maps/president/2024/toss-up/electoral-college; 2024 Electoral College: No Toss-up States, RealClearPolitics, https://www.realclearpolling.com/maps/president/2024/no-toss-up/electoral-college.

3. Kamala Harris: Favorable/Unfavorable, RealClearPolitics, https://www.realclearpolling.com/polls/favorability/trump-vs-harris.

4. See Bureau of Labor Statistics, CPI Inflation Calculator, https://www.bls.gov/data/inflation_calculator.htm.ppear/ .

5. Justin Lahat and Rachel Wolfe, "Americans Are Feeling a Little Better About Economy," *Wall Street Journal*, September 3, 2024, p. A2.

6. Direction of Country, RealClearPolitics, https://www.realclearpolling.com/polls/state-of-the-union/direction-of-country.

7. President Biden Job Approval, RealClearPolitics, https://www.realclearpolitics.com/epolls/other/president_biden_job_approval-7320.html.

8. Tevi Troy, "Uphill Battle: The challenge of vice presidents running to replace their bosses," *Washington Examiner*, October 30, 2024, pp. 13–15.

9. "Kamala on the Afghan Withdrawal," *Wall Street Journal*, August 27, 2024, p. A14.

10. Gallup, Party Affiliation, https://news.gallup.com/poll/15370/party-affiliation .aspx.

11. Daniel Lippman, "No Labels packs it up, won't put forth a presidential ticket," *Politico*, April 4, 2024, https://www.politico.com/news/2024/04/04/no-labels-no -presidential-ticket-00150627.

12. Elizabeth Findell and Natalie Andrews, "Kennedy Pulls Out of Race, Endorses Trump," *Wall Street Journal*, August 23, 2024, p. 1A.

13. James W. Ceaser, Andrew E. Busch, and John J. Pitney Jr., *Defying the Odds: The 2016 Elections and American Politics* (Lanham, MD: Rowman & Littlefield, 2017).

14. Andrew E. Busch and John J. Pitney Jr., *Divided We Stand: The 2020 Elections and American Politics* (Lanham, MD: Rowman & Littlefield, 2021).

15. Jing Pan, "Donald Trump calls tariff 'the most beautiful word in the dictionary,' threatens up to 2,000% tariff to block car imports from Mexico. Would it work?," Moneywise, October 24, 2024, https://moneywise.com/news/economy/ donald-trump-calls-tariff-the-most-beautiful-word.

16. See Io Dodds, "Trump's blitz of anti-trans ads probably worked—but not for the reason you might think," The Independent, December 1, 2024, https:// www.independent.co.uk/news/world/americas/us-politics/trump-anti-trans-campaign -adverts-b2654925.html; Sarah Fortinsky, "Chris Christie: Most effective Trump ad was 'Kamala Harris is for they/them'," The Hill, November 11, 2024, https:// www.yahoo.com/news/chris-christie-most-effective-trump-135946643.html; David Harsanyi, "Trump's Popular 'They/Them' Ad Signals Backlash Against the Left's Culture War," New York Sun, November 18, 2024, https://www.nysun.com/article/ trumps-popular-they-them-ad-signals-backlash-against-the-lefts-culture-war.

17. Richard Rubin, "Harris and Trump Proposals Add to Soaring Federal Debt." *Wall Street Journal*, September 18, 2024, p. A1.

18. "Trump and Harris face off in contentious debate," CNN, September 11, 2024, https://www.cnn.com/politics/live-news/trump-harris-debate-abc-09-10-24#h _bf0713ded98fb1867a0770a9cf09dddf.

19. 2024 National: Trump vs. Harris, RealClearPolitics, https://www .realclearpolling.com/polls/president/general/2024/trump-vs-harris.

20. Garbriel Debenedetti, "David Plouffe on Harris vs. Trump: 'Too Close for Comfort,'" the Intelligencer, October 14, 2024, https://www.msn.com/en -us/news/politics/david-plouffe-on-harris-vs-trump-too-close-for-comfort/ar -AA1sec5K; Sam, Woodward, "Kamala Harris advisers: Internal polling never showed VP ahead," *USA Today*, November 27, 2024, https://www.usatoday.com /story/news/politics/elections/2024/11/27/kamala-harris-advisers-internal-polling /76626278007.

21. Helen Coster and Tim Reid, "Some undecided voters not convinced by Harris after debate with Trump," Reuters, September 11, 2024, https://www.reuters.com

/world/us/some-undecided-voters-not-convinced-by-harris-after-debate-with-trump
-2024-09-11.

22. "Were ABC's Debate Moderators Fair to Trump?," AllSides, September 12, 2024, https://www.allsides.com/story/2024-presidential-election-were-abcs-debate-moderators-fair-trump.

23. "Five Key Takeaways From the Vice Presidential Debate," Newsweek, October 1, 2024, https://www.newsweek.com/jd-vance-tim-walz-debate-election-key-takeaways-1962314.

24. Clay Masters, "'I'm a knucklehead': Tim Walz says he 'misspoke' about Tiananmen Square visit," NPR, October 1, 2024, https://www.npr.org/2024/10/01/nx-s1-5135678/tiananmen-square-tim-walz-debate-2024-jd-vance.

25. "It was a very Midwestern debate. And Vance won." *Politico*, October 2, 2024, https://www.politico.com/news/2024/10/02/vance-walz-who-won-vp-debate-roundtable-00181905.

26. Exit Polls, NBC News, https://www.nbcnews.com/politics/2024-elections/exit-polls.

27. "Read Jack Smith's unsealed court filing," *Politico*, October 2, 2024, https://www.politico.com/news/2024/10/02/jack-smith-trump-court-filing-election-00182235.

28. See Harold Hutchison, "Andy McCarthy Says Latest Jack Smith Evidence Dump Could Taint Jury Pool Against Trump," *Tampa Free Press*, October 19, 2024, https://www.msn.com/en-us/news/politics/andy-mccarthy-says-latest-jack-smith-evidence-dump-could-taint-jury-pool-against-trump/ar-AA1syXon; Isaac Saul, "Jack Smith's new filing on Donald Trump," Tangle, October 8, 2024, https://www.readtangle.com/jack-smith-filing.

29. Joseph A. Wulfsohn, "Harris dodges question on lowering prices by describing 'middle-class' roots: Neighbors 'proud of their lawn'," Fox News, September 14, 2024, https://www.foxnews.com/media/harris-dodges-question-lowering-prices-describing-middle-class-roots-neighbors-proud-lawn?msockid=164edadf2dec6e953cf0ce7a2c426f1f.

30. Ebony Davis, Edward Isaac-Dovere, and Kate Sullivan, "Harris says there's not much she'd have done differently than Biden over the last 4 years," CNN, October 8, 2024, https://www.cnn.com/politics/harris-2024-campaign-biden/index.html.

31. 2024 National: Trump vs. Harris, RealClearPolitics, https://www.realclearpolling.com/polls/president/general/2024/trump-vs-harris.

32. 2024 RCP Electoral College Map, RealClearPolitics, https://www.realclearpolling.com/maps/president/2024/toss-up/electoral-college.

33. 2024 Electoral College: No Toss-up States, RealClearPolitics, https://www.realclearpolling.com/maps/president/2024/no-toss-up/electoral-college.

34. Betting Odds—2024 U.S. President, RealClearPolitics, https://www.realclearpolling.com/betting-odds/2024/president.

35. Diana Glebova, "Cardinal Dolan blasts Harris for skipping Al Smith Dinner, reveals she's 'sending one of those Zooms or something,'" *New York Post*, October 17, 2024, https://nypost.com/2024/10/17/us-news/cardinal-dolan-blasts-harris-for-skipping-al-smith-dinner-reveals-shes-sending-one-of-those-zooms-or-something;

"Best, Worst, and Most Awkward Lines at the Al Smith Dinner," *New York Times*, October 18, 2024, https://www.nytimes.com/2024/10/18/us/politics/trump-harris-al -smith-dinner.html.

36. RCP National Average (2024 vs. 2020), RealClearPolitics, https://www .realclearpolling.com/polls/comparison/2024-vs-2020-president; RCP National Average (2020 vs. 2016), RealClearPolitics, https://www.realclearpolitics.com/epolls /2020/president/us/trump-vs-biden-national-polls-2020-vs-2016.

37. Top Battlegrounds—RCP Average, RealClearPolitics, https://www .realclearpolling.com/elections/president/2024/battleground-states.

38. Gregory Krieg, "Trump loyalists spew racist, vulgar attacks at Harris and Democrats at New York City rally," CNN, October 27, 2024, https://edition.cnn .com/2024/10/27/politics/trump-rally-madison-square-garden-vulgar-attacks/index .html. For a transcript of the event, see "Trump Holds Campaign Rally At Madison Square Garden," Rev, https://www.rev.com/transcripts/trump-holds-campaign-rally -at-madison-square-garden.

39. John Tarantino, Puerto Rico Trash Problem: Understanding the Crisis and Working Toward Solutions, The Environmental Blog.org, October 30, 2024, https:// www.theenvironmentalblog.org/2024/10/puerto-rico-trash-problem.

40. Annie Linskey and Emily Glazer, "Gaffe Puts Focus on Biden Again," *Wall Street Journal*, October 31, 2024, p. A4.

41. Aamer Madhani and Zeke Miller, "AP sources: White House altered record of Biden's 'garbage' remarks despite stenographer concerns," AP, November 1, 2024, https://apnews.com/article/biden-garbage-transcript-puerto-rico-trump-326e2f516a9 4a470a423011a946b6252.

42. Ken Thomas and Andrew Restuccia, "Harris Makes Final Push as Vote Nears," *Wall Street Journal*, October 30, 2024, p. A4.

43. Gregory Krieg, "Trump, with a vest and props, turns his attention to trashing Biden over 'garbage' gaffe," CNN, October 31, 2024, https://www.cnn.com/2024/10 /31/politics/garbage-truck-donald-trump-wisconsin/index.html.

44. Mark Gollom, "Harris casts Trump as threat to democracy in final pitch to vot- ers. Will they listen?," CBC News, October 31, 2024, https://www.cbc.ca/news/world /kamala-harris-closing-trump-1.7367797.

45. Ken Thomas and Gordon Lubold, "Trump Ex-Aides Give Harris Fodder," Wall Street Journal, October 24, 2024, p. A4.

46. Audrey Fahlberg, "White House Press Secretary Says Biden Thinks Trump Is a 'Fascist,'" National Review, October 23, 2024, https://www.nationalreview.com/ corner/white-house-press-secretary-says-biden-thinks-trump-is-a-fascist.

47. Russell Contreras, "Trump's MSG rally draws comparisons to 1939 MSG Nazi event," AXIOS, October 28, 2024, https://www.msn.com/en-us/news/politics/ trumps-msg-rally-draws-comparisons-to-1939-msg-nazi-event/ar-AA1t5mz4. Some critics were already hyping the connection weeks before the event; see PJ Grisar, "Will Trump's Madison Square Garden rally resemble a fascist one from 1939?," Forward, October 10, 2024, https://forward.com/culture/662971/trump-madison -square-garden-rally-1939-german-american-bund-nazi.

48. Threats by Trump against hostile media, which he had long called "enemies of the people," were not new, and they continued after the election. During his first term, he had attempted to go after Amazon, owned by *Washington Post* publisher Jeff Bezos. Six weeks after the election, his appointee Brendan Carr, next in line to head the Federal Communications Commission, wrote a letter to Disney CEO Bob Iger noting the low level of public trust in the major media and a recent $15 million settlement paid by ABC News to Trump. Brian Stelter, "Trump's FCC pick sends stern letter to Bob Iger, blasting 'erosion in public trust,'" CNN, December 24, 2024, https://www.cnn.com /2024/12/23/media/fcc-brendan-carr-bob-iger-abc-letter/index.html#:~:text=Trump %E2%80%99s%2FCC%20pick%20sends%20stern%20letter%20to%20Bob%20Iger %2C%20blasting%20%E2%80%98erosion%20in%20public%20trust%E2%80%99.

49. Ted Anthony, "Washington Post becomes second major US newspaper this week to not endorse a presidential candidate," AP, October 25, 2024, https://apnews .com/article/washington-post-newspaper-endorsement-election-51de8348502aa17 f432504c4764c63f5.

50. Lliam Reilly, "More than 250,000 Washington Post readers cancel subscriptions in revolt over non-endorsement," CNN, October 30, 2024, https://edition.cnn.com /2024/10/30/media/washington-post-cancel-subscription-endorsement/index.html.

51. Joshua Chaffin and Sara Ashley O'Brien, "How Trump Won the Manosphere," *Wall Street Journal*, November 9–10, 2024, p. C1; Anne Steele and Tarini Parti, "Rogan Grabs Spotlight in Election," *Wall Street Journal*, October 26–27, 2024, p. A5.

52. Jesus Mesa, "The Real Reason Why Kamala Harris' Interview with Joe Rogan Was Called Off," Newsweek, November 13, 2024, https://www.newsweek.com/ kamala-harris-joe-rogan-podcast-interview-called-off-reason-1985461.

53. Alayna Treen and Kate Sullivan, "Joe Rogan endorses Trump on eve of the election," CNN, November 5, 2024, https://www.cnn.com/2024/11/04/politics/joe -rogan-trump-endorsement/index.html.

54. 2024 National: Trump vs. Harris, RealClearPolitics, https://www .realclearpolling.com/polls/president/general/2024/trump-vs-harris.

55. Nicholas Liu, "'Bottom has started to fall out': Trump campaign aides fret as Election Day 'confidence has shifted,'" Salon, November 5, 2024, https://www.msn .com/en-us/news/politics/bottom-has-started-to-fall-out-trump-campaign-aides-fret -as-election-day-confidence-has-shifted/ar-AA1tyAH6?ocid=entnewsntp&pc=DCTS &cvid=7143fd923172459eb3f548669317f9e7&ei=33.

56. Tarini Parti, Ken Thomas, and Catherine Lucey, "A Close Race Spurs Fretting by Democrats," *Wall Street Journal*, October 24, 2024, p. A4; Exit Polls, NBC News, https://www.nbcnews.com/politics/2024-elections/exit-polls.

57. 2024 RCP Electoral College Map, RealClearPolitics, https://www .realclearpolling.com/maps/president/2024/toss-up/electoral-college.

58. Betting Odds—2024 U.S. President, RealClearPolitics, https://www .realclearpolling.com/betting-odds/2024/president.

59. Jane C. Timm, "Trump and his allies ramp up election fraud allegations in Pennsylvania," NBC News, October 30, 2024, https://www.nbcnews.com/politics /2024-election/trump-allies-election-fraud-allegations-pennsylvania-rcna177907.

60. Exit Polls, NBC News, https://www.nbcnews.com/politics/2024-elections/exit -polls.

61. Sarah Rumpf-Whitten, "Trump earns endorsement from 'highly respected' Muslim leaders in battleground state," Fox News, October 26, 2024, https://www .foxnews.com/politics/trump-earns-endorsement-highly-respected-muslim-leaders -battleground-state?msockid=04c9eacf7451607b0022fe5c75c8612c.

62. Erin Burnett, "Hear the different messaging on Israel and Gaza from the Harris campaign commercials depending on where you live," CNN, November 1, 2024, https://www.cnn.com/2024/11/01/politics/video/kfile-different-messages -harris-campaign-israel-gaza-ebof-digvid.

63. Louis Jacobson, "How big was Donald Trump's 2024 election victory? 8 charts explain," *Politifact*, November 22, 2024, https://www.politifact.com/article /2024/nov/22/how-big-was-donald-trumps-victory-8-charts-provide.

64. Anna Commander, "Donald Trump Hands Down New Directive to Senate Republicans," *Newsweek*, December 17, 2024, https://www.msn.com/en-us/ news/politics/donald-trump-hands-down-new-directive-to-senate-republicans/ ar-AA1w3FJs?ocid=entnewsntp&pc=DCTS&cvid=6eb08df8296841b9fd56a9e 98defccbe&ei=11.

65. Michael Schaffer, "Trump Won Less Than 50 Percent. Why Is Everyone Calling It a Landslide?," *Politico*, November 22, 2024, https://www.politico.com/news/ magazine/2024/11/22/trump-win-popular-vote-below-50-percent-00190793.

66. For subsequent 2024 demographic result, unless otherwise noted, see Exit Polls, NBC News, https://www.nbcnews.com/politics/2024-elections/exit-polls.

67. Zak Cheney-Rice, "Barack Obama's Tiresome Condescension Toward Black Men," *New York Magazine*, October 12, 2024, https://nymag.com/intelligencer/ article/barack-obamas-tiresome-condescension-toward-black-men.html.

68. Katelyn Caralle, "How Trump flipped the U.S. county with the highest percentage of Puerto Rican voters," *Daily Mail*, November 10, 2024, https://www .dailymail.co.uk/news/article-14065419/trump-flip-county-puerto-rico-voters-2024 -election.html.

69. David Luhnow, Caitlin Ostroff, and Juan Forero, "Trump's Success With Latino Voters Alters Political Terrain for Both Parties," *Wall Street Journal*, November 8, 2024, p. A1.

70. President Exit Polls, *New York Times*, https://www.nytimes.com/elections /2012/results/president/exit-polls.html; Exit Polls, CNN, https://www.cnn.com/elec-tion/2020/exit-polls/president/national-results.

71. Exit Polls, CNN, https://www.cnn.com/election/2020/exit-polls/president/ national-results.

72. Exit Polls National President, CNN, https://www.cnn.com/election/2016/ results/exit-polls; Exit Polls, CNN, https://www.cnn.com/election/2020/exit-polls/ president/national-results.

73. Caitlin Doombos, "Amish turn out for Pennsylvania vote in 'unprecedented numbers': source," *New York Post*, November 5, 2024, https://nypost.com/2024 /11/05/us-news/amish-turn-out-for-pennsylvania-vote-in-unprecedented-numbers -source.

74. For this and subsequent data regarding 2024 exit poll results about issues and candidates, see Exit Polls, NBC News, https://www.nbcnews.com/politics/2024-elections/exit-polls.

75. Isaac Arnsdorf, "Trump Baselessly Blames Assassination Attempt on Democratic Messaging," *Washington Post*, August 3, 2024, https://www.washingtonpost.com/politics/2024/08/03/trump-shooting-democrats-democracy/

76. Gabriel Hays, "Trump says he won new fans after assassination attempt: 'Something happened when I got shot,'" Fox News, December 12, 2024, https://www.yahoo.com/news/trump-says-won-fans-assassination-155900731.html; Jeremy Lott, "The Humanization of Trump," *Washington Examiner*, November 20–27, 2024, pp. 12–14.

77. Exit Polls National President, CNN, https://www.cnn.com/election/2016/results/exit-polls.

78. National Results Exit Poll, CNN, https://www.cnn.com/election/2020/exit-polls/president/national-results

79. Trump Favorable/Unfavorable, RealClearPolitics, https://www.realclearpolling.com/polls/favorability/donald-trump; Kamala Harris Favorable/Unfavorable, RealClearPolitics, https://www.realclearpolling.com/polls/favorability/kamala-harris.

80. "New Report Sees Efforts to Steer Votes," *Wall Street Journal*;, October 24, 2024, p. A4; Trevor Hunnicutt and Jasper Ward, "Chinese hackers targeted phones affiliated with Harris campaign, source says," Reuters, October 25, 2024, https://www.reuters.com/technology/cybersecurity/chinese-hackers-targeted-phones-used-by-trump-vance-new-york-times-reports-2024-10-25; Hannah Rabinowitz, "DOJ announces charges in Iranian plot to kill Donald Trump," CNN, November 9, 2024, https://www.cnn.com/2024/11/08/politics/doj-charges-three-iranian-plot-to-kill-donald-trump/index.html.

81. Dominic Mastrangelo, "Lindsey Graham says 'enough is enough' on Trump bid to overturn the election: 'Count me out,'" The Hill, January 6, 2021, https://thehill.com/homenews/senate/533055-lindsey-graham-says-enough-is-enough-on-trumps-bid-to-overturn-the-election-count-me.

82. Lydia Saad and Margaret Brenan, "Americans' Views of Impeachment, Trump's Record on Issues," Gallup, February 8, 2021, https://news.gallup.com/poll/329423/americans-views-impeachment-trump-record-issues.aspx.

83. "Read McConnell's remarks on the Senate floor following Trump's acquittal," CNN, February 13, 2021, https://www.cnn.com/2021/02/13/politics/mcconnell-remarks-trump-acquittal/index.html.

84. Dominic Pino, "Milton Friedman's Revenge," National Review, November 8, 2024, https://www.nationalreview.com/the-morning-jolt/milton-friedmans-revenge.

85. President Biden Job Approval, RealClearPolitics, https://www.realclearpolitics.com/epolls/other/president_biden_job_approval-7320.html.

86. Joseph R. Biden, Jr., Address Before a Joint Session of the Congress on the State of the Union Online by Gerhard Peters and John T. Woolley, The American Presidency Project https://www.presidency.ucsb.edu/node/370531.

CHAPTER 6

1. John T. Pothier, "Research Note: The Partisan Bias in Senate Elections," *American Politics Quarterly* 12(1), 1984, 89–100, https://doi.org/10.1177 /1532673X8401200105.

2. Frances E. Lee, *Insecure Majorities: Congress and the Perpetual Campaign* (Chicago: University of Chicago Press, 2016), 4.

3. Niels Lesniewski, "2022 Vote Studies: Biden Gets Wins Despite Slim Majority," *Roll Call*, March 23, 2023, https://rollcall.com/2023/03/23/2022-vote-studies -biden-gets-wins-despite-slim-majority.

4. Quinnipiac University Poll, "Nearly 7 In 10 Favor A Limit on How Long SCOTUS Justices Can Serve," May 18, 2022, https://poll.qu.edu/poll-release ?releaseid=3846.

5. Andrew Romano, "Poll: Confidence in Supreme Court Has Collapsed Since Conservatives Took Control," Yahoo News, May 10, 2022, https://news.yahoo.com /poll-confidence-in-supreme-court-has-collapsed-since-conservatives-took-control -122402500.html.

6. Marist Poll, "Overturning Roe v. Wade," June 27, 2022, https://maristpoll .marist.edu/polls/npr-pbs-newshour-marist-national-poll-the-overturning-of-roe-v -wade-june-2022.

7. "Analysis Reveals How Abortion Boosted Democratic Candidates in Tuesday's Midterm Election," Kaiser Family Foundation, November 11, 2022, https:// www.kff.org/other/press-release/analysis-reveals-how-abortion-boosted-democratic -candidates-in-tuesdays-midterm-election.

8. "2022 Exit Polls—House National Results," updated January 10, 2023, https:// www.cnn.com/election/2022/exit-polls/national-results/house/0.

9. 2018 Exit Polls—House National Results," https://www.cnn.com/election /2018/exit-polls

10. "Margin of Victory Analysis for the 2014 Congressional Election," Ballotpedia, n.d., https://ballotpedia.org/Margin_of_victory_analysis_for_the_2014 _congressional_elections; "Election results, 2022: Congressional Margin of Victory Analysis," Ballotpedia, January 12, 2023, https://ballotpedia.org/Election_results, _2022:_Congressional_margin_of_victory_analysis.

11. Janelle Griffith, "Trump-Backed Senate Candidate Blake Masters of Arizona Blames Gun Violence on Black People," NBC News, June 7, 2022, https://www .nbcnews.com/politics/trump-backed-senate-candidate-blake-masters-blames-gun -violence-black-rcna32290.

12. 2022 exit poll, https://www.cnn.com/election/2022/exit-polls/arizona/senate.

13. Andrew Prokop, "The GOP Had Terrible Senate Candidates and It Really Did Sink Them," Vox, November 16, 2022, https://www.vox.com/policy-and-politics /2022/11/16/23458896/republicans-senate-candidate-quality-trump.

14. Rebecca Kaplan, Ryan Nobles, Gary Grumbach, Sarah Fitzpatrick and Julie Tsirkin, "GOP-led House Committees Release Lengthy Report Alleging President Biden Committed Impeachable Offenses," NBC News, August 19, 2024, https://www

.nbcnews.com/politics/congress/gop-led-house-committees-release-lengthy-report
-alleging-president-bid-rcna166954.

15. Donald J. Trump (1st Term), The President's News Conference in Washington, DC, November 7, 2018. Online by Gerhard Peters and John T. Woolley, The
American Presidency Project, https://www.presidency.ucsb.edu/node/332760.

16. Amy Schatz, "In Clips on YouTube, Politicians Reveal Their Unscripted
Side," *Wall Street Journal*, October 9, 2006, https://www.wsj.com/articles/SB11603
5599739286425.

17. Kim Barker, "In Montana, Dark Money Helped Democrats Hold a Key Senate
Seat," Pro Publica, December 27, 2012, https://www.propublica.org/article/in-mon-
tana-dark-money-helped-democrats-hold-a-key-senate-seat.

18. Carl Hulse, "Tester's Fight for Political Survival Is Democrats' Last Stand
on the Great Plains*,"* *New York Times*, October 12, 2024, https://www.nytimes.com
/2024/10/12/us/politics/jon-tester-democrats-great-plains.html.

19. *Meet the Press* transcript, October 1, 2006, https://www.nbcnews.com/id/
wbna15046615.

20. Manu Raju and Clare Foran," What Sherrod Brown Says Went Wrong in His
Senate Race—and for Democrats," CNN, November 24, 2024, https://www.cnn.com
/2024/11/24/politics/sherrod-brown-democrats-workers-ohio/index.html.

21. Brian Arbour, "'All Politics Is Local'? Not Anymore," *Washington Post*,
December 9, 2014, https://www.washingtonpost.com/news/monkey-cage/wp/2014
/12/09/all-politics-is-local-not-anymore.

22. Meredith McGraw, *Trump in Exile* (New York: Random House, 2024), 97–98.

23. Sahil Kapur and Frank Thorp V, "How Ruben Gallego Outperformed Harris, Dominated with Latinos, and Won Arizona," NBC News, November 15, 2024,
https://www.nbcnews.com/politics/2024-election/ruben-gallego-outperformed-harris
-latinos-arizona-senate-election-rcna179344.

24. Hope Karnopp, "Republican U.S. Senate candidate Eric Hovde Misses A Line
in the Pledge of Allegiance," *Milwaukee Journal Sentinel*, April 23, 2024, https://
www.jsonline.com/story/news/politics/elections/2024/04/23/eric-hovde-misses-a
-line-in-the-pledge-of-allegiance-at-slinger-event/73428697007.

25. Matthew Chapman, "'Twisting My Words': GOP Senate Candidate Denies
Saying Elderly People Shouldn't Vote," Raw Story, April 18, 2024, https://www
.rawstory.com/hovde-gop-elderly-voting-twist.

26. Scott Bauer, "Wisconsin's GOP Senate Candidate Hovde Defends Not Knowing Much About the Farm Bill in a Dairy State," Associated Press, October 25, 2024,
https://apnews.com/article/wisconsin-senate-baldwin-hovde-farm-bill-7a854dfb333
e63d4aa3230f05417b610.

27. Mark Z. Barabak, "Column: Champagne Wishes and Caviar Dreams . . . of a
Senate Seat in Wisconsin?" *Los Angeles Times*, May 16, 2024, https://www.latimes
.com/politics/story/2024-05-16/Barabak-Column-Wisconsin-Senate-Republican-Eric
-Hovde-California-Millionaire-Banker.

28. Kyle Kaminski, "National Rankings List Elissa Slotkin as 'Most Bipartisan'
Michigander in Congress," The Gander, May 31, 2024, https://gandernewsroom.com
/2024/05/31/slotkin-most-bipartisan.

29. Emily Guskin, Chris Alcantara and Janice Kai Chen, "Michigan Presidential and Senatorial Exit Polls," *Washington Post*, November 21, 2024, https://www.washingtonpost.com/elections/interactive/2024/michigan-exit-polls.

30. Kellen Browning, "Jacky Rosen Holds Off Sam Brown in Nevada, Keeping a Democratic Senate Seat," *New York Times*, November 9, 2024, https://www.nytimes.com/2024/11/09/us/politics/nevada-senate-election-rosen-brown.html.

31. Angela Alsobrooks, X post, June 28, 2024, https://x.com/AlsobrooksForMD/status/1806705627869438198.

32. Sean Trende, "Maybe I Was Wrong About Maryland Senate Race," RealClear-Polling, April 22, 2024, https://www.realclearpolling.com/stories/analysis/maybe-i-was-wrong-about-maryland-senate-race.

33. Hannah Recht and Eric Lau, "Fewer States Than Ever Will Have Split-Party Senate Delegations," *Washington Post*, November 12, 2024, https://www.washingtonpost.com/politics/2024/11/12/senate-control-2026-map.

34. Edison Research exit polls for 2020 and 2024 at https://abcnews.go.com/Elections/exit-polls-2020-us-house-election-results-analysis and https://abcnews.go.com/Elections/exit-polls-2024-us-house-election-results-analysis.

35. Dave Wasserman, X post, December 10, 2024, https://x.com/Redistrict/status/1866528527287292405.

36. Nicholas Fandos, "Democrats Pass a N.Y. House Map That Modestly Benefits Them," *New York Times*, February 28, 2024, https://www.nytimes.com/2024/02/28/nyregion/redistricting-ny-house-democrats.html.

37. Kadia Goba, "Inside Hakeem Jeffries' New Democratic Machine," Semafor, August 28, 2023, https://www.semafor.com/article/08/28/2023/inside-hakeems-new-machine-new-york.

38. Deirdre Walsh, "How Democrats Are Targeting Red Seats in Blue New York To Help Win Back the House," National Public Radio, October 3, 2024, https://www.npr.org/2024/10/03/nx-s1-5119744/democrats-flip-new-york-house-races.

39. Richard Cohen and Charlie Cook, *The Almanac of American Politics 2024* (Arlington, Virginia: Columbia Books and Information Services, 2023), 268.

40. Cohen and Cook, *Almanac*, 327.

41. Josie Huang, "Anti-Communist Ads in OC House Race Get Pushback in Little Saigon," LAist, October 25, 2022, https://laist.com/news/politics/michelle-steel-jay-chen-communism-china-vietnamese-american-voters.

42. Laura J. Nelson and Melissa Gomez, "Democrats Flip Seat in California's Central Valley in Nation's Final Outstanding House Race," *Los Angeles Times*, December 3, 2024, https://www.latimes.com/california/story/2024-12-03/democrat-adam-gray-ousts-republican-john-duarte-ca13-central-valley-congressional-race.

43. Rachel Livinal, "Did Students Tip the Election for This House Democrat? What The Numbers Show," KVPR, December 9, 2024, https://www.kvpr.org/government-politics/2024-12-09/did-students-tip-the-election-for-this-house-democrat-what-the-numbers-show.

44. Bridget Bowman, Ali Vitali and Kyle Stewart, "House Freedom Caucus Chairman Bob Good Loses Virginia Primary Recount." NBC News, August 1, 2024,

https://www.nbcnews.com/politics/2024-election/house-freedom-caucus-chairman-bob-good-loses-virginia-primary-recount-rcna164672.

45. Scott Wong, "Alabama Republican Becomes the First House Incumbent to Lose a 2024 Primary," NBC News, March 5, 2024, https://www.nbcnews.com/politics/2024-election/barry-moore-jerry-carl-alabama-republican-incumbent-rcna141369.

46. Nicholas Wu, "Cori Bush Becomes Second Squad Member Ousted in A Primary," *Politico*, August 6, 2024, https://www.politico.com/news/2024/08/06/cori-bush-primary-election-loss-00173000.

47. Kevin Frey, "'I Wish I Didn't Pull That Damn Fire Alarm': Rep. Bowman Reflects on His Time in Congress, Primary Loss," Spectrum News NY1, December 13, 2024, https://ny1.com/nyc/all-boroughs/politics/2024/12/13/i-wish-i-didn-t-pull-that-damn-fire-alarm—-rep—bowman-reflects-on-time-in-congress—primary-loss.

48. An influential account of this process was: Morris Fiorina, *Congress: Keystone of the Washington Establishment*, rev. ed. (New Haven: Yale University Press, 1989).

49. Steven S. Smith, "Note 6. Party and Incumbency," Steve's Notes on Congressional Politics, June 10, 2021, https://stevesnotes.substack.com/p/note-6-party-and-incumbency.

50. Nate Moore, "The Blue Dog Blueprint," The Liberal Patriot, December 4, 2024, https://www.liberalpatriot.com/p/the-blue-dog-blueprint.

51. Chris Stirewalt, "The Marvelous Moderation of the Majority Makers," American Enterprise Institute, December 9, 2024, https://www.aei.org/op-eds/the-marvelous-moderation-of-the-majority-makers.

52. Nicole Narea, "Mark Robinson, the North Carolina GOP Nominee for Governor, Is Off the Rails Even by MAGA Standards," Vox, March 6, 2024, https://www.vox.com/politics/24092798/mark-robinson-north-carolina-governors-race-2024.

53. Brian Murphy and Paul Specht, "Robinson Campaign Denies Claims That He Was Regular at Porn Shops Decades Ago, WRAL-TV, September 3, 2024, https://www.wral.com/story/robinson-campaign-denies-claims-that-he-was-regular-at-porn-shops-decades-ago/21606290.

54. Andrew Kaczynski and Em Steck, "'I'm a black NAZI!': NC GOP Nominee for Governor Made Dozens of Disturbing Comments on Porn Forum," CNN, September 19, 2024, https://www.cnn.com/2024/09/19/politics/kfile-mark-robinson-black-nazi-pro-slavery-porn-forum/index.html.

55. Alec Hernández and Jake Traylor, "Trump Calls GOP Candidate with a History of Offensive Remarks 'Martin Luther King on Steroids,'" NBC News, March 2, 2024, https://www.nbcnews.com/politics/2024-election/trump-compares-north-carolina-lt-gov-mark-robinson-martin-luther-king-rcna141523.

56. Sareen Habeshian, "Trump 'Unfamiliar; with N.C. Governor Race Despite Mark Robinson Endorsement," Axios, October 21, 2024, https://www.axios.com/2024/10/21/trump-robinson-north-carolina-governor-race.

57. "NCSL State Elections 2024," National Conference of State Legislatures, December 16, 2024, https://www.ncsl.org/resources/ncsl-state-elections-2024.

58. Wendy Underhill, "2024 State Elections by the Numbers," National Conference of State Legislatures, December 12, 2024, https://www.ncsl.org/state-legislatures-news/details/2024-state-elections-by-the-numbers.

59. "2024 Ballot Measures," Ballotpedia, https://ballotpedia.org/2024_ballot _measures.

60. Mabel Felix, Laurie Sobel, and Alina Salganicoff, "What's Next for State Abortion Ballot Initiatives?" KFF, December 18, 2024, https://www.kff.org/policy -watch/whats-next-for-state-abortion-ballot-initiatives.

61. Sareen Habeshian, "These States Backed Both Trump and Abortion Rights," Axios, November 9, 2024, https://www.axios.com/2024/11/09/abortion-ballot -measures-results-2024.

62. Cayla Mihalovich, "Anti-Slavery Measure Prop. 6 Fails, Allowing Forced Labor to Continue in California Prisons," CalMatters, November 10, 2024, https:// calmatters.org/politics/elections/2024/11/california-election-result-proposition-6 -fails.

63. Sarah Ferris and Katherine Tully-McManus, "The Tangled Strategy to Save Dan Newhouse," *Politico*, September 3, 2024, https://www.politico.com/newsletters/ inside-congress/2024/09/03/the-tangled-strategy-to-save-dan-newhouse-00177193.

64. Ben Winslow, "Poll Shows Struggle for Romney Reelection, A Wide-Open Field for His Replacement," Fox 13 Salt Lake City, September 15, 2023.

65. Donald Trump, Truth Social post, September 13, 2023, https://truthsocial.com/ @realDonaldTrump/111059172309743873.

66. Donald Trump, Truth Social post, June 16, 2023, https://truthsocial.com/@ realDonaldTrump/110556444095989854.

67. Meridith McGraw and Alex Isenstadt, " 'I killed him': How Trump torpe-doed Tom Emmer's speaker bid," *Politico*, October 24, 2023, https://www.politico .com/news/2023/10/24/i-killed-him-how-trump-torpedoed-tom-emmers-speaker-bid -00123329.

68. YouGov, CBS News poll, April 12–14, 2023, https://www.scribd.com/ document/638983487/cbsnews-20230417-2#fullscreen=1.

CHAPTER 7

1. Jason Lange, "Half of U.S. Republicans Believe the Left Led Jan. 6 Violence: Reuters/Ipsos Poll," June 9, 2022, https://www.reuters.com/world/us/half-us -republicans-believe-left-led-jan-6-violence-reutersipsos-2022-06-09/2022; Jennifer Agiesta and Ariel Edwards-Levy, CNN Poll: "Percentage of Republicans Who Think Biden's 2020 Win Was Illegitimate Ticks Back Up Near 70%," CNN, August 3, 2023, https://www.cnn.com/2023/08/03/politics/cnn-poll-republicans-think-2020 -election-illegitimate/index.html.

2. "Trump: Favorable/Unfavorable," RealClearPolitics, https://www .realclearpolling.com/polls/favorability/donald-trump.

3. Aaron Blake, "Trump could be setting himself up for a 'powerful' early failure," *Washington Post*, January 7, 2025, https://www.msn.com/en-us/politics/government/ trump-could-be-setting-himself-up-for-a-powerful-early-failure/ar-AA1x7gWU?ocid =entnewsntp&pc=DCTS&cvid=e76115a0f31a4b6f9e8a25e599c8b646&ei=11.

4. Adam Shaw, "Trump-era southern Border Sees Migrant Encounters Plummet By Over 60% As New Policies Kick In," Fox News, January 28, 2025, https://www.foxnews.com/politics/trump-era-southern-border-sees-migrant-encounters-plummet-over-60-new-policies-kick-in.

5. Betsy Woodruff Ward and Myah Swan, "Trump's immigration crackdown is expected to start on Day 1," *Politico*, November 18, 2024, https://www.politico.com/news/2024/11/18/immigration-100-days-trump-executive-action-00189286.

6. Jing Pan, "Donald Trump calls tariff 'the most beautiful word in the dictionary,' threatens up to 2,000% tariff to block car imports from Mexico. Would it work?," *Moneywise*, October 24, 2024, https://moneywise.com/news/economy/donald-trump-calls-tariff-the-most-beautiful-word.

7. Maia Spoto, "BLM Nonprofit Says Tides Foundation Mismanaged $33 Million (1)," Bloomberg Law, May7, 2024, https://news.bloomberglaw.com/litigation/blm-nonprofit-says-tides-foundation-mismanaged-33-million; Andrew Kerr, "BLM's millions unaccounted for after leaders quietly jumped ship," Washington Examiner, January 27, 2022, https://www.washingtonexaminer.com/news/1400899/blms-millions-unaccounted-for-after-leaders-quietly-jumped-ship.

8. 2024 Exit Polls, NBC News.

9. 2024 Exit Polls, NBC News.

10. Robert J. Donovan, *The Future of the Republican Party* (New York: New American Library, 1964).

11. Regular Class two elections will be held in 20 GOP and 13 Democratic seats. In addition, special elections will be held for two seats being vacated by Marco Rubio (FL) and J. D. Vance (OH).

12. Charles R. Kesler, "Trump, the Republican Party, and American Conservatism: Retrospect and Prospect," in Andrew E. Busch and William G. Mayer ed., *The Elephant in the Room: Donald Trump and the Future of the Republican Party* (Lanham, MD: Rowman & Littlefield, 2022).

13. See Rex Huppke, "Trump picks Musk's money over 'forgotten' Americans of MAGA. Sorry, xenophobes!," *USA Today*, December 30, 2024, https://www.usatoday.com/story/opinion/columnist/2024/12/30/trump-worker-visas-musk-h1b-tweet-immigration/77305420007; Julia Shapero, "Steve Bannon tells Elon Musk to 'sit in the back and study,'" The Hill, December 31, 2024, https://thehill.com/policy/technology/5061472-steve-bannon-elon-musk-visas.

14. Rick Sobey, "Massachusetts Democrat Seth Moulton hits back over progressive 'purity test,' boys in girls' sports,: Boston Herald, November 8, 2024, https://www.bostonherald.com/2024/11/08/massachusetts-democrat-seth-moulton-facing-heat-for-abhorrent-trans-comments-after-election-find-another-job.

15. "Rep. Ritchie Torres on the future for Democrats and the lessons of 2024," *Washington Post*, November 14, 2024, https://www.washingtonpost.com/washington-post-live/2024/11/14/rep-ritchie-torres-future-democrats-lessons-2024.

16. Taylor Walters, "AOC gets dragged for claiming pro-Israel lobby sank Dems in 2024: 'Maybe stop blaming Jews for your problems,'" *New York Post*, November 18, 2024, https://nypost.com/2024/11/18/us-news/aoc-blames-pro-israel-group-for-democrats-2024-election-losses/; Carl Campanile, "Triggered AOC blames sexism

for Trump win as she warns it will be a 'scary' time in US," *New York Post*, November 7, 2024, https://nypost.com/2024/11/07/us-news/triggered-aoc-blames-sexism -for-trump-win-as-she-warns-it-will-be-a-scary-time-in-us.

17. Phillip Elliott, "Democrats Got Clobbered. Bernie Sanders and AOC Think They Know Why," *Time*, November 7, 2024, https://time.com/7173985/trump-bernie -sanders-aoc-election.

18. Steven Hayward, "Chart of the Day: Why Democrats Lost for Dummies," PowerlineBlog, December 31, 2024, https://www.powerlineblog.com/archives/2024 /12/the-daily-chart-why-democrats-lost-for-dummies.php. General Social Survey data reported by the *Financial Times*.

19. Crystal Hayes, "Pelosi blames Biden for election loss as finger pointing intensifies," BBC News, November 8, 2024, https://www.bbc.com/news/articles/ cn7m24zg85eo.

20. Alexander Hall, "Democrats privately gripe about Pelosi's 'damaging' post-election comments: 'She needs to take a seat,'" Fox News, November 15, 2024, https://www.foxnews.com/media/democrats-privately-gripe-about-pelosis -damaging-post-election-comments-she-needs-take-seat; "Obama loses his mojo among Democrats: Party in a reckoning over the failed election efforts; op-eds say— Stop listening to Barack," *Economic Times of India*, December 28, 2024, https:// economictimes.indiatimes.com/news/international/us/obama-loses-his-mojo-among -democrats-party-in-a-reckoning-over-the-failed-election-efforts-op-eds-say-stop -listening-to-barack/articleshow/116769910.cms.

21. Graeme Massie, "Biden still regrets dropping out of 2024 race and believes he could have beaten Trump, says report," *The Independent*, December 29, 2024, https:// news.yahoo.com/news/biden-still-regrets-dropping-2024-005717486.html.

22. Annie Linskey, Rebecca Ballhaus, Emily Glazer, and Siobhan Hughes, "How the White House Functioned with a Diminished Biden in Charge," *Wall Street Journal*, December 19, 2024, https://www.wsj.com/politics/biden-white-house-age -function-diminished-3906a839.

23. Joshua Q. Nelson, "'Embarrassingly wrong': Liberal media figures admit being in denial about Biden's mental decline," Fox News, December 31, 2024, https:// www.foxnews.com/media/embarrassingly-wrong-liberal-media-figures-admit-being -denial-about-bidens-mental-decline.

24. See "Summary H.R. 1—117th Congress," https://www.congress.gov/bill /117th-congress/house-bill/1.

25. Adam Brewster and Caitlin Huey-Burns, "What Georgia's new voting law really does—9 facts," CBS News, April 7, 2021, https://www.cbsnews.com/news/ georgia-voting-law-9-facts.

26. Michael Dorgan, "Pennsylvania mail-in ballots without correct dates will not be counted, court rules," Fox News, September 14, 2024, https://www.foxnews.com/ politics/pennsylvania-mail-in-ballots-without-correct-dates-not-counted-court-rules.

27. Jane C. Timm, "Trump and his allies ramp up election fraud allegations in Pennsylvania," NBC News, October 30, 2024, https://www.nbcnews.com/politics /2024-election/trump-allies-election-fraud-allegations-pennsylvania-rcna177907. In one case, a local judge actually agreed that Bucks County had improperly closed

mail-ballot distribution lines too early; in another, election officials in Lancaster revealed that they had received and rejected hundreds of illegal mail votes.

28. Mark Sherman and Denise Lavoie, "Supreme Court's conservative justices leave in place Virginia's purge of voter registrations," AP, October 30, 2024, https://apnews.com/article/supreme-court-virginia-voter-registration-purge-ba3d785d9d2 d169d9c02207a42893757.

29. 2024 Exit Polls, NBC News.

30. Dave Leip's Atlas of U.S. Presidential Elections, https://uselectionatlas.org.

31. Shane Goldmacher, "How Kamala Harris Burned Through $1.5 Billion in 15 Weeks," *New York Times*, November 17, 2024, https://www.nytimes.com/2024/11/17 /us/politics/harris-campaign-finances.html.

32. See John Fund and Hans von Spakovsky, *Our Broken Elections* (Washington, DC: Regnery, 2021).

33. Philip Timotija, "Musk spent at least $250M to help elect Trump, filings show," *The Hill*, December 6, 2024, https://thehill.com/homenews/campaign/5026691-elon -musk-donates-trump-campaign/; Marshall Cohen, "Elon Musk's daily $1 million giveaway to voters can continue, Pennsylvania judge rules," CNN, November 4, 2024, https://www.cnn.com/2024/11/04/politics/elon-musk-1-million-giveaway/index.html.

34. Stephen F. Knott, *The Lost Soul of the American Presidency: The Decline into Demagoguery and the Prospects for Renewal* (Lawrence: University Press of Kansas, 2019).

35. Drew Friedman, "Trump's promise to revive Schedule F could become a 'prompt' reality," Federal News Network, November 8, 2024, https:// federalnewsnetwork.com/workforce/2024/11/trumps-promise-to-revive-schedule-f -could-become-a-prompt-reality.

36. Valerie Richardson, "Conservatives get the last laugh after Democrats' campaign to demonize Project 2025 bombs," *Washington Times*, December 31, 2024, https://www.washingtontimes.com/news/2024/dec/31/conservatives-get-last-laugh -democrats-campaign-de.

37. Philip Hamburger, *Is Administrative Law Unlawful?* (Chicago: University of Chicago Press, 2014).

38. Herbert Kaufman, *Red Tape: Its Origins, Uses, and Abuses* (Washington: Brookings, 1977), 29.

39. Lindsay Whitehurst, "Judicial independence is under threat, Supreme Court Chief Justice John Roberts warns," *Washington Times*, December 31, 2024, https:// www.washingtontimes.com/news/2024/dec/31/john-roberts-supreme-court-chief -justice-warns-jud.

40. For a detailed examination and dismantling of the Eastman memos, see Joseph M. Bessette, "A Critique of the Eastman Memos," *Claremont Review of Books*, Fall 2021, https://claremontreviewofbooks.com/critique-eastman-memos.

41. 2024 Exit Polls, NBC News.

42. Evan A. Davis and David M. Shulte, "Congress has the power to block Trump from taking office, but lawmakers must act now," *The Hill*, December 26, 2024, https://thehill.com/opinion/congress-blog/5055171-constitution-insurrection-trump -disqualification.

43. David James, "'Did We Just Become Best Friends?' Jeff Bezos Dines at Mar-a-Lago with Donald Trump and Elon Musk," *Entrepreneur*, December 19, 2024, https://www.msn.com/en-us/money/companies/did-we-just-become-best-friends-jeff-bezos-dines-at-mar-a-lago-with-donald-trump-and-elon-musk/ar-AA1waBhw.

44. Ashley Capoot, "Tech Companies Most Threatened By Trump Are Donating to His Inauguration Fund," CNBC, December 13, 2024, https://www.cnbc.com/2024/12/13/tech-companies-most-threatened-by-trump-donating-to-inauguration-fund.html.

45. Adrian Volenick, "CNN and MSNBC Ratings Plunge by Half, Reaching 30-Year Lows—And Billionaires Are Paying Attention," Yahoo Finance, December 15, 2024, https://finance.yahoo.com/news/cnn-msnbc-ratings-plunge-half-203017149.html.

46. Rachel Dobkin, "Donald Trump and Joe Biden's Very Different Christmas Messages," *Newsweek*, December 25, 2024, https://www.newsweek.com/donald-trump-joe-biden-christmas-messages-2006004.

47. Heather Mac Donald, "Luigi Mangione and the American Abyss," *City Journal*, December 23, 2024, https://www.city-journal.org/article/luigi-mangione-unitedhealthcare-ceo-brian-thompson.

48. See survey data at: Mya Jaradat, "Working class: Religious but Not Attending Church," *Deseret News*, June 12, 2023, https://www.deseret.com/2023/6/12/23737197/working-class-religious-but-not-attending-church.

49. Peter Savodnik, "How Intellectuals Found God," *The Free Press*, December 28, 2024, https://www.thefp.com/p/how-intellectuals-found-god-ayaan-hirsi-ali-peter-thiel-jordan-peterson; Gregory A. Smith et al., "Decline of Christianity in the U.S. Has Slowed, May Have Leveled Off," Pew Research Center, February 26, 2025, https://www.pewresearch.org/religion/2025/02/26/decline-of-christianity-in-the-us-has-slowed-may-have-leveled-off.

50. U.S. Chamber of Commerce, "New Study Finds Alarming Lack of Civic Literacy Among Americans," February 12, 2024, https://www.uschamberfoundation.org/civics/new-study-finds-alarming-lack-of-civic-literacy-among-americans.

51. Katie Barrows, "Pew Report: Of All Age Groups, Millennials Most Favor Speech Restrictions," FIRE, November 25, 2015, https://www.thefire.org/news/pew-report-all-age-groups-millennials-most-favor-speech-restrictions; David Inserra, "New Polling Suggests the Kids Are Not Alright on Free Speech," CATO Institute, November 21, 2023, https://www.cato.org/blog/new-polling-suggests-kids-are-not-alright-free-speech.

52. Jack Miller and Michael Poliakoff, "Civic Education: The Phoenix Arises," RealClearEducation, December 27, 2024, https://www.realclearpolitics.com/2024/12/27/civic_education_the_phoenix_arises_638065.html.

Index

About the Authors

Andrew E. Busch is a professor in the Howard H. Baker, Jr. School of Public Policy and Public Affairs and associate director of the Institute of American Civics at the University of Tennessee. He is author, coauthor, or editor of two dozen books on American politics, including most recently *President Reagan's Firing of the Air Traffic Controllers* (2024), *The Elephant in the Room: Donald Trump and the Future of the Republican Party* (2022), and *Divided We Stand: The Elections of 2020 and American Politics* (2021).

John J. Pitney Jr., is Roy P. Crocker Professor of Politics at Claremont McKenna College. He is the author of *After Reagan: Bush, Dukakis, and the 1988 Election* (2019), *The Politics of Autism* (2015), and *The Art of Political Warfare* (2001), and coauthor of numerous books on American politics including *Congress' Permanent Minority? Republicans in the House* (1994) and four previous books in this series: *Epic Journey* (2009), *After Hope and Change* (2013), *Defying the Odds* (2017), and *Divided We Stand* (2021). He is a frequent contributor to the popular press.